David M. (signature)

THE BIBLE AND LAY PEOPLE

There are many books about how people ought to interpret the Bible. This book is about how people in churches actually interpret the Bible, and why they interpret it in the way that they do. Based on a study of Anglicans in the Church of England, it explores the interaction of belief, personality, experience and context and sheds new light on the way that texts interact with readers. The author shows how the results of such study can begin to shape an empirically-based theology of scripture. This unique study approaches reader-centred criticism and the theology of scripture from a completely new angle, and will be of interest to both scholars and those who use the Bible in churches.

Explorations in Practical, Pastoral and Empirical Theology

Series Editors: Leslie J. Francis, University of Wales, Bangor, UK
and Jeff Astley, Director of the North of England
Institute for Christian Education, UK

Theological reflection on the church's practice is now recognised as a significant element in theological studies in the academy and seminary. Ashgate's new series in practical, pastoral and empirical theology seeks to foster this resurgence of interest and encourage new developments in practical and applied aspects of theology worldwide. This timely series draws together a wide range of disciplinary approaches and empirical studies to embrace contemporary developments including: the expansion of research in empirical theology, psychological theology, ministry studies, public theology, Christian education and faith development; key issues of contemporary society such as health, ethics and the environment; and more traditional areas of concern such as pastoral care and counselling.

Other titles in the series include:

The Bible and Lay People
An Empirical Approach to Ordinary Hermeneutics

ANDREW VILLAGE
University of Wales, Bangor, UK

ASHGATE

Published by
Ashgate Publishing Limited
Gower House
Croft Road
Aldershot
Hampshire GU11 3HR
England

Ashgate Publishing Company
Suite 420
101 Cherry Street
Burlington, VT 05401-4405
USA

Ashgate website: http://www.ashgate.com

British Library Cataloguing in Publication Data
Village, Andrew
   The Bible and lay people : an empirical approach to ordinary hermeneutics. – (Explorations in practical, pastoral and empirical theology) 1. Bible – Hermeneutics
   I. Title
   220.6'01

Library of Congress Cataloging-in-Publication Data
Village, Andrew.
   The Bible and lay people : an empirical approach to ordinary hermeneutics / Andrew Village.
      p. cm. – (Explorations in practical, pastoral and empirical theology)
   Includes bibliographical references.
   ISBN-13: 978-0-7546-5801-6 (hardcover : alk. paper) 1. Bible–Hermeneutics. I. Title.
   BS476.V523 2008
   220.601–dc22

2007005500

ISBN 978-0-7546-5801-6

Printed and bound in Great Britain by MPG Books Ltd, Bodmin, Cornwall.

To my family:

Elizabeth, Hannah, Miriam and David

Contents

List of Figures

List of Tables

Preface

Some years ago I found myself preaching to an evening congregation of the evangelical Anglican church where I was assistant curate. The service was in the church hall, a modern carpeted room that held about fifty people that night in a reasonably cosy atmosphere. The passage was from Acts 8, the story of Philip and the Ethiopian eunuch. Fresh from theological college, I began my thoroughly worked-over exposition by looking at verse 26: 'Then an angel of the Lord said to Philip, "Get up and go toward the south"'. Anxious to earth the message in the realities of everyday life, I speculated on what it might mean for us to hear and respond to God's prompting as did Philip. What, I mused, did Philip actually experience? I pointed out that 'angel' means messenger, so we do not actually know what Philip saw or heard. It was at that moment that my well-planned sermon began to unravel. 'Of course we do', came a voice from the third row, 'he saw an angel'.

I had not intended for this to be a dialogue sermon – I had not really got the hang of the monologue yet – but a dialogue it became as the congregation took over and began debating the merits of my proposition. At first I panicked at the loss of control: were the lunatics taking over the asylum, I wondered. But after a while I became fascinated by what I was hearing. Some people had very fixed ideas of angels and were convinced that a glowing, asexual being with wings must have appeared as an apparition and spoken as clearly to Philip as I had to them (well, perhaps more clearly, they would no doubt argue). Others picked up the Old Testament ambivalence about the Lord and the Angel of the Lord: 'Look at Jacob – is he wrestling with an angel or God?' Yet others began to question the whole origin of our picture of angels and whether it was biblical at all. Perhaps Philip had simply 'felt God was saying' in the same way that some of us 'felt God say' when we had words of prophecy during prayer times. After some minutes I had to call a halt, abandoning the gems I had prepared and beating a hasty retreat into the sanctity of open prayer, during which a few pious souls prayed for my hermeneutical enlightenment and deliverance.

The incident intrigued me. I was surprised by the variety of views among what I had until then assumed was a uniformly conservative congregation. I was also pleasantly surprised by the way in which people argued their point, drawing from all sorts of scriptures. I also pondered on what forces had shaped some people's beliefs about angels, and whether this was something they had read somewhere or just absorbed from childhood. More generally, I began to wonder how this congregation read the Bible and what things may have shaped the way they interpreted it. I had been out of college about a year or so, and was hankering after doing some sort of study that would encourage me to keep reading, rather than fossilize my library with the books I read during my ministry training. So I began thinking about biblical interpretation, and began reading some of the books I should have read at college but somehow never did. Anthony Thiselton's *New Horizons in Biblical Hermeneutics* had just been published and was an excellent place to start, leading me on to other books and papers.

The more I read, however, the further I seemed to get from my original question. Everything I read was about hermeneutical theory, philosophy or about applying particular academic methods to certain passages. I struggled to find anything written about how the sort of people in my congregation might interpret the Bible. There was no shortage of books written *for* them by famous evangelists or pastors, or even by Christians like them. But such books were a world apart from the academic ones, and none ever questioned what they did or why they did it. The rift been academy and church was no more clearly evident than in this area of biblical interpretation.

In the end, I decided to investigate for myself, a decision made possible only by my supreme ignorance of the complexities involved in such an enterprise. I brought myself a book on designing questionnaires and set about finding out how ordinary church people interpret the Bible. I interviewed people in the town where I was curate, and from their replies began to shape both key areas of interest and the precise questions I needed to ask. The Bible and Lay People project grew out of this initial interest and has been helped along the way by a host of people. John Nolland and Leslie Francis were able and wise supervisors for my PhD and Leslie in particular has continued to give useful advice drawn from his wide-ranging experience of studying practical theology. He and Jeff Astley edit the series to which this book belongs, and both made helpful comments and gave sage advice on an earlier draft of the manuscript.

Many people participated in the study: incumbents who let me loose on their flocks, those who were willing to be interviewed and those who gamely completed what became a rather long questionnaire. Some wrote to tell me how bad it was, or why they could not find time to complete it, but a larger number expressed interest in the project and encouraged me to continue. I promised to keep the study anonymous, so cannot name them here, but without them the study would not have happened. I also gratefully acknowledge the financial support of the Whitefield Institute and the Bible Society, who funded some of the costs of the research.

Every researcher needs encouragement and support, and I have had it in good measure all along. My parishioners never really understood what I was doing (I refrained from including them in the sample or boring them with sermons about it), but they allowed me time to study, including a three-month sabbatical. Most importantly, my family put up with the extra stress that comes from having a sometimes grumpy and overwrought researcher in the house. My wife Liz has had a long time to get used to it, and she knows exactly when to move from gentle cajoling to outright intimidation to keep me from giving up. All these people helped to make this book possible and I am most grateful for their support.

Note: All biblical quotations are from *The New Revised Standard Version* (Nashville, TN: Thomas Nelson Publishers, 1989).

Andrew Village
December 2006

List of Abbreviations

This book relies partly on the statistical analysis of data. I have used standard abbreviations for statistical variables, which will be readily understood by those familiar with quantitative empirical study. Such people will generally wish to have some sight of the figures upon which assertions are made, so I have given these where necessary. In some cases I have summarized results that are published in more detail elsewhere. For those less familiar with statistics, I have tried to keep the use of jargon to a minimum. It is generally sufficient to know whether or not variables are related in some way, without having to understand all the technicalities of how this was established. For clarity and completeness I have produced a list of the statistical abbreviations used in the text:

α Cronbach's Alpha, a measure of scale reliability

df degrees of freedom

F the F or Fisher's statistic is used to test significance in an analysis of variance

N or n sample size

P or p probability

SD   Standard Deviation of a normally distributed sample

SE   Standard Error of the mean

χ^2 Chi-squared statistic used to test significance in contingency tables. I have presented the results as percentages for ease of comparison, but the analysis is always based on actual frequencies of each cell in the table.

Chapter 1

Introduction

This book is about ordinary churchgoers and their relationship to the Bible. 'The person in the pew' might be one way of describing ordinary churchgoers, though as someone who has worked hard to update the interior of at least one historic church, I like to think that pews are not the only form of church seating. Keeping pews out of the definition reminds us just how varied churchgoing can be. Many people no longer sit on pews, if they ever did, and indeed some do not go to churches or chapels at all. Instead they may meet in homes, village halls, schools and community centres. Churchgoers in the widest sense denotes Christians who gather together to worship, and I use it to distinguish such people from those who either have another or no religious affiliation, or who might see themselves as Christian, but who never attend worship. Most of what follows is applicable to Christians who attend church, rather than to the public at large. This is an important caveat, as we shall see, because the way in which you might go about studying how the general public relates to the Bible is quite different from the way you study churchgoers.

By 'ordinary' Bible readers I have in mind those who have not been trained in academic biblical scholarship. More specifically, I am distinguishing between those in churches who are called to preach or teach from the Bible and those who are recipients of that teaching and preaching. The division is not that neat, of course, because familiarity with academic biblical scholarship is not always a prerequisite for a Bible-based ministry and because those receiving such ministry may themselves be highly trained biblical scholars. Nonetheless, in general, those who are selected for ministry in churches will have been trained in the methods and insights of biblical scholarship and those to whom they minister will have not.

For some ministers, exposure to academia is like exposing the back of a duck to water: they emerge virtually unscathed and return to minister as if nothing had happened. Others are changed beyond recognition, emerging with new insights and new jargon that may forever separate them from their roots. Some indeed never make it back into churches because they are drawn into the world of the academics, circulating entirely within it and rarely, if ever, having to communicate their knowledge to ordinary people. For most ministers, however, training expands and shapes the way they understand the Bible, so that preaching is an exercise in reading with trained insight and then trying to convey a message to those without that insight.

What of the background of people who receive ministry? It is important to recognize at the outset that 'ordinary' does not mean 'ignorant', any more than 'trained' means 'knowledgeable'. Ordinary churchgoers may include those with postgraduate degrees and professional qualifications that far exceed those of the person in the pulpit. What distinguishes the ordinary from the trained in this context is primarily exposure to a particular way of reading the Bible: the way of the academy. That still leaves scope for enormous variation among people who attend church. They vary in gender, age and educational background. There will be different personalities and each person will have had his or her own unique experiences. They will not be randomly dispersed across congregations because some will choose to attend churches of a particular style or denomination. All of these factors, and others, might affect how ordinary churchgoers encounter and interpret the Bible.

The reason why I embarked on the study of ordinary Bible readers is that the academy, for all its sophisticated developments in biblical scholarship in the last fifty years, remains largely ignorant of what other people do with the Bible. Only in the last few years has academic scholarship begun to be aware of the peculiarities of its own approach to the Bible and the fact that 'ordinary' readers exist at all. If the academy is to understand this alien group of readers, it has to do so in its own terms. As we shall see, postmodernism has permitted academics a great deal of licence in what can now legitimately be called 'academic readings'. But no matter how much they may want to personalize or contextualize their readings, they are still academics reading the Bible. They share information using a style that is conventional and particular to a given discourse. Even when they seek to make their findings or insights more widely available, they are instantly identified as belonging to the community of scholars.

It seems to me that the only honest way for the academy to try and understand ordinary readers is to use its own tools to observe and reflect on this phenomenon. If some biblical scholars abandon any sense of rational, objective enquiry under the banner of postmodernity, then what they might gain in opening dialogue with non-scholarly communities they will lose by stepping out of the academic discourse. The academy cannot pretend to be what it is not, but that does not mean that biblical studies must be wholly secular or wholly confined to traditional methods of literary study. Practical or empirical theology offers a way for the academy to look beyond its own concerns in ways that it can understand. That, as I see it, is what practical theology is about: looking objectively with whatever empirical methods seem appropriate to a given field, and bringing that knowledge as datum into the field of theology. For this particular enquiry the datum is what ordinary churchgoing Christians do with the Bible, and what shapes the way they read it. The theological areas affected by this are those that revolve around the status and role of the Bible in faith communities and how this might relate to other ways in which God communicates with people.

Empirical approaches to Bible reading are rare. The reason for this seems to be that approaching the subject from this angle is both difficult and dangerous. I want to argue that neither of these is a sufficient reason for avoiding the subject. The difficulties will be all too apparent to anyone who has experience of trying to measure human religious attitudes, beliefs or behaviours. Human beings are complex entities, and the apparently simple task of describing human religion is daunting enough, let alone trying to measure or explain it. The temptation is either to oversimplify, and thereby create artificiality, or to under-simplify and thereby create confusion. One response to such difficulties is to write off the field of enquiry as being an impossible area to study. I encountered that response from some people who warned me not even to think of embarking on this project, and I suspect some before me who had toyed with this subject decided that this was the wisest course of action. Yet every discipline has to start somewhere, and experience in the natural sciences shows over and again that what seemed impossible a few years ago has become an everyday reality. For example, until quite recently it would have seemed absurd that we could tell anything about the composition of the earth's atmosphere millions or billions of years ago. Scientists could speculate on what *might* have been going on, but empirical measurement was out of the question. Until, that is, someone worked out how to measure the oxygen isotopes in microscopic bubbles in rocks nearly four billion years old. The chain of discovery that allows any such measurement must be vastly complicated: it relies on understanding what isotopes are, the particular isotopes of oxygen, the behaviour of different isotopes in different atmospheres and the ability to extract and analyse unimaginably small amounts of material trapped in vast quantities of rock. So the ability to understand this particular phenomenon, the evolution of the earth's atmosphere, has itself evolved over a long period in which increasingly complex measurements had to be made. As techniques and understanding improved, so did the complexity of the questions that could be asked. Understanding has developed through a circular process of asking questions, finding techniques to measure what was needed to answer those questions, and using the results to shape new questions. These questions in turn could be answered only by developing more sophisticated techniques and methods.

Empirical study of Bible reading is in its infancy, and the sorts of questions we might want ask seem impossible to answer at the moment. Those questions that we can answer often give such obvious results that there seems little reason for bothering in the first place. That does not mean that it is pointless even trying, because complex questions cannot be answered until the simple questions have firm answers. Firm answers to simple questions usually raise other questions that were not even thought of initially. Those who first identified oxygen as an element[1] could not even have begun to conceive of measuring the earth's atmosphere billions of years ago, but without their crude experiments the journey of discovery would not even have started.

One of the aims of this book is to ask questions that might simulate ways of finding answers. Research in this field requires an ability to transform general ideas into specific questions and specific questions into instruments that will give useful answers. This is difficult work and there will doubtless be wrong answers and blind alleys along the way. But difficulty is not a reason for dismissing the enterprise; it is the challenge that makes the enterprise worthwhile in the first place.

The second reason why empirical approaches to Bible reading are scarce is that they enter dangerous territory. For those for whom the Bible is sacred scripture (and I count myself among them), asking 'ordinary' people how they interpret the Bible might seem to carry the implication that popular practice should overrule sound doctrine. Perhaps if we give credence to what ordinary people do with the Bible we risk being enslaved by bad practice: will the lunatics indeed take over the asylum? The Christian faith is built upon centuries of biblical and theological study that have

---

[1]   The discovery of oxygen is usually ascribed to Joseph Priestley in 1774 or Carl Wilhelm Scheele two years earlier.

shaped the way that theology is taught, ministers are formed and congregations are led. Even in churches that trace their roots back to the Reformation, the Bible has not always been wrestled from the grip of the institutional church. Even when it was, some might argue, it fell into the hands of academic theologians who did an even better job of keeping it away from ordinary people.

Asking what people do is not the same as approving what is done, but I can imagine that some ministers might find any examination of Bible reading in their congregations a threatening exercise. Simply posing a question can be a dangerously liberating experience in some contexts. But there is also a wider danger if the results of such study show how infrequently the Bible is read or how 'unsound' interpretative practice is among lay people. Theologically and theoretically the Bible has a key, if not central, place in most Christian denominations. Where illiteracy is widespread there may be some justification for little direct engagement of ordinary churchgoers with the biblical text. But if this continues to be widespread even when people *could* read the Bible, what does this say about role of scripture in Christian life? Are those who choose to not read the Bible for themselves doing 'wrong'? Are they less able to understand or communicate with God? Is biblical knowledge essential, or merely helpful, for ordinary Christians? These are dangerous questions to ask, especially if empirical data give us answers we would rather not have known.

If empirical approaches to Bible reading are dangerous for the church, they may be no less so for the academy. It may be true that some areas of academic biblical study are largely immune from worries about what ordinary people make of the Bible. Historical-critical approaches have deliberately drawn a line between what the text meant and what it might mean today, and the latter has never really entered into discussion. Literary critics who search the text for the 'implied' reader are not pretending that such a reader has any connection with 'real' readers. For some such critics, finding out that lay people have no knowledge or interest in such scholarship would come as no surprise and would make little difference to how they went about their study. Those who work from faith-based positions might find it depressing that truths revealed by scholarly study have not penetrated very far into the church, but that might be a problem of communication rather than fundamental approach. However, the growing legions of reader-response critics might be more worried if none of their work seemed at all relevant to ordinary churchgoers. After all, the whole notion of privileging the reader over author or text has led to varieties of scholarship that are meant to relate to the concerns of 'real flesh and blood readers'. Such intent leads inexorably to the kinds of questions that empirical study is best placed to answer: what do ordinary readers make of the Bible? However, few reader-response critics have ventured to ask those questions or to seek objective answers. Most are content to examine their own interpretations more self-consciously or to indulge in some armchair speculation on what may happen with ordinary readers. This might be partly due to the difficulties of collecting data, but perhaps it is also because the answers revealed by such data could prove threatening. On the one hand, if academic readers have preoccupations that are wholly different from those of ordinary readers, it raises doubts as to whether they have begun to understand the meaning of reader response at all. If, on the other hand, scholars have spent the last two centuries or so refining their method simply to end up interpreting the Bible as ordinary people always have done, the worth of the whole scholarly enterprise is called into question. Perhaps it would be best to leave ordinary readers well alone.

Another reason for the lack of empirical studies of Bible reading might be that they require a cross-disciplinary approach. The increasingly scientific nature of psychology and sociology takes these disciplines further away from the more philosophical and theological concerns of modern academic biblical exegetes. The world of behavioural studies, attitude measurement and statistical analysis is as far away from the world of philosophical hermeneutics as that world is from the concerns of ordinary Bible readers. There are several different worlds to bring together in this sort of exercise and they have varying histories of interaction.

First, there are the two worlds of traditional theology and philosophical hermeneutics. These have a long history of association, and indeed biblical hermeneutics has been a driving force in the discipline of general hermeneutics. After all, for some at least, a great deal hangs on what exactly the Bible means because they believe it to be the source of ultimate meaning. Anthony Thiselton (1980; 1992) has probably done more than anyone else to show how the philosophies that shaped general hermeneutical thinking have constantly challenged and engaged with Christian understandings of scripture. Developments in secular hermeneutics have inevitably influenced the way that theologians have understood the Bible. In some cases the interaction has been long and mutual; in others the secular approach has proved to be incompatible with the fundamental philosophical stance of Christianity.[2] Whatever the view taken about this interaction, it is a well-established one that has found a legitimate place in the academy and, to some extent, in church circles. The relationship of theology and hermeneutics has relevance for a study such as this because these discourses create the theoretical frameworks that might shape an empirical enquiry. They indicate some areas that might be relevant to how ordinary readers interpret the Bible. In addition, the wider philosophical currents of secular society may impinge directly on how churchgoers view the Bible and its place in the world. Postmodernity, for example, is more than a theoretical way of thinking about the world; it is also a description of how some people in society actually relate to the world.

A second cross-disciplinary requirement for this study is to link the worlds of academic theology and empirical science. Traditionally these worlds live separate lives within the academy: the one often located in the hallowed halls of the older buildings that were part of the university's foundation, the other at the more recent 'science site', constantly growing and building new laboratories. For theologians, the task is to build on the mountain of theological tradition, working by deduction from established principles and weighing the evidence of text and reason. For those schooled in empirical study, the task is to observe, manipulate and draw conclusions on what is, rather than what ought to be. For many people, these seem to be two separate worlds, and some have tried very hard to keep them so. But the difference is perhaps not as great as it might at first appear. For both co-exist in the same academic world where they rely on a discourse that weighs ideas against evidence and

---

[2]   See, for example, Thiselton (1992: 114) for a discussion of postmodernist and deconstructionist approaches in relation to theological interpretation.

probability. Both, though they may believe otherwise, are shaped by the prevailing dogma (or paradigms) of their disciplines; dogma that governs what can and cannot be done under the name of theology or science.

There are several areas where science and theology engage with each other. One involves theologians engaging on their terms with what it means to maintain faith in, or alongside, the world revealed by science rather than scripture. This is familiar ground to theologians, even if the scope and nature of the task is changing rapidly as science invades the sacred spaces once thought to be solely the domain of the spiritual. There is also ground that is unfamiliar to both disciplines, involving as it does philosophical musings on the incomprehensible frontiers that currently lie beyond the reach of conventional science: the parallel universes, multiple dimensions of space or time and the incongruities of the physical world that defy rational explanation (Hodgson 2005). And then there is the field of empirical or practical theology, where theologians are pretty much the away team, playing on the other team's familiar turf. Empirical approaches to religion can be quite varied. Some are essentially scientific and confine themselves to observing, hypothesizing and testing ideas about the phenomenon of religion, much as any other behavioural science. Others are more firmly rooted in theology, and see empirical data as something that guides and shapes our understanding of how God operates in the world. The tension between those who see the engagement as essentially scientific or essentially theological is a sign of the difficulty of trying to reconcile these two worlds of discourse. This book is based on an approach that insists that whatever is done theologically with the evidence, that evidence itself must be gathered with the tools and integrity of empirical science.[3]

There is one final area where two different worlds must be brought together in this kind of exercise, and that is the attempt to link the academic to the non-academic. More specifically in this case, academic theology must interact with the beliefs of ordinary churchgoers. This is not quite the same as bringing together university and church, for these worlds have a long history of engagement; indeed they were inseparable for centuries. People of faith continue to insist on a place for faith in the academy, and academic theology has penetrated into the heart of many church institutions such as theological colleges. Bringing academically trained and ordinary Christians together is not akin to engaging with the enemy; it is more a case of bringing the foot soldiers into contact with the generals. Both are on the same side in the battle, but their understanding and experience of it are poles apart. This poses difficulty for those who are based in the academy who try to understand the world of discourse of ordinary churchgoers. There is a strong temptation to impose on them ideas and thought patterns that arise from academic theory rather than the genuine reality of a non-academic world. Engagement requires a 'bottom up' approach as well as a 'top down' one, but that can be difficult unless the investigator has some

---

[3]   Francis (2002) outlines the distinction between this approach, which he has developed, and the more theologically-rooted approach of the Nijmegen school developed by Hans van der Ven (1998). For further discussion of the definition and purpose of practical or empirical theology, see Ballard and Pritchard (1996), Cartledge (1999) and Woodward and Pattison (2000).

connection with the world of ordinary churchgoers.[4] This engagement needs to hear and understand the world of ordinary churchgoers, without compromising the detachment that is required for a truly empirical approach.

Bringing those three worlds together into some sort of dialogue is the difficult and dangerous task of this book. My experience as scientist, parish priest and university lecturer probably makes me as fitted as most to rush in where angels fear to tread. That does not mean I am bound to succeed in wearing several different hats at once, only that I might at least know what it is like to wear each of those hats one at a time.

Methods of Empirical Research

This section is intended for those who may be interested in the theological or hermeneutical issues raised in this book, but who are not familiar with empirical approaches to the study of religion. Those who are familiar with handling quantitative data using statistical analyses may wish to skip to the next section.

People who study human behaviour (psychologists, sociologists, anthropologists and the like) tend to fall into two main camps that might be termed 'quantitatives' and 'qualitatives'.[5] Those who use quantitative methods generally simplify a phenomenon into constructs that can be measured by numerical scaling. This, they claim, adds more rigour and the quantification allows statistical prediction because variations in the scaled construct can be related to variations in other factors. Those who prefer qualitative methods believe that too much is lost in the initial simplification of constructs, so that researchers end up predicting something that either does not exist or, if it does, that has no meaning to the people being studied. Qualitative study involves thorough observation that tries to record everything said in open interviews or done during a behavioural interaction. All of this information is coded, and the researcher looks for significant patterns or events. This approach still requires some level of simplification and quantification, if only to identify the significant, frequent or repetitive. It is still the task of the researcher to extract key trends from the mass of observations. This, argue the quantitatives, is the Achilles heel of the method because it is all too easy for researchers to see what they want to see and shape the data to fit their preconceived ideas.

Both approaches have their uses and, ideally, each researcher needs to decide what would work best for a particular investigation. Combining approaches offers powerful tools of analysis, but in practice it is unusual to find studies that do this well. Researchers are creatures of habit, and the methods we have used before, and

---

[4]   Jeff Astley (2002) discusses these issues in his book *Ordinary Theology*. He explores the way that religion is 'learnt' and how this relates to the study of theology. In a chapter entitled 'Studying Ordinary Theology' he stresses the need to use empirical methods to test observation and intuition. 'Serious "looking and listening" are needed to test the intuitions that we all have about what and how ordinary people believe and feel' (p. 103).

[5]   I am aware of the wide and complex debate on the value of these two approaches, and that they are not as separate as this summary might suggest. Jeff Astley (2002) has a useful discussion of these methods in relation to the empirical study of 'Ordinary Theology'.

with which we are familiar, will tend to be the ones to which we turn first. When I embarked on this study I bought several tomes on qualitative techniques in social science and considered the possibility of doing the whole study by detailed interviews and observation of Bible-study groups. This would be a perfectly valid approach, which I have since learnt others have undertaken. But I was not approaching the area with an entirely blank page. Before I trained for ordination I had spent fourteen years as a research scientist, studying the ecology of birds of prey. Ecologists are used to having to scrabble about collecting information that is hard to come by and that requires sophisticated statistical techniques to sort out. Wrestling with ways of quantifying and analysing behaviour was in my blood, so it was hardly surprising that I settled for a more quantitative approach.

With hindsight, I think that was the right approach anyway. The losses due to simplification are, it seems to me, outweighed by the ability that quantification gives to test relationships and identify causal factors. Bible reading is a complex business that could be shaped by many different factors: our beliefs, gender, age, education, experience and church community, to name but a few. Many of these are interrelated, so quantitative analysis is probably the best way of sorting out which factors are primary and which are secondary. For example, in Britain there are links between age, sex and educational qualifications. In general, educational experience for the over twenty-fives declines with age, and is higher in older men than in older women.[6] The rise in educational standards since the Second World War means that younger people are more likely to have experience of university education than their parents or grandparents. If in a sample of churchgoers there is a trend between age and Bible reading, this might be due to age as such, or it might actually be due to educational experience, with the age relationship being a spurious side effect. Quantitative statistics allow the researcher to decide which of these is likely to be the most important factor.

A word of caution is required at this point, as all those trained in statistical inference will no doubt be aware. Numbers have a strange mesmerizing effect on researchers. They lull us into a false sense of security and lead us beside apparently still waters that are not always what they seem to be. There are a number of issues surrounding the use of statistics in this book that need to be borne in mind. First, statistical analysis is largely about looking for patterns and relationships within a dataset. A dataset is a collection of information that may or may not represent the reality of what is being studied. In the physical sciences there is usually a close relationship between the numbers and the quantities being measured. We expect the reading on an ammeter to reflect accurately the amount of current flowing through the circuit. This accuracy eludes social science a lot of the time. The measures devised to quantify human attitudes, beliefs or aspirations are unlikely to ever fully represent such complexity. So they cannot always identify subtle differences or shades of opinion, and sometimes (perhaps often) they will give different quantities

---

[6]   The *Labour Force Survey* made by the Department of Education in 2003/2004 showed that in the 25–29 age group, 29% of both men and women had a degree or equivalent qualification. In the 50–59 age group, however, the proportions were generally lower, but higher in men (17%) than in women (11%). (Summerfield and Gill 2005: Table 3.16).

for something that is actually the same. As I mentioned earlier, the crudity of datasets is not a good reason for abandoning the attempt to quantify, but it is as well to remember that the scales and measures used in this book are approximations to reality, not a substitute for it.

A second reason for caution is the limit imposed by the nature of analytical studies. Quantification allows the use of statistical analyses that can compare and contrast or look for patterns of relationship. Is this quantity bigger than this one? Are these two scales related, so that a high score in one predicts a high (or low) score in the other? Which factors are most closely related to each other? What this sort of analysis cannot do is say for certain what *causes* these patterns. If people in evangelical churches read the Bible more frequently than those in other traditions, is this because they go to an evangelical church, or did they select an evangelical church because they read the Bible frequently? Or perhaps both choice of church and Bible reading frequency are themselves shaped by other factors such as basic beliefs about Christianity. Scientists faced with such possibilities would generally want to perform an experiment by holding all other factors constant, manipulating one variable and measuring what happens to the other. We might ship a randomly selected busload of evangelicals to the nearest Anglo-Catholic church for a few months and see if they start to read the Bible less often. Attractive as this might seem to the obsessive researcher, there are limits on what is possible when working with real people and their social systems. Manipulation of this sort is rarely possible, so the best that can be hoped for is to measure as many relevant variables as accurately as possible, and to use statistical analyses to decide which are likely to be directly or indirectly related. In the case of Bible reading frequency we may, for example, notice that not all people in evangelical churches read the Bible every day, but some people in Anglo-Catholic churches do. If we measure what people believe about the Bible, we might see that this is more closely related to how often it is read than is church tradition. If this were the case, it would be reasonable to infer that beliefs about the Bible might shape reading frequency and might also be one factor that determines where people worship. But this will always remain a best guess rather than a certainty.

A third reason for counselling caution in the face of quantification is the very nature of statistical analysis. What excites statisticians are 'significant' results or even 'highly significant' results. These are terms used to denote particular levels of probability: they are expressions of how certain we can be that a relationship exists or of how confident we can be in the result. For the untrained, this is a rather odd way of speaking. In the 'real' world, something is either true or it is false. Either this is larger than that or it is not. Either these two things are correlated or they are not. But this is not so in the world of statistics because statistics work on samples, not whole populations. So, for example, I might want to find out how often Anglo-Catholic and evangelical Anglicans read the Bible. It is impossible to survey every Anglican of either persuasion, so I would need to ask a number of people from each tradition, and assume that what they said reflected what was true of the people I did not survey. How much confidence I put in the result would depend on a number of factors. If I was able to sample the majority of Anglicans in each group, I would be happier with the outcome than if I sampled just half a dozen of each. Furthermore, if the difference between the two groups was large, I probably would begin to notice this after I had gathered a relatively small number of answers from each tradition. If, on the other hand, there was a lot of overlap, so that average frequency of Bible reading was only slightly higher in one group than the other, I would want to sample a large number of people to ensure that I had an accurate picture of each tradition. Notice that neither of these issues depends on how accurately people answer my questions, nor whether my sample might be biased in some way (if, for example, all the frequent readers in evangelical churches were keen to answer, while all the rest hid under the pews to avoid embarrassment). They are simply a function of the nature of what is being quantified. The higher the proportion of the actual population sampled, the more accurate results will be. The bigger the actual difference in what is being measured, the smaller the sample size needed to show a difference.

Statistical analyses use the properties of samples to calculate how likely an inference is to be true, given the distributions of the samples. It calculates the probability that the difference or relationship observed could have arisen just by chance. If that probability is very low (say less than 1 in 20) then it is very likely (but not impossible) that what is measured represents a real difference in the whole population. That is what statisticians call a 'significant' result. It is not, however, a certain result. It does not follow that because analysis shows that a result is statistically significant, it must have significance in reality. Occasionally, purely by chance, the numbers will fall in such a way that they appear to show a difference where none exists. Using probability levels of 1 in 20 (5%) and 1 in 100 (1%) means results will be unlikely to mislead, but it does not mean they cannot mislead.

These caveats are an important reminder that empirical analysis of human attitudes, beliefs and behaviours is not exact science. Attaching numbers to human attributes does not endow the numbers with magical powers to explain everything. But it may enable them to explain some things. They allow the researcher to have confidence that some things that seem to be so are actually so. They can also allow things that are not obvious from simple observation or intuition to emerge from the complex web of interactions that make up human social systems. As such, statistics are good slaves but bad masters.

Empirical theology has to operate within the methodology and demands of the social and psychological sciences. These are disciplines that demand analytical and statistical rigour. Assertions must be based on data that are properly collected and carefully analysed using standard and accepted statistical techniques. Such techniques are likely to be incomprehensible and utterly irrelevant to people interested in the hermeneutics of ordinary readers. Several chapters in this book refer to data that I have presented in more detail elsewhere, and those interested in statistical details may want to refer to these. In most cases, I have used standard statistical terms and analyses with little or no explanation on the assumption that those who are not statistically minded can ignore the figures and concentrate on the main findings. It is important, however, for those whose prime interest is theological rather than empirical to be aware of the inherently empirical nature of my approach, along with the strengths and weakness of such an approach.

The Bible and Lay People Study

This book deals with various topics related to the hermeneutics of ordinary readers. Most of these topics are related to one particular study, which I refer to as the Bible and Lay People study. This section gives the background to this study and describes the study sample.

Selection of Study Variables and Pilot Studies

Empirical studies of religion fall into two main types. Surveys measure the frequency or extent of beliefs or practices among a particular group or population. Examples might be the frequency of church attendance or the age structure of church congregations. Surveys require careful sampling in order to ensure that the frequencies reported in the study sample accurately reflect the frequencies at large. For this reason they work best with short questions that ensure high response rates. Surveys are good for measuring the prevalence of behaviours or beliefs, but they cannot always identify the factors that shape those behaviours or beliefs. Analytical studies, on the other hand, are less interested in absolute frequencies and more interested in identifying the underlying factors that explain or predict behaviour and beliefs. An analytical study of church attendance would want to show why some people attend more often than others and whether it is possible to predict their attendance from other factors such as age, gender or church tradition. For an analytical study it is important to include a wide range of participants but not necessarily a wholly representative sample. So for church attendance it would be important to investigate both frequent and infrequent attendees, but the numbers in each cohort would not necessarily have to reflect their frequency among church members. Indeed, it is sometimes necessary to over-represent a minority group in order to accumulate a large enough sample for meaningful analysis. The aim of the Bible and Lay People study was to investigate the factors that shape biblical interpretation, rather than simply to describe the frequency of Bible reading or particular types of interpretation. So from the start I aimed at an analytical survey that required detailed investigation of a range of lay people rather than a short survey.

The study began in 1994 with around 20 extended interviews with people from churches in and around Northampton, England. These were open ended and allowed participants to talk freely about their experience of the Bible, their beliefs about it and how they interpreted it. The aim was to identify issues that were relevant to lay people, and to begin to narrow the focus of study. The Bible is a big collection of books that vary enormously in content and style. 'How do you interpret the Bible?' is probably too general a question to elicit meaningful responses. The results of the interviews suggested that the best way of narrowing the focus of the study was to use a test passage and build questions around it. Miraculous healing leant itself as a subject for the test passage for several reasons. Most Christians have at some stage prayed for someone to be healed, so the idea of God healing is familiar both through the biblical text and through religious practice. On the other hand, people's beliefs about miraculous healing, and their experience of healing prayer, is very varied.

This allowed the opportunity to relate interpretation of a biblical passage to people's experience.

The next stage was to create a questionnaire that would measure a variety of variables connected with biblical interpretation. Some would be measures of the way that people interpreted the passage (or the Bible in general) and others would be variables that explained or predicted the way that the Bible was interpreted. In technical terms, the former are *dependent* variables and the latter are *independent* variables. The aim was to record a range of responses for each variable and then look to see which variables were related, and in particular which predicted or explained biblical interpretation. The choice of dependent variables was shaped by several factors. It was important to allow topics to emerge from the concerns of ordinary people, and not to allow the agenda to be entirely theory driven. Imposing academic models on ordinary readers is precisely what the study was trying to avoid. On the other hand, a great deal of effort has gone into theoretical hermeneutics and it would be wrong to ignore ideas that might be important to lay people even if they were unaware of them. What emerged was a balance between the two that was also dictated by the practical consideration of what could be measured reliably and what was feasible to achieve in a single study. It was clear from the initial pilot interviews that topics such as literalism and historicity, which are perhaps less important to contemporary academic biblical studies, are still key issues for lay people. At the same time, key theoretical notions such biblical horizons were not ideas that many interviewees talked about directly, though this did not mean that they were unimportant.

There was a similar need to balance the choice of which independent variables to measure. While it is easy enough to record peoples' age, gender or educational experience, measuring such things as beliefs about the Bible or miraculous healing requires more than a single question. One area that may be important for biblical interpretation is personality. In particular, it has been suggested that psychological type theory could influence the style and content that people prefer when a Bible passage is expounded (see Chapter 6). After some initial doubts about the feasibility of including personality in the study, I was persuaded to include a measure of psychological type in the questionnaire.[7]

The initial interviewing was followed by a number of pilot questionnaires that were administered to various groups in order to hone the instruments that would be used in the final sample. Psychologists call this 'operationalizing the constructs', which is a way of expressing the fact that it is one thing to theorize that a variable might be important, it is another to measure that variable. For example, people may vary in how literally they interpret the Bible, but how do you quantify this? You could ask a simple question such as 'How literally do you interpret the Bible?' but this may lead to a variety of unhelpful answers. Not only might this depend on which bits of the Bible are under consideration, but the same answer may mean different

---

[7]   I am indebted especially to Leslie Francis, who began supervising the project about halfway through, for persuading me that personality was not the imponderable variable I had thought it might be. He had already published material on personality and scripture, and his experience in this field was invaluable.

things from different people. I might consider myself to be a very literal interpreter, but those of a more fundamentalist persuasion might think otherwise. The situation is even more complicated for less tangible constructs such as attitudes towards the Bible or beliefs about it. There are many different ways of quantifying apparently abstract ideas, some of which have been well tried and tested by psychologists, sociologists and market researchers. One method used in the Bible and Lay People study was to create summated rating scales. These involve asking a variety of questions around the same topic, with each question having a numerical scale for answers. The scores for the different questions are then summed to give an overall score that is a measure of response on that topic. Likert scales (Likert 1932) are often used to measure attitudes or opinions and are built on this principle. A scale consists of a number of statements (items) with which respondents may agree or disagree, and their responses can be scored numerically. Reliability analysis can be used to identify items that cohere and seem to be measuring the same basic attitude or opinion.[8]

Data from the initial interviews were used to construct questions and scale items that were given to churchgoers in Anglican and other denominations in a series of three pilot studies between 1996 and 1998. These allowed individual scales to be developed and tested before they were used in the final questionnaire. Early on I decided to use a test passage from Mark 9:14–29, the healing of a boy with an evil spirit (see the Appendix). This could be interpreted in a variety of ways, partly depending on whether the boy was seen as being demon possessed or suffering from epilepsy. As well as testing responses to a specific passage, the questionnaire also quantified more general beliefs about the Bible and miraculous healing.

The Final Questionnaire

In its final form the questionnaire consisted of five sections:

The test passage
Participants were asked to read the passage (from the New Revised Standard Version, but with all chapter and verse marking removed) and then asked questions about it. These included whether they had heard it before, whether they could imagine themselves in the story, and questions relating to biblical horizon. In addition, there were also a number of interpretations of the test passage that were designed to appeal to different personality types.

---

[8]   Those interested in the technical details of summated scale construction and reliability analysis should consult general texts on questionnaire design (Aiken 1996; Oppenheim 1992) or specialist texts (Lee 1993; Spector 1992). Likert items used in this study had a five-point response scale ranging from strongly agree to strongly disagree. Responses were numerically scored to create scales, which were tested for their reliability. The standard measure of scale reliability is known as Cronbach's Alpha, which indicates how closely scores for individual items on a scale are correlated. Alpha ranges from zero to one, and values of around 0.8 or above are generally thought to indicate a reliable scale.

Beliefs about the Bible

The second section enquired about more general beliefs concerning the Bible, morality and religious pluralism. Some items measured beliefs themselves while others sought to test how dogmatically beliefs were held. There was also a section on general biblical literalism.

Miraculous healing

The third section contained items that related to miraculous healing and praying for healing. These investigated both beliefs about healing (by asking participants to respond to imaginary scenarios) and the participants' experiences of miraculous healing or praying for healing.

General background information

The fourth section gathered information on church tradition (present and past), sex, age, occupation, educational experience, church attendance and Bible reading. The latter included both a measure of Bible reading frequency and the use of Bible reading aids such as study notes or commentaries. There was also a group of questions that asked about charismatic practices such as speaking in tongues, prophecy and visions. The aim was to build up a picture of the religious background and experience of each participant that might shape the way that they interpreted the Bible.

Psychological type

The final section was the Keirsey Temperament Sorter (© Keirsey 1995), a published questionnaire consisting of 70 forced-choice questions (Keirsey 1998; Keirsey and Bates 1978) that assessed personality type according to a model first suggested by Carl Jung in the 1920s.

The result was a questionnaire of over 200 questions that suited the analytical design of the study. The final sample was likely to be biased towards those who had the time and inclination to complete a long questionnaire about Bible reading, and these were likely to be mainly Bible readers. Although an analytical study does not require a totally representative sample, it does require that the range within the sample covers most of the range in the population. For this reason it was necessary to select carefully a variety of churches from different traditions for the final survey.

The Final Sample

The final sample was drawn solely from worshippers in Anglican churches in England. Limiting the sample to Anglican churches gave some coherence to the sample, in that all the worshippers would presumably have at least some common liturgical and ecclesiastical background, but it also enabled some quite diverse church traditions to be included in the study. The Church of England has a long tradition of different parties and factions, which live together in a sometimes uneasy alliance (Baker 1996; Furlong 2000; Hylson-Smith 1989, 1993; Randall 2005). The majority of churches use worship that is derived from the Book of Common Prayer and its modern equivalents. Services combine a stress on the word and sacrament and there is usually a common pattern to the liturgy and music. Many of these congregations call themselves 'middle of the road' or 'traditional' Anglicans, but for the purpose of this study I refer to them as broad church.[9]

The two main wings of the Church of England are the Anglo-Catholic and the evangelical. Anglo-Catholic congregations stress the liturgy and sacraments, rather than the word, and draw inspiration from Roman Catholic rites and practices. Although members can be conservative, there is a strong tradition of liberalism among many Anglo-Catholic congregations. Evangelicals, on the other hand, tend to be less liturgical and sacramental and place greater emphasis on preaching and Bible exposition. They may use forms of liturgy based on Anglican worship, but are less likely to stick rigidly to particular patterns or clerical dress codes.[10] In recent times, Anglican evangelicals have been more influenced by the Charismatic Movement than other parts of the Church of England.

From 1999 to 2001 I approached a number of Anglican churches in central and southern England and asked if they would be willing to participate in the study. I selected them on the basis of proximity to where I lived, contacts with incumbents or lay people, or their church tradition. Participating congregations agreed to distribute questionnaires directly to members of the electoral roll and by leaving copies in church for a number of weeks.[11] Each questionnaire contained a stamped addressed envelope that allowed participants to return them directly, rather than via a collection box at church.

Questionnaires were distributed in eleven different congregations and 404 were returned. This formed the basic sample for the study. Although it was not wholly representative of the Anglican Church in England, it spanned a wide range of people and covered much of the variation found among ordinary churchgoers in the denomination. One way of checking the representational validity of the Bible and Lay People study sample was to compare it to larger samples from national surveys of all denominations in England made at roughly the same time. The two best are the *Church Attendance Survey* (CAS) of 1998 (Brierley 2000) and the 2001 *Church Life Profile* (CLP), which sampled around 100,000 churchgoers in England (Escott 2001). Although these may not themselves be wholly representative, they at least give some indication of the validity of the Bible and Lay People sample. Participants in the latter study were asked to identify the tradition of their church. Of the 399 who answered this question, 30% chose evangelical; 9% chose charismatic or charismatic evangelical; 34% chose broad church and 27% chose Anglo-Catholic. There are no official figures for the number of people in different church traditions in the Church of England and the most reliable data to date is probably that in the CAS. The CAS

---

[9]   This is to conform to the phrase used in the Church Attendance Survey (Brierley 2000).

[10]   An exception might be 'low church' evangelicals who use the Book of Common Prayer.

[11]   The electoral roll is the nearest equivalent to a membership list in the Church of England. It is completely revised every six years, updated each year and generally reflects the more active attendees. However, some people on electoral rolls rarely attend, and some regular worshippers are not on the roll.

asked people to assign their church to particular categories and then estimated by assuming everyone in the church would agree with this. For Anglican churches, the 16,281 replies were divided 28% Anglo-Catholic or Catholic, 22% evangelical and 50% for the remaining four categories (Brierley 2000: Table 41). This suggests the Bible and Lay People sample may have underestimated the 'broad church' group that were neither Anglo-Catholic nor evangelical, but this comparison is heavily dependent on how people understood some rather ambiguous terms in the CAS.

Of 400 who indicated their sex in the Bible and Lay People study, 63% were women and 37% were men, which is close to the estimate of 61% women in Church of England congregations estimated from the CAS, and to the 65% women for all denominations in the CLP. To compare the age distribution it was necessary to make some adjustments to the age categories. The results (Fig 1.1) suggested that the Bible and Lay People sample had a higher proportion of people in their 30s–50s and fewer younger and older people compared with CAS. This might have been because of the relatively high proportion of participants from evangelical churches where this age group predominated.

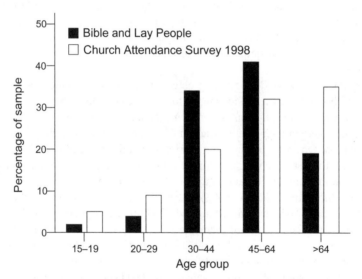

Fig 1.1   Age profiles of the Bible and Lay People sample

The educational experience of participants varied widely: some had no formal educational qualifications while others had postgraduate degrees (Table 1.1). Again, I am not aware of any official estimates of educational experience among the Church of England congregations, so it is hard to tell if this sample is typical. A poll of readers of the *Church Times* in 2001 found that 63% of 5,762 lay Anglicans from England were graduates (Francis, Robbins and Astley 2005). Churchgoers tend to be more educated than the population at large, and the CLP reported 37% of men and 30% of women with degrees or equivalent among the total sample of all denominations, compared with figures of 16% and 13% for the equivalent age group (roughly 16–65) for the population as a whole. The equivalent figures for the same age group in the Bible and Lay People study were 72% of 119 men and 55% of 202 women, suggesting that this was a relatively well-educated sample, even by church-going standards. Even so, a third of the sample had no qualifications beyond School Certificate, Ordinary Level or General Certificate of Secondary Education.[12]

Table 1.1 Educational experience of people in the Bible and Lay People study

Highest qualification	AC %	BC %	EV %	All %
No qualification	4	12	4	6
O-Level	24	37	22	26
A-Level	7	11	13	11
Degree or diploma	38	36	46	41
Postgraduate	28	5	16	15
N =	93	109	200	402

Note. AC = Anglo-Catholic; BC = Broad church; EV = Evangelical. Columns do not always add up to 100% due to rounding errors.

Overall, it appeared that the study sample, while not wholly representative of the Church of England, did cover a sufficiently wide range of people of different traditions, sex, age and educational experience to enable a meaningful analysis. It would be wrong to use the results to indicate the frequency of beliefs or behaviours in the Church of England as a whole, but this was a sample that embraced much of the variation you would find if you visited a variety of congregations. It is this sample that formed the basis for the empirical study of biblical interpretation among lay people.

[12] These are all national qualifications for 16-year-olds used in England at various times in the twentieth century.

Chapter 2

Biblical Studies in Academy and Church

The story of how the Bible has been understood within the church and academy is long and complex. There are many different ways of telling this story, each dependent on the particular interests and aims of the narrator. For some it is about philosophies shaping culture and religion; for others it is about the development of method in hermeneutics; for yet others it is about the struggle between the academy and the church for the 'ownership' of these texts. No one perspective can embrace all the complexities, and what follows is no exception. There is now a plethora of stories recounting this same history from different perspectives and for different purposes.[1] The common view is that academic biblical studies evolved rapidly over the last thirty years as the historical-critical method was joined first by literary-critical approaches and latterly by a concentration on readers. I will look briefly at developments from three different but closely related viewpoints: philosophical, methodological and theological. The aim will then be to speculate on how these developments might or might not impact on ordinary churchgoers and what they mean for an empirical study of Bible reading.

Philosophy and Culture Shaping Biblical Studies

From one perspective, biblical study in the academy has followed developments in Western culture since the Enlightenment. It was the rise of modernity that began to separate the interpretation of the Bible from the 'dogmatic clutches' of the church and to allow the text to be examined rationally and objectively. In practice, this meant historically and, in common with approaches to all ancient literature, the dominant aim was to understand the origins of the text, and especially the intentions and context of the author. By the middle of the last century, academic study of the Bible was almost entirely driven by this philosophical paradigm (Bray 1996: 223).

From about the 1960s, various cultural changes began to challenge the assumptions of modernity. Several writers have pointed out that these changes came from different quarters and lacked a simple cause (Lyon 1999). What did unite them was a rejection of those things associated with modernity: the idea of the 'meta-narrative', the notion of objectivity and the supremacy of rationality. The term used to describe this flux is 'postmodernity', which is notoriously difficult to pinpoint or

---

[1]   Perhaps the most thorough overview from the perspective of hermeneutical theory is Thiselton (1992). Other accounts can be found in Segovia (1995a; 1995b), Bray (1996), Thiselton (1998), and Metzger and Coogan (2001) among many others.

define.[2] However they are defined, postmodern beliefs, attitudes and understandings have certainly shifted the focus of academic biblical scholarship. The search for objective, rational truth has been replaced, or at least eclipsed, by the notion of different 'readings' of scripture that fight shy of any claim to universal truth.

In terms of biblical hermeneutics, Thiselton (1992: 11; 1998) identifies the work of Hans-Georg Gadamer as giving a decisive impetus and philosophical underpinning to much of what followed. Although Gadamer was not usually considered a postmodern philosopher as such, his challenge to the already crumbling edifice of objective criticism was timely and decisive (Weinsheimer 1985: 16). Gadamer stressed both the contingency of each 'actualization' of a text and the importance of tradition in allowing communities to make practical evaluations of texts. His ideas have sparked both developments and counter-arguments that have led to the growing importance of hermeneutics as a discipline of philosophy. This philosophical debate has mingled with ideologically driven cultural movements such as feminism, Marxism and post-colonialism. The result has been the kind of interpretation typified by what Fernando Segovia (1995b) terms 'cultural studies'. In contrast to its modernist predecessors, this approach sees interpretation as the interaction of texts with readers who come from particular social locations, and who therefore create particular and local meanings.[3]

Biblical studies with a postmodern basis have by no means achieved the sort of monopoly previously enjoyed by historical criticism. Instead, different methods are used by different schools, or even within the same school. Scholars are increasingly aware of the assumptions underlying their own particular approach, and there is a reluctance to universalize findings and opinions. The mingling of these powerful currents has left the world of biblical studies in something of a flux: the word 'crisis' has more than once been linked to the discipline. This perhaps reflects the fact that a once-dominant philosophical paradigm has been toppled, but by no means eliminated. Without a single, accepted philosophical basis for establishing meaning, consensus is hard to achieve and those who practice in the guild today have to accept that, for a growing number of scholars, how the Bible is read and interpreted depends strongly on who is reading it.

Changing Methods in Biblical Studies

This changing philosophical and cultural climate has spawned a wide range of new methods for studying the Bible in the academy. These are now so well documented and described that only a brief summary is needed here.[4]

---

    2   See, for example, Lyon (1999: 7–24) or Alvesson (2002: 18–46). Adam (1995: xii) reminds us that defining postmodernity is a preoccupation more suited to modernity.

    3   Postmodern academic study of the Bible is not a 'method' as such, but a range of styles of reading. The characteristics of these ways of reading have been summarized by Adam (1995; 2004), Aichele et al. (1995), Brueggemann (1997), Fowler et al. (2004), Jobling et al. (2001), Keegan (1995) and Segovia (1995b).

    4   Useful description and discussion of some of these methods can be found in Adam (1995), Anderson and Moore (1992), Barton (1998), Coggins and Houlden (1990), Gillingham

Historical-critical studies such as source, form or redaction criticism sought the world 'behind' the text. The text was mined for clues that revealed its origin, construction and purpose, much as an archaeologist excavates an ancient burial mound in order to recreate the lives of the occupants from the clues they leave behind. These were the methods of rational modernity, driven by a belief that the history thus created was, by and large, an objective account that was free from religious censorship or observer bias. If the information generated by such an enterprise seemed distant or irrelevant to the faithful, that was deliberately so. The chief aim was to show what the text meant then, not what it might mean today.

Historical methods were then joined by literary studies, which took their lead from the New Criticism and Structuralism developed by secular literary scholars in the early to midtwentieth century. Spurred by Wimsatt and Beardsley's seminal article 'The intentional fallacy',[5] these scholars abandoned the search for the author's intention and focused instead on the world 'within' the text. The aim was to understand how the words, structures and images in the text combined to shape meaning. The approach was still very modernist, with the assumption that literary structures of meaning were objective entities that pointed to the understandings passed from author to readers. Literary critics soon realized that these were not necessarily the *real* author or *real* readers, but their counterparts implied by the text and constructed by scholarly analysis. This sort of analysis began to find a home in biblical studies in the 1970s and 1980s. Although the more extreme forms of Structuralism failed to make much headway, narrative and poetic analyses have become widespread and commonplace.

The rise of reader-centred approaches has had a much more complex history. One strand evolved from literary critics who became interested in how texts actually affect readers and guide them in the reading process. Thus began an interest in real 'flesh and blood' readers rather than their implied counterparts. Another strand arose from ideological challenges to the hegemony of white, male, European biblical scholars who assumed that their way of reading the text could be understood by all. Feminist, liberation, black (now African-American) and post-colonial approaches all stressed the importance of the social location of readers (Segovia and Tolbert 1995a, 1995b). These literary and ideological approaches have been joined by others that either directly draw on postmodern insights (Adam 1995; Aichele et al. 1995), or are heavily influenced by the individuality of the reader (Kitzberger 1999).

The result is that the study of the Bible in the academy in the late twentieth and early twenty-first centuries has become a many-headed beast. Those who in the early days prophesied the end of historical criticism were unduly optimistic (or pessimistic, depending on their views), and historical approaches continue unabated, boosted by a growing interest in evidence beyond the biblical texts and from insights from social science (Esler 1994; Richter 1995; Whitelam 1998). What has changed is the loss of the monopoly of method and the consensus of what counts as legitimate

---

(1998), Haynes and McKenzie (1999), Hayes (1999), McCartney and Clayton (1994), Shillington (2002) and Tate (1997) among others.

   [5]   Wimsatt and Beardsley (1971). This article has been reproduced in many places, but was first published in the *Sewanee Review* in 1946.

criteria for academic study of scripture. While the majority of work is still very much within the style of academic discourse, some of the material is rooted almost entirely in subjectivity.[6]

Theological Approaches to Biblical Studies

One of the effects of the rational study of the Bible associated with modernity was the desire among some scholars to separate study of the text from the claims of systematic theology. Most writers on the subject point to the work of Johann Philipp Gabler in the late eighteenth century as giving the initial rationale and method to this process. Gabler's strategy was to start with a historical study of the text, then to compare different ideas presented by different authors and finally to distil from this comparison the universal and timeless truths that would shape the development of systematic theology (Childs 1993: 4–5). In practice, the enterprise of creating such a synthesis proved an impossible dream. As scholarship grew it spawned increasingly specialized disciplines which separated the study of theology from the study of the Bible, and which made it difficult for one person to study both Old and New Testaments. Biblical theology seemed to require a unity of thought that was hard to attain in the ever-fragmenting world of scholarship (Fowl 1997: xiii). Perhaps for this reason, the creation of a 'biblical theology' in the twentieth century was marked by a number of false starts. Attempts to counter the perceived weaknesses of liberal Protestant theology or historical criticism were themselves prone to attack on philosophical or methodological grounds.[7]

Joel Green (2002) contends that all these attempts to revive the link between biblical studies and theology failed because they were based on the same 'linear hermeneutics' espoused by Gabler. The linearity is the assumption that biblical study proceeds along isolated stages of identifying past meaning and then creating a theology for today. Green represents a growing number of theological interpreters who point out the impossibility of creating a biblical theology by starting with the detached, critical stance of historicism.[8] This counter-reaction to the rejection of 'confessional' reading within the academy has partly drawn on postmodern understandings of the

---

[6]   A good example are some of the essays collected in *The Personal Voice in Biblical Interpretation* (Kitzberger 1999). These draw on the method of 'autobiographical criticism' (Anderson and Staley 1995), which makes individual experience the key to interpreting the text.

[7]   Morgan (1990) refers to Karl Barth and especially Rudolf Bultmann as offering the most influential synthesis of biblical scholarship and modern theology in the twentieth century, though he is scathing about subsequent developments in the English-speaking world. The rise and decline of the Biblical Theology Movement in the United States is described from an interesting, postmodern perspective by Penchansky (1995).

[8]   Green makes this distinction clear when he writes: 'Reading the Bible as Christian scripture means acknowledging the relation between the words of scripture and the ongoing presence of the crucified Christ, who is Lord of the church. Such a hermeneutic finds its orientation not in an objective reading of biblical texts but in the creative and redemptive aims of God that come to their most visible expression in Jesus of Nazareth, the Word become flesh' (Green 2002: 19–20).

importance of reader stance in creating meaning from texts. Given the now widely accepted view that a neutral stance is neither possible nor desirable, many Christian scholars are suggesting that confessional (that is theological) readings treat the Bible in a way that the texts themselves demand. This is reading 'with the grain' rather than 'against the grain'.[9]

Some interpreters have gone so far as to suggest that theological interpretation is the *only* legitimate way to approach sacred texts. Francis Watson (1994) sparked a lively debate by suggesting that this way of reading scripture should be the sole interest of academic study of the Bible. Philip Davies (1995) was quick to counter this with the opposite view that faith-based study of the Bible has no place in secular, state-run universities. While not all theological interpreters would go as far as Watson,[10] there is a drive to reconnect biblical and theological studies in a way that is unafraid to argue that sacred scriptures read without a sense of their sacredness cannot be understood in any meaningful way. This movement is important because it has begun to reverse the separation of biblical scholarship from faith communities, a separation that was in danger of leading the academic community into a narrow, reductionist view of the nature of biblical interpretation.

Implications for Ordinary Churchgoers

The developments I have just described have been mainly issues within the discourse of academic biblical studies rather than within the church at large. Just how far these currents of change have affected the religious community of ordinary churchgoers is unclear. If philosophical movements have rocked the foundations of the academic study of the Bible, have they had an equally dramatic effect on the religious life of ordinary people? An example of how difficult it can be to link philosophical or cultural movements to religious faith is the long-running and intense debate about secularization and the decline in church attendance in western Europe. 'Secularization theory' has its roots in the nineteenth century with the work of Auguste Comte, Emile Durkheim and Max Weber. It was developed in the twentieth century by Bryan Wilson (1966) and Peter Berger (1969), and has more recently been championed by Steve Bruce (2002). The theory has been elaborated in many directions, but at its core is the idea that religious affiliation has declined in western Europe because people have become secularized by modernity. This perception of an inevitable decline of religious belief and practice in the face of growing human knowledge, rationality and technology has been vigorously challenged from several directions (Cox 2003).[11]

---

[9]   Recent works include Ford and Stanton (2003), Fowl (1997; 1998), Green and Turner (2000), Vanhoozer (1998) and Watson (1994; 1997).

[10]   Stephen Fowl (1997: xxviii, note 10), for example, positions himself somewhere between the two, and elsewhere argues that faith communities should use the results of secular scholarship where they are helpful, but not if they are unhelpful (Fowl 1998: 179–190). He terms this 'plundering the Egyptians'.

[11]   Some, such as Robin Gill (1993; 2003), have cast doubt on the extent of the decline; others, such as Callum Brown (2001), argue that other social forces were more important in

Whatever the merits of these different arguments, the question remains as to whether modernity is inevitably inimical to religious faith, and therefore whether or not present-day churchgoers represent a shrinking cohort of people with a pre-modern world view in a modern world. If the latter is true, then modernity may not have penetrated the rank and file of regular churchgoers, which in turn implies that they are unlikely to understand modernist approaches to biblical interpretation. If, on the other hand, modernity is not the chief cause of decline, those who remain in churches may be no more or less 'modern' than the rest of society.

Some scholars certainly assume that the majority of ordinary citizens in the West have acquired the outlook of modernity and can only understand the Bible on these terms. Rudolf Bultmann's famous attempt to demythologize the Bible was in order to make the ancient text have meaning for modern people, on the assumption that modernity was the dominant mindset of the time (Bultmann 1972). This may not, as we have seen, be the case. My impression from worshipping in a variety of churches over the last thirty years is that the kind of scholarship associated with modernity, with its heavy emphasis on rationality and rejection of the supernatural, does not play well in many congregations, where mention of the latest ideas of theologians is the surest way of getting a laugh in an otherwise dull sermon. Modernist study of the Bible has seemed to reduce its meaning and value as a sacred text in ways that often appear incomprehensible or risible to those at the heart of the faith community. However, it may also be the case that churches have lost precisely those people who need to find modernist ways of appropriating biblical truths and retained those who continue to prefer a pre-critical use of the Bible.

Postmodernity has been the subject of much discussion in the church. In biblical studies, some have hailed it as an opportunity for faith-based studies to stand on equal ground with secular studies, while others see its rejection of absolute truth as diametrically opposed to the fundamental tenets of Christianity (Brubaker 1997; Gulley 1995; Harrington and Patten 1994; Keegan 1995; Lyon 2000; Menzies 1994; Noble 1994, 1995; Vanhoozer 2003; Wilkinson 1997). The impact goes much further than biblical studies, however, and more and more commentators are aware of the problems and possibilities raised for the church in general by postmodernity (Braaten and Jenson 2002; Dockery 1995; Goodliff 1998; Johnston 2001; Lyon 2000; Murray 2004). It is unlikely that many churchgoers are aware of these academic debates between modernists and postmodernists, but this does not mean that they are unaffected by the different world views. Modernity is not a natural world view: subjectivity is reflexive, objectivity must be learnt. This means that education may be an important factor in determining how far ordinary Bible readers have appropriated a modernist outlook. Postmodernity may also have to be learnt (perhaps a better term is 'absorbed') from the multiple sources of information available to an increasing proportion of people in the developed and developing worlds. The chronological

---

leading to secularization. Gill, Hadaway and Marler (1998) analysed British survey data from the 1920s to 1990s and concluded there has been a decline in belief in God and in traditional Christian beliefs among the general population, but not a decline in belief in the transcendent. This move from traditional Christian belief to a more general spirituality has been noted by other researchers (e.g. Heelas and Woodhead 2004).

link between the growth in postmodernity, youth culture and media technology may partly explain why this world view seems to be associated with the more media-savvy, younger generations (Osgerby 2004). If postmodernity is mainly associated with younger people there may be a complex interaction between world view, age and educational experience. Older people with experience of higher education may be trained in the objectivity associated with modernity, but this may be increasingly less so among younger graduates and postgraduates. Both groups may nonetheless share a critical ability not found in those who have little experience of handling texts, and whose last formal Bible study was in Sunday school. Church congregations, no less than the community of scholars, may now represent a rich collage of differing world views and outlooks.

What of the methodological changes that have swept biblical scholarship in recent years: how much difference have they made to ordinary Bible readers? Since I have earlier defined 'ordinary' as 'not trained in biblical scholarship', the obvious answer would be 'not at all'. However, it might still be the case that approaches developed by academics gradually filter into congregations through leaders, teachers and preachers who are trained in seminaries that are part of the academic community. Ordinary churchgoers may pick up these ideas and approaches to the Bible through church Bible studies, Bible reading notes or from the pulpit, without actually being trained to use or critically evaluate them.

Scholarship certainly does influence the hierarchy of churches, as illustrated by the way that historical study has gradually become part of church scholarship in many mainstream churches ranging from Pentecostalism (see Chapter 8) to the Roman Catholic Church. The Pontifical Biblical Commission (PBC) report shows how far the Roman Catholic Church has mellowed from its initial hostility to the historical-critical method.[12] By the 1990s there had been a remarkable metamorphosis, so that the PBC reflects a generally accepting attitude to historical criticism and an open, but cautious, attitude to other 'scientific' methods of interpretation. Ironically, the real venom is reserved for 'fundamentalist interpretation', which is singled out for special attack:

> [Fundamentalism] accepts the literal reality of an ancient, out-of-date cosmology simply because it is found expressed in the Bible ... The fundamentalist approach is dangerous, for it is attractive to people who look to the Bible for ready answers to the problems of life. It can deceive these people, offering them interpretations that are pious but illusory ... Without saying as much in so many words, fundamentalism actually invites people to a kind of intellectual suicide. It injects into life a false certitude, for it unwittingly confuses the divine substance of the biblical message with what are in fact its human limitations. (Houlden 1995: 45–6)

The criticisms of fundamentalism made by the PBC are reminiscent of attacks on the Catholic Church by historical-critical scholars,[13] and show how much the

---

[12] The report is reproduced and reviewed by Houlden (1995).
[13] James Barr (1973: 105), renowned for his attacks on fundamentalism, writes: 'the official Roman Catholic position has for a long time had remarkable similarities to the fundamentalist position'.

church began to embrace historical interpretation in the last half of the twentieth century. This acceptance of the need to take into account historical issues when reading the Bible is now widespread in all mainstream denominations. It surfaces, though not necessarily in full academic guise, in more popular material such as Bible study notes and in films and television documentaries. A quick scan of Bible notes produced by organizations such as the Bible Reading Fellowship or the Scripture Union shows that commentators often refer to the historical background of the text in order to draw out contemporary lessons for their readers. Mel Gibson's film *The Passion of the Christ* (2004) was controversial for many reasons, not least because it seemed to make a claim for historical authenticity that could hardly be imagined in earlier Hollywood portrayals of the life of Jesus (Beal and Linafelt 2006; Garber 2006). Television documentaries that try to recreate the history of biblical events and interpret them in modern terms have developed their own particular genre in recent years.[14] Although these examples might not be classed as historical-critical, they nonetheless show a desire to understand the history that underlies the Bible.

Historical ways of understanding the Bible are increasingly common in churches, though as we shall see in Chapter 4, they may not necessarily have much currency among some churchgoers. Literary approaches are also surfacing, though again not in academic guise. There are a few popular Bible commentaries that are based on a literary reading, and there is a growing stress on the use of story in preaching.[15] It is probably too early to judge the impact of more overtly postmodern approaches to Scripture on ordinary churchgoers, and reactions among church scholars have been mixed.[16] Some have hailed this liberation from modernity as a great opportunity for the church to wrestle biblical study back from the hands of experts by giving respectability to the kind of reading that has always gone on in churches. Some scholarly work does seem to support this view, but others most certainly does not. Some of the articles in Kitzberger (1999) illustrate this well. Maria Co writes as a Filipino steeped in the tradition of Ignatius of Loyola, and her reading of John's gospel involves a typically Ignatian use of the imagination to enter into the world of the text. Such a reading, she says, runs counter to her training in doctoral studies but clearly reflects her early exposure to texts in the context of faith, prayer and contemplation. While this approach may be a radical departure for an academic

---

[14] I have in mind programmes such as *Son of God*, produced by the BBC in 2001 and presented by Jeremy Bowen, and more recently *The Miracles of Jesus*, produced by the BBC in 2006 and presented by Rageh Omar. Both programmes examined in detail the historical background of Jesus of Nazareth and were used in Christian circles to encourage debate and evangelism.

[15] Some recent guides to preaching (e.g. Edwards 2005; Frymire 2006; Massey 2006) are an example of a trend that is probably driven both by the general postmodern tendency to convey truth through story, and the more specific growth of literary approaches to biblical interpretation.

[16] Something of the tension within evangelical circles can be seen in the articles edited by Dockery (1995), especially Dan Stiver's response to Anthony Thiselton (pp. 239–53). In Pentecostalism, the debate is evident in the issues of *Pneuma, The Journal of Pentecostal Studies* published in 1993 and 1994. See especially Cargal (1993), Harrington and Patten (1994) and Menzies (1994).

critic, it would raise few eyebrows if adopted in a church Bible study. These slightly detached essays are in stark contrast to the much more personal approach of, say, Jeffrey Staley or Stephen Moore in the same volume. Moore's 'Revolting revelations' begins with a summary of various parts of his life including drug taking, Christian conversion, current agnosticism/atheism and a previous homosexual affair. From this starting point he tackles the book of Revelation in the form of a frank conversation with himself that includes explicit sexual material and some four-letter words that would certainly not go down well in the average congregation. While some (but by no means all) fellow scholars might find his approach interesting, refreshing and entertaining, this method of dealing with scripture seems to have little to do with any attempt to understand or to help lay people interpret the Bible.

The postmodern trend that links the text so closely to those who read it also jeopardizes the objectivity and universality of truth claims that most churchgoers would want to affirm for their scriptures. For this reason, some have warned that these methods of biblical study may be a Trojan horse containing ideas that could fundamentally undermine traditional Christian forms of understanding scripture.

Implications for an Empirical Study of Bible Reading

The various changes in philosophy and methodological approach that have swept over academic biblical studies have several implications for anyone undertaking an empirical study of Bible reading among ordinary churchgoers. The first is the need to be aware of the philosophical background of empirical study, which is very much the child of modernity. Empirical study, and especially quantitative empirical study, is an exercise in objectivity and rationality. It quantifies in order to objectify and assumes that this helps to dispel some of the bias and self-delusion that can accompany subjective engagement. As we have seen, this sort of method runs counter to current fashions of biblical study in the academy, as well as to the sort of pre-critical use of the Bible likely to be encountered in churches. The central goal of this study risks being dismissed by academics and churchgoers alike. I have persisted with such an approach in the belief that the current fashion may be just that, and that the value of empirical study may remain when postmodernity it has run its course. One has only to look at the extraordinary success of the biological, medical and physical sciences to see that empirical method, for all its faults, is a powerful way of describing complex systems. However, the recent developments in the philosophy of hermeneutics are a useful reminder that in this area of endeavour, as much as any, it is important to understand the limitations of method.

A second implication arises from the complexity of biblical interpretation in both academy and church. The possibility now exists that churchgoers have been influenced by a wide range of world views and philosophies. Just as biblical studies are now highly heterogeneous in the academy, so churchgoers may bring to the Bible a wide range of beliefs, experiences and practices. Such diversity is perhaps unusual historically, but seems to be typical of this period of history as cultural movements evolve and collide. A single empirical study of a phenomenon such as 'ordinary Bible reading' cannot possibly describe all of this complexity and diversity. Whatever is found could well be countered by other results from different samples, or by looking at different aspects of the same group. This does not undermine the task, but it is worth bearing in mind that whereas uniform systems are easily described by a handful of studies and small samples, complex systems take longer to understand or analyse. It has been clear for some time that academic biblical studies are in a state of flux: the same may true for the role of the Bible in church congregations.

A third implication of this diversity is the need to be cautious in interpreting empirical data of ordinary Bible reading. Although pre-critical and postmodern approaches to the Bible may appear to be rather similar, postmodernity is nonetheless the child of modernity. Postmodern interpreters are *post*-critical rather than *pre*-critical: that is, they are aware of the issues of objectivity and rationality, even if they choose to interpret from a particular, subjective standpoint. The discourse of postmodernity in the academy has been a hermeneutic of suspicion, questioning the motives embedded in texts and the use to which they are put by their interpreters. Approaching the Bible with a critical mindset has the inevitable effect of alienating it from the reader. If, as Paul Ricoeur suggests, the aim is to reach a stage where the distant, critically-dissected text once again speaks with primal power and energy, this 'second naivety' has a different origin and nature from the 'first naivety' of the pre-critical reader. Although academics may be all too aware of the water that has flowed under the bridge, this does not mean that others are. Empirical study is often about observing effects in order to uncover causes. Sometimes the same effect can have two very different causes, and this might be true in biblical interpretation.

In what follows, I try to quantify effects, test ideas about causes and then draw some theological conclusions from what I have observed. Such theological speculation would not be warranted if this were simply an exercise in empirical description. However, description by itself might not connect with those who toil in the fields of biblical study in academy or church. The theological aspect of empirical theological description requires some degree of prescription, as well as simple description (Astley 2002: 108). Clear empirical description would be a good starting point, and one that will require much more than this study to complete, but the end result has to make some connection to both the academic scholar and the churchgoer. To do this requires some sort of theological engagement with the empirical data. I have tried to do this in each of the following chapters, alongside drawing some practical implications for churches from the empirical findings. In the final chapter I draw some of the main findings together, and suggest how an empirical approach to Bible reading might begin to inform a theology of scripture.

Chapter 3

The Bible and Ordinary Readers

Attitude, Belief and Behaviour

A person's relationship to a sacred text such as the Bible encompasses a number of different aspects. Among these are their attitude towards the Bible, their beliefs about the Bible and their use of the Bible. It would not be surprising if these were related to each other: people who have negative attitudes towards the Bible are unlikely to believe that it has any divinely ordained authority, and probably read it seldom if ever. Those who believe it to be the word of God will presumably have a positive attitude to it and will be more likely to read it. This broad generalization hides a more complex picture in which attitudes, beliefs and practices are distinct aspects of a holistic relationship to scripture. Before examining some empirical evidence about this relationship, it is helpful to clarify what is meant by each of these concepts.

An attitude is a basic disposition towards something or somebody. Psychological theories about attitude have a long and complex history (Fishbein and Ajzen 1975), but most psychologists and sociologists would agree that attitudes refer to feelings or dispositions directed towards objects in the broadest sense. In technical terms, an attitude is a 'bipolar affective dimension', which defines a disposition that can be positive, negative or neutral. Attitudes towards the Bible might include a positive reverence, respect and submission to the text, or a negative profanity, disrespect and rejection. Even indifference could be seen as an attitude towards the Bible, implying a neutral disposition somewhere in the middle of a bipolar scale. The key point is that attitudes tend to be directed towards something, and evaluate it in a way that is rooted more in our emotions than in our thoughts. Attitudes are hard to measure directly and psychologists usually infer a person's attitudes from other things such as behaviour, intentions or beliefs.

Beliefs are specific ideas or thoughts about something. In technical terms, belief occurs when an attribute is linked to an object: existence may be linked to God, trustworthiness to your vicar or the presence of life to Mars. In the case of the Bible, beliefs might relate to how it came to be written, its veracity, its role in the life of the church and its authority for individual believers. Beliefs about the Bible have shaped the history of the Christian faith, and lie at the heart of the main fault lines within the Church. Ordinary readers may be largely oblivious of the theological debates about the Bible, but most are likely to have some beliefs about it. These may or may not be linked to their attitude towards the Bible. Conservative and liberal Christians may have different beliefs about the Bible, but share a positive attitude towards it. Similarly, two people who believe that the Bible is the revealed word of God may have a very different attitude to it: one may be liberated by the revelation of divine love; the other may live in fear of judgement by an all-powerful deity.

Behaviour refers to specific physical responses such as what we do with our time, how we spend our money or how we vote. The behavioural aspects of our relationship to the Bible include how and when we encounter the Bible and the behaviour that stems from that encounter. I use 'encounter' because many Christians never actually read the Bible for themselves. This has been true throughout history and is no less true today in 'literate' societies. Many churchgoers in Britain encounter the Bible mainly when it is read liturgically in church. A smaller number may study it in groups, or read it during personal devotions. Very few people read the Bible in the manner of those trained in the academy. If you are reading this sort of book, your behaviour suggests you are not an 'ordinary reader', and you are likely to read the Bible more often than most churchgoers. You may also have a different way of interpreting the Bible, related to your interest in it and whatever academic training you have had. More generally, the frequency of Bible reading, and the context in which it takes place, might tell us something about how it is likely to be interpreted.

We could broaden the definition of behaviour to include things that are done or said in response to encountering the Bible. Those who believe that God speaks to them through the Bible are likely to want to respond to what it says. How the text is used is a key part of the relationship between believers and their scripture, be it as a lamp to guide their path, a shield to defend their faith or stick with which to beat their enemies. This book is mainly trying to explore some of the things that might shape the way that readers make sense of the Bible. The issue of the consequences of Bible reading, in terms of the attitudes, beliefs or behaviours it induces, is not the main subject of this book, though as we shall see, it is not always easy to separate causes and consequences in this field of study.

The Relationship of Attitudes, Beliefs and Behaviours

So how might attitudes towards, beliefs about and use of the Bible be related? Beliefs are likely to be related to attitudes, but this relationship may not be simple. Some social scientists see beliefs as manifestations of underlying attitudes. For others, beliefs are what create attitudes in the first place. Either way, one would expect a fairly close relationship between a particular belief and the attitude to which it relates. However, social scientists have often failed to predict *particular* beliefs from *general* attitudes. One of the more influential models linking beliefs, attitudes and behaviours assumes attitudes are shaped by *sets* of beliefs (Fishbein and Ajzen 1975). This model has been successful in explaining why it is that attitudes can be based on beliefs, even though people sometimes believe things that are contrary to their attitudes. Thus someone may have a very high regard for the Bible because they believe that it is the inerrant word of God, divinely inspired and the final authority in all matters of faith and conduct. Having a 'Bible-believing' attitude does not necessarily mean that people believe everything in scripture should be obeyed. Other beliefs may mitigate basic beliefs about the Bible so that, for example, current practices overrule first-century ones when it comes to what to wear, or not wear, in church. This is not a 'mistake' or an 'error', it is simply the reality of how beliefs normally relate to attitudes.

Attitudes and beliefs are generally thought to shape our behaviour but, again, the link is far from straightforward. Psychologists and sociologists have often found it difficult to predict specific behaviour from general attitudes. Fishbein and Ajzen suggested that attitudes shape our intentions, and it is intentions that lead to specific behaviours. They suggested that individual attitudes interact with 'social norms' in order to shape specific intentions. In other words, we match our own views about doing something with what other people will think about us doing it. In their model, intentions can predict action fairly well, provided the intention and action are narrowly defined and close in time. The intention to 'vote in tomorrow's election' will probably predict tomorrow's behaviour better than a general attitude that 'people ought to use their vote'.

Research on religion has often tended to assume that beliefs, attitudes and behaviour are closely linked. This produces a simpler picture in our minds, but it may not accord with reality. Are 'Bible-believing' Christians the only ones who have a positive attitude towards the Bible? Does frequent reading or hearing of the Bible automatically imply more conservative beliefs about it? The rest of this chapter reviews what information there is on attitudes, beliefs and reading practices associated with the Bible.

Attitude towards the Bible among Ordinary Readers

Empirical evidence on people's attitude towards the Bible comes from two main types of survey: those measuring attitude towards Christianity (or Judaism) in general, and those specifically measuring attitude towards the Bible. The former tell us something about how much the Bible is part of religious life, but may tell us rather little about the scope and nature of attitude towards the Bible. The latter give more detail, but there have been few specific surveys to date.

In the latter half of the twentieth century there was a growing interest in studying religion among psychologists and social scientists, particularly in the United States. This spawned a host of inventories and questionnaires designed to assess attitudes towards, and beliefs about, religion.[1] Many of these contained items about the Bible because researchers assumed that attitude towards the Bible was linked to attitude towards Judaism or Christianity in general. Although many scales of religiosity contain items about the Bible, rather few of them have yielded useful information about attitude towards the Bible. Many items measure beliefs about the Bible, or Bible-reading practice (to which I will turn later), but not many have tried specifically to ask about attitudes. Those that do measure attitudes have not always reported item results independently, so it is not possible to tell anything specific about attitude towards the bible. An exception is the now widely used 'Attitude Toward Christianity' scale (Francis 1978; Francis and Stubbs 1987). This scale was originally developed for use with children, was later converted for use with adults, and has been applied to a wide range of people. It contains two items about the Bible:

---

[1]   Hill and Hood (1999) is a thorough compendium of measures of religious attitudes and beliefs.

'I find it boring to listen to the Bible' and 'I think the Bible is out of date'. Both these items are tapping into attitude towards the Bible, rather than what someone believes about the Bible or how often they might read it. The rest of the scale contains similar sorts of items that refer to church-going, prayer and the reality of God.

One way relating attitude to the Bible with attitudes to other aspects of religion is to look for correlations between answers to the 'Bible' items and answers to other items. The first thing to note about the Francis scale is that it is a one-dimensional scale, so that all the items are positively correlated with one another. This tells us that a positive attitude towards the Bible is linked, as we might expect, to a positive attitude towards other aspects of Christianity. However, a more detailed look suggests that the link is not as close as it might be. Correlations between the Bible items and others in the Francis scale have been reported from several different groups of people (teenagers, undergraduates and adults) and different countries including the UK, USA, Australia and Canada (Francis 1992; Francis et al. 1995; Francis and Stubbs 1987). In each case, the correlations between the two Bible items and the rest are among the lowest four of the 24 items. A lower correlation from a single sample would not indicate anything, but the fact that both items are *consistently* lower across such a range of samples suggests that attitude towards the Bible might be a distinct subset of attitude towards Christianity in general.

The correlations do not show if attitude towards the Bible is more positive or negative than other attitudes. Where actual scores have been reported (Francis 1989) the indication is that people may have a more positive attitude to the Bible than to other aspects of religion, and this seems to be borne out by studies that have specifically measured attitude towards the Bible. In the 1970s, the Bible Society sponsored a series of surveys in the UK that assessed matters related to the Bible. This culminated in a door-to-door survey across the country, which used a Thurstone-type scale developed by the society called the 'Attitudes to the Bible Scale' (Harrison 1983; Hartberg 1980).[2] This scale consisted of 14 items referring to beliefs about the Bible ('The Bible is God's message to all mankind') and items that reflected more general attitudes to the Bible ('The Bible seems like a very boring book'). The survey sampled 1136 people across England and provided a useful snapshot of attitude towards the Bible among the general population in the early 1980s.

At that time, around 80% of households had a Bible and about 12% of the population read the Bible at least once a week. In general, attitude towards the Bible was favourable and, compared with other similar scales, indicated a slightly more favourable attitude to the Bible than to God or the church. There was little difference in attitude between regions or social classes, but there were other differences that reflected general trends in religious attitudes: women were generally more favourable than men, and older people more favourable than younger ones. What was perhaps more surprising was the high regard for the Bible among people who hardly, if ever, attended church. Among such people, around 62% agreed that the Bible was 'God's

---

[2] A Thurstone scale contains items that range evenly between those that indicate a very positive attitude to those that indicate a very negative attitude. Scales are calibrated using a panel of judges, so that there is some confidence that a high score on the scale indicates a positive attitude and a low score a negative one.

message to all mankind'. So even those who probably knew little about what the Bible says had a high regard for what it represents.

This high regard for the Bible was reflected in a more recent and ad hoc survey reported by David Clines (1997) at the University of Sheffield. He sent students on his Bible and the Modern World class to survey people in the town. They too found that more people owned a Bible than actually read it, and that there was a surprisingly high regard for the Bible, even among people who knew little about it.

Attitudes to the Bible are bound to be more positive among regular churchgoers than the population at large, but it would be wrong to assume that all churchgoers can easily explain what they feel towards the Bible and why. In 1988 a group of researchers in Durham sampled congregations across the Anglican diocese (Fisher et al. 1992). The survey included several items that related to attitudes towards the Bible. These centred on whether the Bible is an accurate guide to history, science, theology or ethics, and whether it is relevant today. Strictly, these sorts of questions probably measure belief about the Bible, rather than attitude towards it, but they were sufficiently general to indicate something about overall attitude towards the Bible. The researchers found that around half the sample of 445 agreed that the Bible was *not* an accurate guide to history, science or ethics. Fewer (27%) agreed that it was not an accurate guide to theology and nearly three-quarters disagreed with the notion that the Bible was irrelevant for today. What struck the researchers was the relatively high numbers in each case that were uncertain. This seemed to imply a high proportion (perhaps a third) of committed Anglican churchgoers whose attitude towards the Bible was not clearly formed one way or the other. Perhaps this stemmed from people who had not had to grapple with such issues before, a fact supported by the relatively low use of the Bible in this sample.

I am not aware of any other studies that have tried to measure attitude towards the Bible among the general population, either in Britain or elsewhere. The situation in Europe is probably very different from that in the United States, and within Britain attitudes towards the Bible may be changing rapidly. The high regard for the Bible among the general population may be declining rapidly now that it is no longer read or heard by most people. The perceived threat of terror that pervades Western societies at the moment has, rightly or wrongly, perceived links with religion. Religion in general is being blamed for many ills and divisions in today's world, and it seems likely that the scriptures of religions are going to be held in lower esteem than they were. In post-Christian, secular societies the Bible occupies an anachronistic niche. Although much of the current judicial and ethical structures of society arose from those who saw the Bible as the chief guide for public morality, the Bible and its religion are being sidelined in western Europe.

Beliefs about the Bible among Ordinary Readers

I have mentioned earlier the interrelatedness of attitudes and beliefs, so that much of what was said in the previous section could also be applied here. However, beliefs about the Bible are going to be more specific than attitude towards it, and such beliefs have been forged over a very long history. The preoccupation of clerics and academics with the nature of the Bible has spawned enough material in the last decade alone to fill several libraries, and it is not the purpose of this book to add to these particular debates. However, scholarly and theological debates do set the parameters for the beliefs of ordinary Bible readers, and have shaped the way that empirical studies have approached the subject.

The key beliefs that are likely to be important to ordinary Bible readers are those that are central to the debate between conservative evangelicals and liberals. These include beliefs about the origin of the Bible, its inspiration, inerrancy, literal truth and authority. These beliefs are likely to be linked because those who believe that the Bible is entirely human in origin may agree that it was inspired (in the sense of any other inspired human activity) but are unlikely to see it as entirely without error or as having final authority over their lives. Those who believe that the Bible writers were inspired in a unique way are more likely to believe that the Bible is without error.

Having said this, there has been considerable debate, even within evangelical circles, on just what these different ideas encompass,[3] and the difference between terms is sometimes hard to express. Much of the debate within evangelical circles has involved misunderstandings caused by using the same word for different beliefs, so that even guides intended for lay people require precise definitions and pedantic scrutiny of opposing arguments.[4] When scholars try to define exactly what is meant by terms such as inspiration, inerrancy and infallibility the result is such careful qualifications that some have suggested dropping terms like inerrancy altogether.[5] This minefield of complexity surrounding traditional beliefs about the Bible means that care must be taken in assessing such belief among lay people, who may use terms differently from academics or differently from each other.

Most of the information we have on what ordinary people believe about the Bible has been gathered as part of wider research interests, rather than by dedicated design. Items referring to the inerrancy or authority of the Bible have featured in a number of different questionnaires, mainly from the United States. Most studies were seeking to distinguish Christian belief from unbelief, and belief about the Bible was assumed to be correlated with other Christian beliefs. A good example is the 'Christian Orthodoxy Scale' (Fullerton and Hunsberger 1982), in which two of the 24 items refer to belief about the Bible.

A major problem with these kinds of questionnaires is that they assume that there is a single dimension of belief about the Bible that is related to religious (Christian) belief in general. Those who score high on belief in the existence of God, divinity of Christ or other key doctrines also score high on belief in the inerrancy and authority of the Bible. However, there are Christians who might uphold many orthodox

---

[3]   This debate has been most evident in the United States. The collection of essays in Conn (1988) gives some background to these debates, especially the bibliographic postscript by John Muether. Other useful collections are Geisler (1980), and Phillips and Okholm (1996).

[4]   For example, see Belcher (1980).

[5]   Feinberg (1980) illustrates the complexities of defining the term 'inerrancy': his definition comes with three qualifications and no fewer than eight 'misunderstandings' that need to be avoided.

doctrines yet do not have a traditional or evangelical view of the Bible. Liberal belief is easily confused with unbelief, a point made by Leslie Francis (1984), who attempted unsuccessfully to separate liberal belief from unbelief in a study of college students and ordinands. An earlier study by Hunt (1972) had developed the so-called 'Literal, Anti-literal and Mystical' (LAM) scales in a similar attempt to find a way of assessing committed yet non-literal belief. Hunt suggested that there were two alternatives for those who could not accept literal belief in some or all of the main Christian doctrines or biblical narratives. Anti-literal belief was characteristic of those who rejected literal belief and therefore saw no veracity in any of the religious claims of the Christian faith. This amounts to a non-religious stance or unbelief, at least with respect to Christianity. Others might reject literal belief, but nonetheless hold a faith position because they interpret stories symbolically and find the Bible is true, but not always literally true. Hunt termed this 'mystical belief', while others who followed up his work have used the term 'metaphorical' (van der Lans 1990). This sort of belief seems closest to liberal belief about the Bible. The key finding arising from using LAM scales is that it is necessary and possible to distinguish conservative from liberal beliefs about the Bible without confusing liberal belief with lack of belief.

The other area where beliefs about the Bible have featured as part of wider research concerns has been in studying religious affiliation among American Protestant denominations. The mobilization of the political right in the United States in the 1980s led to a spate of research on right-wing, fundamentalist Christianity (Boone 1989; Carpenter 1997; Jelen 1989b; Wilcox 1992). The need to identify the political voting patterns and aspirations of this section of the population encouraged researchers to try and develop simple ways of identifying different strands of conservative Christianity. Hitherto, most sociologists had simply grouped religious affiliations into broad categories such as Roman Catholic and Protestant. These divisions were poor predictors of voting patterns, not least because the term 'Protestant' covered anything from liberal Presbyterians to fundamentalists.

A search began to find questionnaire items that would discriminate between different Protestant groups on doctrinal grounds. Belief about the Bible seemed to be a likely candidate, but there was conflicting evidence about this. Nancy Ammerman (1982) suggested that belief about the creation story discriminated between fundamentalists and other evangelicals: fundamentalists, she argued, believed the story happened exactly as written whereas evangelicals preferred a less literal interpretation. However, using just one Bible story (the Genesis creation narrative) proved to be too narrow a focus because it was poorer at identifying fundamentalist believers than was a more general question about biblical literalism (Dixon et al. 1992). Smidt (1989) reviewed the questions used in various American surveys of Christian belief, and found that the exact phrasing of questions about the Bible had important consequences for interpreting the results. Questions about infallibility, inerrancy, inspiration and literalism might not clearly differentiate between evangelicals and other Protestants unless they were combined with other items about Christian belief and evangelism practice. The problems in multiple definitions of the same term seemed to rule out the use of doctrinally-loaded words in questionnaire items.

Another problem was that the nuances of different terms might be important to some groups and not others. Jelen (1989a) found that the distinction between literalism and inerrancy was lost among a large sample of white Protestants, who tended to answer questions about these beliefs in the same way. However, a telephone survey of 271 African Americans in Washington, DC suggested that the difference between a literalist and inerrant view of the Bible was indeed an understood and meaningful distinction among this group of lay people (Jelen et al. 1990).

The inability to find a workable group of reliable and universally valid doctrinal questions that would easily identify different religious groupings seems to have led to a loss of interest in this particular line of enquiry. The resurgence of political interest in the religious vote during George W. Bush's second-term election may lead to a revived interest in redefining the biblical beliefs of different Protestant groups in the USA, as evidenced by the Baylor Religion Survey (2005). What is clear in the meantime is, first, that using items with terms such as 'inerrancy', 'infallibility' and 'inspiration' in surveys may not necessarily clarify exactly what people believe about the Bible. Second, questions may need to be tailored to particular groups because some will be more aware and interested in distinctions in meaning than are others. Third, there may be a range of beliefs even within those who share the same broad outlook or denominational affiliation.

The Bible Scale in the Bible and Lay People Study

A central aim of the Bible and Lay People study was to develop a measure of belief about the Bible that was appropriate for Anglican churchgoers in England. It had to assess belief across the likely range of conservative to liberal belief in the denomination, though it was not necessary to accommodate total scepticism or disregard for the worth of the Bible because this is a very unlikely position for any churchgoer. Pilot interviews and searches of the literature suggested that the key poles of the conservative–liberal axis in the Church of England could be characterized thus:

Conservatives understand the Bible as the inspired word of God, authoritative to the life of believers, which contains sufficient and exclusive truth for salvation. The Bible is believed to give a true account of events as recorded, and passages have a meaning that is universally true and clearly evident to those who have faith. Additional conservative beliefs include a rejection of divorce, homosexuality, sex before marriage or abortion as right ways to behave, and a rejection of other religions as means of access to God or to salvation.

For liberals, the Bible is inspired truth about God, important in the life of believers, but not necessarily authoritative in all matters. It contains a mixture of literal and symbolic truth and some human errors. What the Bible means may depend on who is reading it, and its truth stands alongside truth about God from other religions. There may be an acceptance of divorce, homosexuality, sex before marriage and possibly abortion as desirable, unavoidable or morally neutral behaviours, and an acceptance of the validity of other belief systems, especially other religions.

The key differences in terms of Bible belief concern the extent to which the Bible might be literally versus symbolically true, the extent to which it might contain errors of fact, the degree to which its truths are exclusive to Christianity or available from other faiths, and the extent of biblical authority. The issues of inerrancy, infallibility and inspiration were important, but it seemed unlikely that most participants would be familiar with the detailed distinctions made by some scholars.

I developed a large pool of items and tested them in pilot studies. Of these, twelve seemed to cover the range of beliefs about the Bible in the Church of England (see Table 3.1). What do the items in this 'Bible scale' tell us about ordinary churchgoers in the Church of England? There are two ways of investigating the results: one is to look at individual items and the other is to analyse the score for the scale as a whole. Examining individual items gives some idea of the range of beliefs among lay Anglicans in England. The marked differences between different traditions means that the overall results depend strongly on how many people of each tradition were in the final sample. Nonetheless, looking at results within each tradition gives some idea of the frequency of different beliefs.

Table 3.1   Items used in the Bible scale

Items	AC %	BC %	EV %	All %
The Bible contains some human errors*	89	71	46	63
I have never found the Bible to be wrong about anything	12	24	51	35
Science shows that some things in the Bible cannot have happened*	49	42	20	33
The Bible contains truth, but it isn't always true*	82	63	35	53
If the Bible says something happened, then I believe that it did	17	37	61	45
The people who wrote the Bible created stories to explain things they didn't understand*	39	32	18	27
You can't pick and choose which bits of the Bible to believe	30	51	69	55
Once you start doubting bits of the Bible you end up doubting it all	9	21	36	26
Some parts of the Bible are more true than others*	84	64	40	57
The Bible is the final authority in all matters of faith and conduct	32	57	82	64
I use the Bible as the only reliable guide for life	19	42	57	44
Christians can learn about God from other faiths*	77	73	44	59
N =	92	109	199	400

Note. The table shows the percentage of participants who agreed or strongly agreed with each item in the scale. *These items were reverse scored. AC = Anglo-Catholic; BC = Broad church; EV = Evangelical.

There were three items that stressed slightly different aspects of the idea of inerrancy: 'The Bible contains some human errors', 'I have never found the Bible to be wrong about anything' and 'Science shows that some things in the Bible cannot have happened'. From the first two, it seems that around half (46%) of evangelicals believed that the Bible contains human errors and approximately the same proportion (51%) had never found it to be wrong. The equivalent figures for Anglo-Catholics were 89% and 12% respectively. People were generally less sure that science had shown the Bible might be wrong: 20% of evangelicals and 49% of Anglo-Catholics. In each case, those in broad churches fell between the other two traditions. These findings are very much as expected,[6] though it is interesting that a relatively high proportion of evangelicals were willing to admit some human error in the Bible.

The issue of literalism was tested by three items: 'The Bible contains truth, but it isn't always true', 'If the Bible said that something happened, then I believe that it did' and 'The people who wrote the Bible created stories to explain things they didn't understand'. The first of these was a phrase I heard from lay people several times in the pilot interviews and, despite its apparent lack of clarity, it seems to express well the difference between symbolic, mystical or metaphorical truth and literal truth. A large majority of Anglo-Catholics (82%) agreed with this statement, whereas only 35% of evangelicals did so. The majority of evangelicals (61%) believed that, in general, biblical events actually happened, compared with only 17% of Anglo-Catholics. Overall, there was less certainty about the possibility that some biblical narratives may have had an aetiological origin (i.e. created to explain natural phenomena). Generally there was a low level of belief in biblical literalism, though this was much higher among evangelicals than among Anglo-Catholics.

The two items on biblical authority reflected statements that are familiar in some church circles. 'The Bible is the final authority in all matters of faith and conduct' is a statement often used by evangelical organizations as a test of true faith, and it was perhaps not surprising that 82% of people from evangelical churches agreed with it. Perhaps more intriguing might be the 18% who disagreed or who were not certain. Over half (57%) of respondents from broad churches and almost a third (32%) from Anglo-Catholic churches also agreed with this belief, showing that the Bible carries important authority for many churchgoers in the Church of England. The other item, 'I use the Bible as the only reliable guide for life', picks up on notions of the Bible as a yardstick for behaviour. It also links to notions of exclusivity (the word 'only') so there is some ambiguity in using it in isolation. Nonetheless, it is interesting that whereas 57% of evangelicals agreed with this, only 19% of Anglo-Catholics did so.

An issue that emerged from the initial pilot interviews was the notion that the Bible should be accepted as a whole. Evangelicals often used the term 'cherry-picking' in a derogatory way to denote the practice of selectively attending to, or ignoring, parts of the Bible. Technically this might be referred to as the issue of canonicity

---

[6]   The *Church Times* survey of 2001 (Francis, Robbins et al. 2005) found that 11% of laity believed the 'Bible was without error'. This is similar to the 11% of Anglo-Catholics in the Bible and Lay People study who could not agree that the 'Bible contained some human errors'. The *Church Times* sample contained a higher proportion of Anglo-Catholics and lower proportion of evangelicals than the present study.

or integrity, and there were three items that touched on this area of belief. The first, 'You can't pick and choose which bits of the Bible to believe', arose directly from the cherry-picking image and over two-thirds (69%) of evangelicals agreed, compared with less than a third (30%) of Anglo-Catholics. The idea that 'Some bits of the Bible are more true than others' was accepted by 84% of Anglo-Catholics but only 40% of evangelicals. Although it is difficult to define what is meant by something being 'more true', most ordinary churchgoers in this sample seemed intuitively to understand the term as pointing to the variability of different Bible writings in terms of genre and authority. A related concept was the 'all or nothing' nature of the Bible: the idea that once ground was conceded, the entire edifice would crumble. This was often said by evangelicals when they spoke of the reason why they believed things from the Bible that other people found implausible. Generally few people agreed with the rather extreme statement that 'Once you start doubting bits of the Bible you end up doubting it all', but over a third (37%) of evangelicals did so.

A final aspect of belief about the Bible that relates to the liberal–conservative debate is the notion of the exclusive truth of the Bible. I piloted a number of items, but only one, 'Christians can learn about God from other faiths', made into the final scale. Although not directly related to the Bible, it picks up idea that knowledge of God is available outside the Bible. Whereas 77% of Anglo-Catholics and 73% of those from broad churches agreed with this, only 44% of evangelicals did so.

These results give a snapshot of the kind of beliefs held by some 400 Anglicans in the Church of England at the end of the twentieth century. A few things emerge:

First, there are sharp and consistent differences between people from Anglo-Catholic and evangelical churches. In every case, the former held a higher proportion of people with more liberal views and the latter a higher proportion with more conservative views. In virtually every aspect of belief about the Bible, these two traditions seemed to be at opposite ends of the scale. Admittedly, the items were carefully chosen to cover the range of opinion within the Church of England, but even so, the fact that people who share the same denominational affiliation, historical roots and authorized liturgy can have such diverse opinions on the Bible highlights the extraordinary ability of the Anglican Church to maintain communion. Applying the same questions to people from other denominations would indicate if the range encountered in this study spans the full range of Christian belief among ordinary readers of the Bible, or if there are more extreme views at either end of the scale. The latter might well be true because, despite the differences, a significant proportion of Anglo-Catholics upheld the final authority of scripture and a significant proportion of evangelicals allowed for the possibility that the Bible might contain errors.

The second thing to note is that in every case results from broad churches fell between those of the other two traditions. Again, this was expected to some extent because the items were developed for use among the majority of Anglicans in England. This intermediate position was not because people in broad churches were more undecided, it was because they held beliefs less strongly or less consistently across items. Broad-church belief was sometimes closer to Anglo-Catholic belief and sometimes to evangelical belief. On the issues of inerrancy and exclusivity, most broad-church Anglicans tended to side with more liberal than conservative belief. The opposite was true (though to a smaller extent) when it came to beliefs about the authority or canonicity of the Bible. Over the Church of England as a whole, broad churches probably represent the majority of congregations, which implies that, in general, churchgoers are willing to concede the possibility that the Bible might contain errors and might not be the sole source of information about God, but they would still see it as carrying final authority in some areas of their lives.

Looking at the Bible scale item by item gives a picture of the sorts of things people in the sample believed about the Bible. The next question to ask is whether the different aspects of belief about the Bible are related. Testing this involves using the statistical techniques of factor analysis and reliability analysis. Running these tests for the 12 items in Table 3.1 showed that responses to these items among the final sample of participants were strongly correlated and that the sum of scores for all the items gave a reliable single measure of the extent of conservative versus liberal belief.[7] Demonstrating the reliability of a scale is important because it gives confidence in using a person's individual score in statistical analyses.

Another important question is whether this scale really is measuring conservative versus liberal belief and not just Christian belief versus unbelief. The first line of evidence was that those who scored high on biblical conservatism also scored high on moral conservatism and religious exclusivity (Village 2005a). Those with low (liberal) scores on the Bible scale were correspondingly less morally conservative and held more plural religious beliefs. Another line of evidence was to ask how often people attended church and see if this related to their score on the Bible scale. If low scores equate to unbelief, rather than liberal belief, then we would not expect any frequent churchgoers to have low scores because unbelievers are unlikely to attend church often. There was no correlation between the Bible score and attendance among people from Anglo-Catholic or broad churches, showing that a low (liberal) score on the Bible scale was possible for people who were highly committed church attendees. There was, however, a positive correlation in evangelical churches (see Fig 3.1), suggesting that the Bible scale might be measuring Christian commitment in general in these churches. In evangelical churches, where belief about the Bible is central, those with more liberal views might well feel marginalized and therefore not attend as often as they could. In other churches, what someone believes about the Bible does not seem to prevent them taking a full part in congregational life.

The most important outcome of developing a one-dimensional scale of Bible belief is that it can be used to investigate such belief in more detail. The answers to each item can be numerically coded so that in each case a score of 1 equals the most liberal answer and a score of 5 the most conservative. Summing all scores of all twelve items gives the Bible score, which has minimum possible value of 12 (i.e. a score of 1 for each item) and a maximum value of 60 (i.e. a score of 5 for each item). This Bible score is then a measure of general liberal or conservative belief in the Bible. The question is no longer simply *what* do ordinary people believe about the Bible, but *why* do they believe what they do. In other words, what factors determine whether someone will have a more liberal or more conservative belief?

---

[7]   For the Bible scale, Cronbach's $\alpha = .91$, showing a very high degree of reliability (Village 2005a).

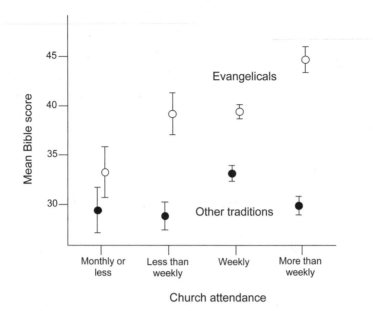

Fig 3.1   Mean (± SE) Bible score against church attendance

We have already seen that church tradition is a strong predictor of Bible belief, and it is not surprising that mean scores were lowest in Anglo-Catholic churches (28.5, SD = 6.4), intermediate in broad churches (33.4, SD = 8.6) and highest in evangelical churches (40.2, SD = 8.6). This does not add a great deal to our understanding, however, because it is almost axiomatic in the Church of England that Anglo-Catholic churches are going to be more liberal and evangelical ones more conservative. A more useful analysis of variance showed that the main factors correlated with Bible scores besides church tradition were education levels and church attendance (see Table 3.2).[8] Bible scores were negatively correlated with education levels in all

Table 3.2   Analysis of variance of the Bible scale

Source of variation	df	F
Church tradition	2	29.1***
Church attendance	3	3.4*
Education	1	7.7**
Tradition–Attendance	6	3.4**
Error	383	(61.4)

Note. From Village 2005a. Church tradition and church attendance were entered as factors and education level entered as a covariate in a general linear model. Value in parenthesis is the mean square error. $^* p < .05$; $^{**} p < .01$; $^{***} p < .001$.

---

[8]   The 'Tradition–Attendance' source of variation in Table 3.2 assesses whether the relationship between the extent of conservatism and church attendance varied between traditions. The fact that it was statistically significant confirmed the observation in Fig 3.1 that the Bible score increased with attendance in evangelical churches but not elsewhere.

traditions, which seems to represent the liberalizing effect of general education on biblical conservatism. There were no significant effects of gender or age on Bible scores.

The Bible scale was not only useful in indicating different sorts of Bible belief within the Church of England, it was also a good measure of biblical conservatism versus biblical liberalism. Including it in analyses in subsequent chapters allows an assessment of how general belief about the Bible interacts with other factors in shaping biblical interpretation among lay people.

Use of the Bible by Ordinary Readers

Earlier in this chapter I mentioned the sometimes tenuous link between attitudes, beliefs and behaviours. People do not always act according to what they believe, and religious life is no exception. We have seen that the available evidence suggests that people generally have a positive attitude towards the Bible and that the Bible and Lay People study suggested quite varied beliefs among this particular sample of Anglicans. We might predict from this that the Bible will have high use in churches, but the way it is used will vary according to tradition. The data I will present here comes from general surveys of the frequency of Bible reading and more specific information from the Bible and Lay People study.

The few surveys of Bible reading among the population at large suggest that it may be read more often that expected in an apparently post-Christian society. The Bible Society survey in 1982 found that 12% of people in England read the Bible privately at least once a week, whereas 35% had never read it and 26% had not read it for at least a year (Harrison 1983). The 1990 and 1992 surveys reported in Clines (1997) asked slightly different questions, but the equivalent figures were around 19–23% who had read the Bible in the last week, 20–54% who never read it or read it long ago, and 14–37% who had read it in the last year. Both these figures imply that millions of people read the Bible every week in Britain, though there are problems in projecting the figures in this way. The Harrison survey was conducted by Gallup, and was probably reasonably accurate at the time, but is over 20 years out of date. The Clines surveys were very impromptu and cannot be generalized to the whole population.

Similar national surveys have been conducted in the USA, the most recent being the Baylor Religion Survey (2005). This was a Gallup poll of 1721 people across the USA that included a question on reading sacred texts. The available results are not broken down by religion, so it is difficult to tell which answers refer to people in general reading the Bible in particular.[9] One table gives figures for 'Protestants' and 'Catholics' and this is presumably the Christian element of the sample reading the Bible. Of these 1353 participants, 25% read weekly or more, while 43% read once

---

9   The data were downloaded from the Association of Religion Data Archives (<http://www.thearda.com>) from the tables of the Baylor Religion Survey. The questioned asked was: 'Outside of attending religious services, about how often do you read the Bible, Koran, Torah, or other sacred book?'

or twice a year or less. There was a marked difference between the two groups, with Protestants much more likely to read weekly than Catholics.

These national surveys are difficult to interpret because it is not clear what is involved in 'reading the Bible': there is a big difference between the sort of devotional reading associated with the daily 'quiet time' and the casual reading or looking up quotes that many people may do from time to time. It is difficult to know if such surveys tend to attract mainly religious people, though this should not have been a problem with the Gallup polls. If they are in any way representative they suggest that a relatively high proportion of people read the Bible on a fairly regular basis. The high proportion in the USA might be expected, given the generally high levels of church attendance, but in Britain the numbers seem much higher than might be predicted from church attendance. There is clearly a need for a more up-to-date and thorough survey in Britain.

Churchgoers are likely to read the Bible more often than the public at large. The survey mentioned earlier from Durham was of Anglican churchgoers, but even here only 35% read it weekly or more, 48% read it only occasionally and 7% had never read the Bible (Fisher et al. 1992). Surveys of regular churchgoers by the Bible Society suggest around 30–40% read weekly or more and a similar proportion seldom, if ever, read the Bible (Brierley 1999: Table 6.4.2). The *Church Times* survey found that 76% read the Bible weekly or more, 18% less than monthly and 1% never (Francis, Robbins and Astley 2005: 22). Taken with national surveys, the data indicate that Bible reading is surprisingly frequent among the population at large, given the generally low church attendance, and perhaps surprisingly infrequent among some churchgoers, given the importance of scriptures historically for the Christian faith. A key point is that church attendance without Bible reading is not at all uncommon.

The people surveyed in the Bible and Lay People study were probably the more frequent users of the Bible because it is they who would be more likely to complete a questionnaire about it. So the overall results are probably less useful than the comparisons between traditions or correlations with other variables. Participants were asked how often they read the Bible and given seven possible replies representing increasing extent of reading (see Table 3.3). Over half (53%) of the total sample of 400 read the Bible more than once a week, which probably represents those who read it daily, or try to. The overall pattern was for a bimodal distribution, with people either never, or hardly ever, reading the Bible or doing so almost daily. Regular but infrequent use seemed rare, and this might suggest that Bible reading among lay Anglicans tends to be an 'all or nothing' phenomenon.

It is unlikely that half the members of the Church of England read the Bible every day, and it would be wrong to overgeneralize the results. They do, however, show the marked differences between traditions, with more than twice as many evangelicals reading more than weekly (69%) compared with broad-church Anglicans (32%). Bible reading seemed particularly low in broad churches, with just under half the sample (44%) reading no more than a few times a year. This probably represents the true picture for much of the Church of England. Daily reading was slightly more frequent in Anglo-Catholic churches (40%), which I suspect was mainly through following the lectionary during the daily offices. Overall, there was no statistically significant

Table 3.3   Frequency of Bible reading in the Bible and Lay People study

How often do you read the Bible?	AC %	BC %	EV %	All %
Only heard at church	8	14	3	7
Hardly ever	15	12	4	9
Few times a year	22	18	6	13
Monthly	5	2	4	4
Fortnightly	3	8	5	5
Weekly	7	14	10	10
More than weekly	40	32	69	53
N =	92	109	199	400

Note. AC = Anglo-Catholic; BC = Broad church; EV = Evangelical.

difference in reading frequency between Anglo-Catholic or broad churches, the main difference being the much greater frequency in evangelical churches.

People were also asked for more details of how exactly they read the Bible, and were given several options, which were not mutually exclusive (see Table 3.4). Just under half (47%) would sometimes look up subjects, while 40% sometimes used notes. Fewer people reported using other tactics such as reading book by book (18%), reading wherever the Bible happened to fall open (17%), returning to favourite passages (16%) or using commentaries (17%). There were fewer differences between traditions in reading method, the only statistically significant one being the much greater frequency of using Bible reading notes among evangelicals compared with others.

Table 3.4   Ways of reading the Bible in the Bible and Lay People study

When you read the Bible, do you:	AC %	BC %	EV %	All %
Read book by book	24	16	17	18
Open and read	13	21	16	17
Look up subjects	50	54	42	47
Go to favourite passages	14	20	14	16
Use Bible notes*	21	26	55	40
Use commentaries	14	11	21	17
N =	92	109	199	400

Note. Participants could choose more than one response. Percentages are based on the total number of participants, some of whom did not read the Bible and did not select any of these options. AC = Anglo-Catholic; BC = Broad church; EV = Evangelical. *Evangelicals were significantly more likely to use Bible notes than were other traditions ($\chi^2 = 41.8$, $df = 2$, $p < 0.001$).

Examples of which notes or commentaries were used are listed in Table 3.5 as a percentage of all participants. Bible notes mentioned included those produced by the Bible Reading Fellowship (*New Daylight*), Scripture Union (*Daily Bread*) and Crusade for World Revival (*Everyday with Jesus*). Notes from the Scripture Union were most frequent and were mentioned by 14% of all participants. Commentaries were used less frequently and included a wide range. A few people mentioned what might be classed as 'critical' commentaries, but the most popular were established titles such as those by Matthew Henry, Arthur S. Peake and William Barclay. These are devotional commentaries that are probably the most readily available in Christian bookstores.

Table 3.5   Bible reading notes and commentaries used by participants in the Bible and Lay People study

Bible reading notes	%	Commentaries	%
Bible Reading Fellowship	6	Commentaries in a Bible	3
CWR Everyday with Jesus	6	Bible Speaks Today	1
Scripture Union	14	Tyndale Press	1
Other notes	6	William Barclay	2
		Matthew Henry	2
		Peake	<1
		Other commentaries	5

Note. Participants could choose more than one response. Percentages are based on 404 participants, some of whom did not read the Bible or did not use notes or commentaries, so did not select any of these options.

Overall, these results seem to be much as expected, confirming the generally low frequency of Bible reading in non-evangelical churches and the devotional, rather than critical, material used to guide Bible reading. Although the sample in the Bible and Lay People study did include a high proportion of frequent readers, it also included some who rarely if ever read the Bible.

What factors predicted the frequency of Bible reading? Beliefs about the Bible are a likely candidate, and there was a strong positive correlation between reading frequency (on a 7-point scale) and the Bible score ($r = .43$, $df = 395$, $p < 0.001$), indicating that people with more conservative views about the Bible generally read it more often. This has to be tempered by looking at the relationship *within* church traditions. As we saw earlier, tradition and Bible score are themselves highly correlated, so we would expect that tradition would not explain any more of the variance in reading frequency if we have already allowed for the effects of Bible score. However, tradition does have some additional predictive power on Bible reading frequency because the correlation between frequency and Bible score is absent in Anglo-Catholic churches (see Fig 3.2).

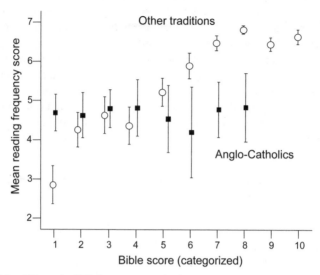

Fig 3.2   Mean (± SE) frequency of Bible reading against Bible score

The reason for this difference is not known for certain, but it may be because the way in which the Bible is encountered and read in Anglo-Catholic churches is fundamentally different from other traditions. I suspect that in broad and evangelical churches the main encounter is in the 'quiet time', a daily period of prayer and reflection that is traditional among evangelicals in particular. Those who have strong conservative beliefs about the Bible will tend to have quiet times and have them more frequently than those with more liberal beliefs. In Anglo-Catholic churches, the encounter may be more through the practice of the daily office, which could be equally likely among people of more liberal or conservative beliefs. This is a question raised by the results that would benefit from further research.

There was no relationship between the frequency of Bible reading and age, sex or general levels of education. Those with some experience of theological education at university (certificate, diploma or degree level) read the Bible more frequently than those with equivalent educational experience in other subjects. There was also a strong relationship between attendance and frequency of reading which held across all traditions (see Table 3.6).[10]

Including general education in the model shows that the effect of theological education is specific, and not merely because those with higher education qualifications in theology by definition have high education levels. Education was not by itself significantly related to Bible-reading frequency, though those with no formal education qualifications did read less often than others.

---

[10]   The source of variation 'Tradition–Bible score' in Table 3.6 is an interaction term. The fact that it was statistically significant confirms that the relationship between reading frequency and Bible score shown in Fig 3.2 differed between Anglo-Catholics and other traditions.

Table 3.6   Analysis of variance of Bible-reading frequency

Source of variation	df	F
Church tradition	2	7.1**
Theological education	1	9.9**
Church attendance	3	21.1***
Bible score (categorized)	9	5.9***
Tradition–Bible score	17	2.8***
Education	1	3.5
Error	360	(2.7)

Note. Bible score was categorized into ten levels and entered as a factor with church tradition, theological education and church attendance. Education level was entered as a covariate in a general linear model. Value in parenthesis is the mean square error. $^*p < .05$; $^{**}p < .01$; $^{***}p < .001$.

The best predictor of whether someone used Bible study notes was church tradition, with evangelicals being much more likely to do so than other traditions.[11] This relationship remained after allowing for differences in education levels and Bible score, so it appears to be directly associated with practices in the churches of each tradition. Evangelical churches seem to encourage the use of Bible reading notes more than those in the other traditions. Many of the notes mentioned tended to come from evangelical or conservative-evangelical organizations and this may be a self-perpetuating state of affairs. If it is mainly evangelicals who use notes, publishers are unlikely to produce the kind of material that would suit other traditions, so there is less opportunity to encourage people from more liberal traditions to read in this way.

The use of commentaries was much more unusual and predicted by quite different factors. As might be expected, those with some experience of theological education were more likely to use commentaries.[12] Use of commentaries was also more likely among more conservative readers, at least in broad and evangelical churches. Thus mean Bible scores were higher in those who used commentaries, but there was no such difference for Anglo-Catholics.[13] So the people most likely to use commentaries were conservatives in broad or evangelical churches who had had some theological education.

---

[11]   For those who read weekly or more, 37% of 43 Anglo-Catholics, 51% of 49 broad-church members and 63% of 156 evangelicals used notes, a highly significant difference ($\chi^2 = 14.9, df = 2, p < 0.01$).

[12]   Among frequent readers, 46% of 59 people with some theological education used commentaries, compared with 18% of 189 without such education, a highly significant difference ($\chi^2 = 19.6, df = 1, p < 0.001$).

[13]   For broad-church and evangelical congregations, the mean Bible score for 52 people who used commentaries was 44.2 (SD = 7.8), compared with 39.6 (SD = 8.3) for 153 people who did not ($t = 12.2, p < 0.01$).

Theological and Practical Implications

Attitude towards the Bible

What people in general think of the Bible is relevant both for society at large and for Christians in particular. Britain is in ethical and moral transition as old certainties and norms for a host of attitudes and behaviours including sexuality, marriage, the beginning and ending of life, and treatment of the planet are being challenged or eroded. We have created enquiries and commissions to help us find answers to such questions because, even where the biblical norms are fairly clear, some believe they are no longer a satisfactory basis for a national consensus. If different sections of society are going to have their say of how we make laws, it would seem important to know the extent to which society as a whole feels the Bible should figure somewhere in our deliberations.

This is not simply a question of asking the church for moral advice. The 70% or so of people who registered their religion as 'Christian' in the 2001 UK national census[14] do not necessarily constitute 'the church'. They are unlikely to know much about what the Bible actually says and might even have a rather negative attitude towards it. Or they may not. They might consider that the Bible is a crucial resource for society and that it should still be regarded as sacred scripture. If there is a widely held positive attitude towards the Bible, then that is something that should at least be borne in mind when decisions are made and laws are formulated. Is the Bible simply part of our past, or does it have a role in our future?

The attitude of the general public to the Bible is of particular importance to the church. In the latter part of the twentieth century, churches in Britain finally woke up to the implications of the changing place of religion in society. There was widespread understanding that survival was at stake (Brierley 2000) and what was needed was mission rather than institutional maintenance.[15] The notion of bringing nominal Christians 'back to church' suddenly seems out of place for generations that have never had any church contact at all. The majority of children are not baptized, church weddings are being replaced by secular ceremonies and more and more funerals are in crematoria rather than churches. Conversion is no longer a return to the familiar, it is a step into the unknown.

If the religious profile of the nation is changing with each generation, then understanding this profile is important for a church that wants to persuade people to accept the Gospel. If mission activity is to be effective, it needs to know how unchurched people regard the Bible. Paul's approach at the Areopagus in Athens (Acts 17:16–34) has been suggested as a paradigm for evangelism today[16] because it is tailored to his audience, in this case Greek philosophers, for whom the prophecies

---

[14]   Table KS07 *Religion, Census 2001: Key Statistics for the rural and urban area classification* (Office for National Statistics, 2004).

[15]   In the Church of England there have been a range of reports that that looked at the nature and role of church in a changing society. These have included *Faith in the City* (1985), *Faith in the Countryside* (1990) and *Mission-Shaped Church* (2004).

[16]   For examples, see Flemming (2002) and Losie (2004).

in Jewish scripture would be meaningless. So Paul does not appeal to this authority, but begins with something to which they could relate by developing the notion of an 'unknown' God. Paul's technique is to reveal this God as the creator God who governs the world, to whom all people are innately drawn. This is a very different approach from, say, Peter on the day of Pentecost, where a Jew speaks to Jews who hold a common scriptural inheritance. Here, prophecy from Joel that would have had the familiar ring of scripture to Peter's audience is used to interpret the manifestation of the Holy Spirit (Acts 2:16–21).

Christians who perceive the Gospel as primarily a biblical message will want to appeal to the Bible as they seek to persuade others to accept that message. How will such an appeal play in society today? Is there enough residual respect and acceptance of the Bible to allow evangelists to quote it as a commonly accepted authority? Or does that authority need to be established in the first place? Does the Gospel have to be demonstrated in action before it will be recognized on the page? The highly successful *Alpha Course* (Gumbel 1994) is based on an evangelical approach that arose in the stable of post-war British evangelicalism associated with people such as John Stott and David Watson. Its success might seem surprising, given that it uses the Bible as a key authority for the veracity of the message. However, this authority has to be established near the start of the course,[17] and the message of scripture is placed alongside the work of the Holy Spirit in individuals, which is seen as a key factor in the conversion process. It would be interesting to know how crucial a person's initial attitude to the Bible is in shaping their reaction to the course. Is a basic positive attitude to the Bible important in shaping outcomes, or does the course succeed even with those who have a negative attitude when they start?

This example shows how understanding basic attitudes to the Bible in the population at large can shape the way we approach mission and evangelism. Theologically it takes us back a step and asks in what sense God might work by changing attitudes. Are people's attitudes already determined before they weigh the particular claims and demands of the Christian message, and if so, by what? If a positive attitude towards the Bible is a crucial prerequisite to Christian conversion, how does the church shape such attitudes in society? Conversely, it would be useful to know what creates negative attitudes and whether this is something for which churches are chiefly responsible. If people absorb negative attitudes from secular sources, then perhaps the answer lies in tackling any ill-informed or one-sided bias that drives the dissemination of such attitudes. The public face of the church becomes crucial, and the call of Jesus to allow the light to shine (Matthew 5:16) becomes imperative. If, however, negative attitudes towards the Bible arise because those who claim to be 'Bible believers' show no hint of the love or charity it demands, or if those who claim to be Christians follow a religion without recourse to their scriptures, then the church has a very different task indeed. If the *church* is the chief promoter of negative attitudes towards the Bible then the accusations of Jesus

---

[17]   Session 1 *Who is Jesus?* has a section that reviews textual criticism and the New Testament evidence.

against the religious authorities of his time have a particular modern relevance.[18] Empirical evidence in this area might help Christians to see that which they would otherwise choose to ignore.

Beliefs about the Bible

Empirical study is beginning to show that the theological concerns that have ignited academics and church scholars do have some importance for ordinary churchgoers, though for many the issues are less complex. The broad definitions of liberal and conservative are basic categories that define and shape the beliefs of most lay Christians, but there is no simple bipolar distribution of belief. Those that do not fall clearly into either camp are not necessarily people who have uncertain or no beliefs about the Bible; rather they are combining aspects of liberal and conservative belief. This suggests a reasonably sophisticated process of giving more or less weight to different aspects of Bible belief (inerrancy, authority, etc.) and, within a given aspect, giving more or less weight to particular propositions about the Bible.

Theologically, there have always been those who have sought to expound a view of the Bible that is neither strongly liberal nor strongly conservative. These views are characterized by the acceptance of the 'situatedness' of scripture and the way that it reflects the world view and concerns of its human authors. The possibility of symbolic rather than literal interpretations is accepted, as is the practice of drawing on extra-biblical information in making decisions about the original meaning or current applicability of a passage. The issue remains as to where to draw the line between event and fictional story, especially when it comes to the central Christian narratives of the incarnation and resurrection. I will discuss these sorts of issues in more detail in Chapter 4. Here I want to address the issue of the appropriateness or otherwise of various lay beliefs about the Bible.

Deductive arguments about Bible beliefs begin with certain propositions that are held to be true and upon which other truths are built. A good example would be the way in which evangelicals have tried to predicate biblical authority on biblical inerrancy and inerrancy on verbal inspiration.[19] Empirical approaches are more inductive, in that they look at what *seems* to be the case before trying to decide what *ought* to be the case. Looking at the range of beliefs about the Bible among lay people raises the question of whether there is a single, 'correct' approach to the Bible, or whether diversity is both inevitable and a God-given necessity.

If what matters to God is whether followers of Jesus Christ have the correct beliefs about scripture, then it would seem that some followers have got it seriously wrong. Those who take a strongly conservative view would probably argue that scripture

---

[18]   Examples are Jesus' accusation in John 5:39–40 against those who sought to kill him that 'you search the scriptures because you think that in them you have eternal life; and it is they that testify on my behalf. Yet you refuse to come to me to have life.' In a similar vein, the woes directed at Scribes and Pharisees in Matthew 23 are about the way they used scripture selectively to justify their unjust behaviour. Jesus is equally hard on those who would want to abandon the scriptures (in this case the Torah) altogether (Matthew 5:17; 22:23).

[19]   See, for example, Freeman (1996).

is the word of God and that those who doubt its inerrancy and exclusive sufficiency for salvation cannot meaningfully understand the nature and purposes of God at all. Those who take a strong liberal view of the Bible might counter that conservatives have a view of scripture that misunderstands its true nature, fails to give due weight to the human fallibility it represents and therefore leads to unnecessary acceptance of harmful notions. In either case, the aim of the church would presumably be to promote true beliefs about scripture which would then transform the discipleship and mission of God's people. Beliefs about scripture would thus be the cornerstone on which the Christian faith is founded.

I do not intend to argue this case through, let alone try to prove that one view of scripture is the correct one. Instead I simply raise the question whether beliefs about scripture should have such pride of place. That does not mean that they are not important, in the sense that what someone believes about scripture has major consequences on how they engage and respond to God. But perhaps God judges people not by what they believe the Bible to be, but what they do with that belief. For Christians, every kind of belief about the Bible (including disbelief) carries with it a responsibility to use the belief consistently and openly and to justify decisions made and actions taken. Different beliefs will tend to lead to different sorts of challenges. Those who hold scripture as the inerrant word of God are faced with the challenge of honestly reconciling different biblical viewpoints and working out what to do with words that appear to fly in the face of the message of the one who is claimed to be the living Word. Those who see the Bible as a record of sometimes flawed human beliefs about God face the necessity of demonstrating how they fall under the authority of the God they worship, and why their claims about God should carry any weight. Even those who never read the Bible, or claim that it contains little that is relevant to them, must base their beliefs and actions on something.

The Bible contains a view, or views, of God and accounts of how humans relate to God. It is nonsense to claim that what it says is of no importance for those who worship God, but perhaps there is no single 'correct' way of relating to it. All beliefs about the Bible contain the possibility of misuse, be it unconvincing efforts to create coherence, or a cavalier disregard of demanding texts. What might be more important is that beliefs are appropriate and shape lives that are pleasing to God.

The idea of appropriateness can be seen in relation to the finding on education levels and Bible belief. Education will crop up as a key factor shaping many different aspects of the hermeneutics of ordinary readers. In terms of Bible beliefs, there is strong evidence that experience of higher levels of education is associated with a shift from more conservative to more liberal beliefs about the Bible. This is not inevitable, as we shall see in the case of biblical literalism, but it is a general trend. The theological questions this raises are whether this represents the liberation of God's people enslaved by ignorance, the pollution of minds with a secular world view, or neither of these possibilities. Education is not always something people can choose to have or not have; it is more often something they may or may not have. If they do not get it, is a particular kind of Bible belief more appropriate than another? Do those who have been educated have a responsibility to take on beliefs about the Bible that are appropriate to what they have experienced? I return to this issue in reference to the specific issue of literalism in Chapter 4.

Bible-Reading Practices

It is no surprise to find that a generally positive attitude to the Bible among the population at large is not necessarily reflected in the specific behaviour of actually reading it. The generally low rates of Bible reading in at least some Anglican traditions were confirmed in the Bible and Lay People study and are an important reminder to professional biblical scholars and conservative church people that there are committed Christians who do not read the Bible very often. One might question the use of 'committed' here, because in all three traditions infrequent Bible reading was also associated with infrequent attendance, a standard measure of religious commitment. Nonetheless, the empirical results demand some theological reflection on what faith might mean for those who rarely read the Bible.

Bible-reading practice is shaped partly by belief (conservatives read more frequently and are more likely to use commentaries), partly by experience (theological education increased the frequency of reading and the use of commentaries) and partly by church tradition (Anglo-Catholics show different trends from the other traditions and evangelicals are more likely to use Bible study notes). Clearly, those traditions that believe the Bible to be central to faith do a better job of encouraging Bible reading and Bible study. In these traditions, not reading the Bible in a particular way is viewed as a failure to live as true disciples, and those who do not do so are likely to be less committed members (at least as expressed by attendance). In other traditions there is less expectation to read, and encounter with the Bible comes through different ways. Corporate engagement through liturgical reading and preaching may be more important than private reading. Is there a theological case for justifying low rates of Bible reading among some ordinary churchgoers, or is this a sinful neglect?

Any answer to this question needs to take into account that private Bible reading is a relatively recent phenomenon in Christian life (Marshall 1995). It has presumably relied on the changes associated with the Reformation, which coincided with changes in the availability of printed texts in vernacular languages and in a gradual rise in literacy. For much of Christian history, and for many Christians today, direct access to scripture is impossible or something alien to the rest of their lives. Even in 'literate' societies such as Britain, many people cannot read or find books an alien medium.[20] There are several different ways in which the church deals with this. In some traditions there is a strong reliance on clergy or lay readers to mediate the word through liturgy or preaching. In others, the stress is on the direct influence of the Holy Spirit on the lives of believers.[21] The advantage of the former traditions is the possibility of trained readers guarding against the abuse or misuse of scripture and acting as interpreters for those who need to know the content and intent of scripture. Oral or visual communication is no less powerful or important than written

---

[20]   Less than 1% of adults in England can be described as illiterate, but 16% have literacy levels at or below those expected of an 11-year-old. A 2004 survey found that 34% of adults did not read books. (National Literacy Trust website <www.literacytrust.org.uk> November 2006).

[21]   The pentecostal and charismatic traditions are an interesting case in point, and one that I discuss in more detail in Chapter 8.

communication in such circumstances. The disadvantages are that those who cannot read are reliant on the trained elite, who may fail to convey scripture accurately or faithfully. Part of the drive behind the Reformation was a struggle to escape the abusive practices of those who held the keys to scripture.

There is no space here to develop the full implications of this, for it covers wide and deep areas that have long history of debate. What can be done is to raise questions that others might explore. A first question concerns the relationship of the Bible to illiterate Christians, especially in traditions that stress the primacy of scripture. It is difficult for those who can read to imagine life for those who cannot. Perhaps too easily we overlook the very different way in which many people know scripture: they *hear* it, or hear it expounded. They rely heavily on memory, and hence may need to hear scripture in familiar language, even if that language is sometimes archaic.

A second question is the responsibility of lay people to engage with the scriptures of their faith. If disciples *can* be instructed and inspired directly by reading scripture, *must* they be so? If faith and salvation are possible for the illiterate, is it right for literate Christians who have full access to scripture to eschew the reading and study of those scriptures? Are those who can read but prefer not to committing some sort of sin, or are other forms of religious life legitimate for all? Salvation must be available to those who have to rely on others to read scriptures, for to argue otherwise is to create a literary elitism, but perhaps more is expected of those have the ability and experience to read and understand. Perhaps the Gospel principle expressed in Luke 12:48, 'From everyone to whom much has been given, much will be required; and from the one to whom much has been entrusted, even more will be demanded', is important here. The ability to read is a great gift and, whatever else literate Christians read, it would seem odd to ignore the foundational documents of their faith. The empirical evidence of low levels of Bible reading among some apparently literate Christians points to the importance of organizations that encourage and promote Bible reading among lay people.

A similar issue relates to those who have responsibility for mediating scripture to those who do not read it for themselves. There are warnings in scripture that the role of mediating the Gospel is one that carries particular demands and should not be undertaken lightly (for example, Mark 9:42, James 3:1). If many churchgoers encounter scripture only when it is read in church (as direct Bible reading, within liturgy or during sermons), the performance of these tasks is crucial. Readings that are inaudible or dull are missing an important opportunity, and churches need to value and encourage those with the gift of liturgical reading.

Further Research

Attitude towards the Bible

There is scope for a repeat of the sort of survey that was done by the Bible Society in the early 1980s, that would allow a snapshot of attitudes to Christianity in general, and the Bible in particular, among the population of Britain. Has low use but positive attitude towards the Bible been replaced by non-use and negative regard? Or does the Bible retain some special place in the hearts and minds of ordinary people? These are questions that should be addressed to the population as a whole, and would therefore require the sorts of careful randomization of sampling that is used in national surveys. Informal polls are better than nothing, but they will not begin to deal with the diversity and complexity of the country as a whole.

The study in Durham raised the issue of attitudes towards the Bible among committed churchgoers. Armchair observers might suggest that it would be a waste of time measuring attitudes within churches because these are bound to be uniformly positive. Empirical theologians might not be so sure, and the researchers in Durham found evidence to suggest that attitudes could be more varied than might be expected. Admittedly, the questions used in that survey were more about beliefs than attitude, and they may have got a different impression if they had used questions such as 'I think the Bible is boring' or 'I think the Bible is out of date'.[22] Nonetheless, there was some evidence that attitudes among sections of churchgoers may be ambivalent at best and downright negative at worst. A more wide-ranging and thorough study of attitude towards the Bible among churchgoers would need to sample a range of denominations and would need to use instruments that clearly separated basic attitudes from specific beliefs. If this sort of study found committed churchgoers with negative attitudes towards the Bible it would raise questions about why this was so, and what the consequences of such attitudes were for the expression of Christian faith.

Beliefs about the Bible

The Bible scale seems to be a reliable and valid way of measuring liberal versus conservative belief, at least among Anglicans in England. In theory it should be related to the literal and mystical dimensions of Hunt's LAM scale, and one test of construct validity would be to run the scale with the original or modified LAM scales. Validity of the scale could also be tested by applying it to a wider range of denominations, including those that may have more liberal or conservative congregations than the ones that took part in the Bible and Lay People study.

Another question is whether there might be other aspects of Bible belief that are not embraced within the general notion of liberal versus conservative.[23] In denominations where churchgoers are more conservative, more nuanced dimensions of belief might be apparent. Variations in belief about inerrancy may exist that are not at all related to belief about biblical authority. To tease out such variations quantitatively it would be necessary to develop a more sensitive instrument specifically for use in more conservative churches. This would entail either a completely different scale, or the addition of extra items to the existing one. Such an exercise might be worthwhile for someone studying, say, fundamentalist churches, but I suspect the Bible scale as it is will probably cover the key areas of belief in most denominations.

---

[22]   In fact the nearest equivalent question, about the relevance of the Bible for today, showed a strong positive attitude, though even here only 71% agreed the Bible was relevant.

[23]   In technical terms this is the question of whether Bible belief is a single or multi-dimensional construct.

The issue of canonicity and biblical authority might be most usefully examined among congregations at the more liberal end of the scale. It is among this group that churchgoers are likely to be making decisions on the present-day validity and utility of different Bible passages. Do ordinary readers simply ignore Bible teachings that conflict with their own, or do they have criteria, explicit or implicit, that help them to decide if any given passage carries the weight of biblical authority? Presumably the directions offered by the Bible interact with other sources of authority in the life of believers, and these may need to be considered at the same time as the Bible. The notion of the canon of scripture has been a much debated subject in churches and the academy, both in terms of which parts to include or exclude and in terms of the influence of the canon on biblical interpretation. Ordinary Bible readers are sometimes sensitive to the dangers of picking and choosing bits of the Bible, but whether this is a true 'canonical awareness' remains to be seen.

The other area where research could be directed is to look at beliefs about the Bible among the non church-going public. In some ways this is a less attractive and more difficult proposition. People who never read the Bible or seldom think about it may not have any beliefs about it at all. Examining attitudes towards the Bible, rather than belief about it, might be a more rewarding approach. Nonetheless, there may be some merit in seeing whether people with little or no religious affiliation have any clear or coherent beliefs about the Bible and its significance for society.

Use of the Bible

Frequency of Bible reading is a relatively common item on national surveys of religion. In multicultural societies, this question can be confused with the reading of sacred scriptures in general (as mentioned earlier for the Baylor Religion Survey). This is unhelpful because the nature and role of scriptures is not necessarily equivalent between religions and may vary in different societies. To understand the place of the Bible in society at large it is necessary to know the background of the sample (religious affiliation and religious commitment) and the nature of the encounter with scripture. I have found that asking for a wide range of frequencies is probably less useful than looking for key distinctions. Few people *regularly* read once a month and the key divisions are probably between those who read it seldom if ever, those who read it occasionally and those who read it daily as part of their devotional life. Care needs to be taken to distinguish those who may not read it privately, but who hear it read in church or in study groups. Frequency needs to be related to *significance* and this might require a broad definition to include people who may feel the Bible is important for society at large, even if they never read it and have little knowledge about it.

Chapter 4

Biblical Literalism and Ordinary Readers

Biblical Literalism in Academy and Church

Biblical literalism is the belief that events in the Bible happened as described: Jesus rose from the dead, David slew Goliath with a sling and stone, Noah built an ark and so on. It is not an all-or-nothing belief, because even the most radical liberal is bound to accept that some of the events described must actually have happened, and even the most conservative fundamentalist will concede that the Bible can speak metaphorically in places. The issue is about where to draw the dividing line between what is essentially fact (even if coloured by the perception of the reporter) and what is essentially fiction (even if based on something that actually happened).

There is a tendency for some in academia to caricature the average churchgoer as a naive literalist who lives in a fantasy world in which prophets survive being swallowed by giant fish, water can suddenly become wine, and storms can be stilled instantly by the voice of divine command. Such a person, it is assumed, has never done a serious reality check on their beliefs, nor yet understood the richness and diversity of biblical writing. In the other direction, academic theologians are well known in church circles for turning biblical scepticism into an art form. Put enough of them in a room for long enough and they will eventually decide that nothing at all in the Bible ever happened. Press reports of the Jesus Seminar and their little coloured balls seemed to sum up the whole foolish enterprise.[1]

Reality, of course, defies such simple stereotyping, even if each extreme position is based on a grain of truth. Both academy and church are more diverse than these caricatures admit and both embrace a wide range of views on literalism. Academics have long grown used to dealing with non-literal interpretations of the bible. Ironically, perhaps, the most influential and sustained onslaught on literalism in the last century came from Rudolf Bultmann, a churchman committed to trying to make the Christian message meaningful for 'modern man' (Bultmann 1972). His ideas were not new and the veracity of supernatural events reported in the Bible has been questioned for centuries. What he gave was a philosophical justification and methodology for extracting the message from the grip of the mythological world view of the original authors and applying it in existential terms to the lives of modern

---

[1]   The Jesus Seminar sought to assess scholarly opinion on the veracity of each of the reported sayings or actions of Jesus in the synoptic gospels (Funk 1998, 2001; Funk and Hoover 1993). Assessment was by voting, using different coloured balls to represent different degrees of certainty. Natural scholarly caution meant that only a handful of sayings achieved full consensus as originating with Jesus, which was often perceived by outsiders as the typical product of scholarly unbelief.

believers. His demythologizing was not without its critics at the time (Macquarrie 1960), and has largely been abandoned by academics now, but it shaped a whole generation of academic biblical interpreters.

Other changes in biblical studies have made literal interpretation either irrelevant or redundant in most academic circles. Bultmann wrote at a time when historical criticism held sway in biblical studies. Historical criticism has preoccupied itself with the history of the text as much as the history to which it points. Form critics like Bultmann viewed texts as creations of religious communities that were sufficiently detached from the primary events they described to make those events unclear and virtually inaccessible. Similarly, redaction criticism looked at the way texts were selected and shaped by authors, rather than the veracity of the originating event. This interest in the communities that created texts, rather than the history in the text, has also shaped the related discipline of social-scientific criticism, which uses the insights of modern sociology to explain the nature of the communities that created biblical writings (Barton 1995; Esler 1994; White and Yarbrough 1995).

The decline in the monopoly of historical critical approaches to the Bible coincided with a rise in more sceptical attitudes to the objectivity of history in general (Jenkins 1995; Munslow 1997). Modern views of biblical history question the veracity of even the apparently 'historical' writings, which might be based on core events but which are also heavily overlaid with interpretation and polemic. Events are interpreted in the telling and retelling so that it is difficult to separate fact from spin. To be sure, there are those who resist the idea that history is irreducibly subjective (for example, Fulbrook 2002), and this is certainly true within biblical studies. But scholarship has largely moved on from the need to link the biblical text with historical event,[2] not least because of wider changes in biblical studies in the academy. These changes include literary approaches to biblical events that see the importance of stories not in whether or not they actually happened, but in the power of narrative to convey deeper or wider meaning. The text encapsulates conventions and codes that may or may not be shared by author and reader, and which act to convey the all-important message. The underlying event, if there was one, is not the main focus of interest. So too the growing attention to readers stresses the interaction of text and reader at the expense of the history behind the text. While the reader's perception of the literalism of an event might be an issue here, it is rarely discussed by academics. What counts is the power or otherwise of the passage to speak to the particular context of the reader.

The effect of these influences has been to produce biblical scholarship that has a varied but somewhat indifferent attitude to biblical literalism. Some academic writers such as Don Cupitt (1997) tend to see all religious language as essentially metaphorical, implying that rather little of the Bible should be taken as literally true. The stress is on the values and ideas encapsulated and expressed in religious

---

[2]   The field of biblical archaeology makes a fascinating case study of the way in which scholarship has moved away from seeking to 'prove' biblical history. Davis (2004) reviews changes in this arena of discourse, and concludes that the swing away from classical biblical archaeology to a more biblically neutral 'Syro-Palestinian archaeology' has perhaps gone too far.

language, and this represents, perhaps, the endgame of Bultmann's programme of demythologizing. In this extreme form, the divine is a purely human invention that has reality only in the language in which it is expressed and encapsulated. So taking the Bible literally at any level would seem to be a naive and pointless exercise.

Non-literal views of the Bible are widespread among secular academic scholars, but what about those whose constituency includes the church and for whom the Bible is not just any other Ancient Near East literature? As we have seen in Chapter 2, Francis Watson is someone who has argued for the primacy of the church as a locus for interpreting the Bible, and for a legitimate place for confessing scholars in secular universities. He has argued for the importance of biblical narrative, but concedes that history recorded in the gospels is not pure description but narrative history written in the context of the 'historic Christ-event' (Watson 1997: 52).

Evangelical scholars who work at the interface of academy and church are probably most aware of walking a tightrope between academic respectability and the need to be true to their church roots. The tension is most visible when dealing with the issue of biblical literalism, especially those events which would be almost universally interpreted non-literally by academics but literally by many ordinary churchgoers. The Genesis account of creation has long taken centre stage in debates about biblical truth, and seems to function as a litmus test of soundness in some church traditions. Evangelical scholars writing for faith-based constituencies need to be more cautious in challenging the historicity of Genesis 1–3 than those who engage with secular or liberal academic theologians. Don McCartney and Charles Clayton, writing in the USA for conservative 'students and thoughtful lay people', are forthright in asserting that the Genesis story actually happened as described: 'the fall of Adam in Genesis 3 is of religious significance precisely because it actually happened in real space and time' (1994: 212). Stephen Travis, an evangelical scholar writing a Bible study guide for lay people in Britain, shifts the focus way from historicity without actually denying it: 'People often argue about how the Genesis story is to be squared with modern science and the theory of evolution. But Genesis 1 is not about *how* the world was made but about *God's intention* in making the world. It is not in competition with science' (1994: 15, author's italics). John Goldingay, writing from a similar background but for a more academic readership, wrestles with the place of fiction in historical story in his book *Models of Scripture* (1994). He has little hesitation in regarding Genesis 1–3 as 'not history in the sense that we normally give that word', but is more cautious about other contentious issues. For example, in rebutting Marxen's view that the empty tomb stories arose by inference when the disciples saw Jesus was alive, he writes: 'In my view the stories are closer to factuality than that … but this is not to imply that in principle scripture cannot contain stories that are "fictional" yet true in the sense that they give us accurate insight into the actual Jesus' (Goldingay 1994: 69).

In general, then, academic biblical scholars tend to downplay the issue of literalism and have moved biblical interpretation to different pastures. This does not bother ordinary churchgoers much unless there is visible a clash of the worlds of academia and church, when literalism can become a key issue. An example of this is the furore that accompanied the appointment of David Jenkins as Bishop of Durham in 1984 (Dyson 1985; Harrison 1985). As professor of theology in a university department, he was well used to the notion of demythologizing biblical stories that were created by people with a different world view from our own. By the 1980s, such ideas were common currency for academic theologians and if anything rather passé. But for a bishop-elect to speak of the resurrection as 'no mere conjuring trick with bones' was too much for many churchgoers within and beyond Anglicanism. Stressing the effects of resurrection for the believer at the expense of the historical reality of bodily resurrection seemed to imply the latter did not, or could not, happen.

The reactions to Jenkins's consecration were mixed. Many ordinary churchgoers were probably confused and angered to hear a bishop apparently denying the reality of the central miracle of the Christian faith. Remarks taken out of context were open to misunderstanding and may have reinforced the notion that academic theology simply fosters unbelief. Some interpreted the lightning bolt that struck the site of his consecration the day after the event as a clear sign that God is perfectly capable of controlling his creation, whatever wayward bishops might believe. On the other hand, there were also many who welcomed what was, for them, a refreshing approach to dealing with the conundrum of biblical miracles. Such people may have struggled to accept that some biblical events could have happened, but found little alternative between literal belief and unbelief. For them, as for a slightly earlier generation who read Bishop John Robinson's *Honest to God* (1963), allowing room for non-literalist belief within the church must have seemed like a breath of fresh air.

This diversity of reaction suggests that the beliefs of lay people about biblical literalism might be more varied than they appear. Not only are some inherently more literal interpreters than others, but also any one person is likely to have diverse views of different sorts of biblical events. Few are likely to question whether or not Jesus really was crucified, but how many would accept that he walked on water or fed 5,000 people with a couple of loaves and few fish? Literalism is not about accepting the whole of the Bible as literally true or not literally true. It is likely to involve some sort of hierarchy of events that range from clear fiction to clear fact. In that sense it is not all that different from the ideology that drives the Jesus Seminar, though perhaps few on either side of that debate would see the links.

One exception to this might be the sort of literal belief associated with Christian fundamentalism. Here, the Bible functions as a shibboleth for group identity (Boone 1989), and literalism may be caught up in this process. The core of fundamental belief is the authority of scripture, which stems from its divine origin. Inspiration implies inerrancy and infallibility, as expressed in statements of faith such as the Chicago Statement.[3] Literalism is not one of these core beliefs, but stems directly

---

[3]   The statement was produced in 1978 at the launch of the International Council on Biblical Inerrancy, which was a colloquium of evangelical scholars and leaders that completed its work in 1988. The first statement on inerrancy contained Articles of Affirmation and Denial, which included the following from Articles 11 and 12: 'We affirm that Scripture, having been given by divine inspiration, is infallible, so that, far from misleading us, it is true and reliable in all the matters it addresses. We deny that it is possible for the Bible to be at the same time infallible and errant in its assertions. Infallibility and inerrancy may be distinguished, but not separated. We affirm that Scripture in its entirety is inerrant, being free from all falsehood, fraud, or deceit. We deny that Biblical infallibility and inerrancy are limited to spiritual, religious, or redemptive themes, exclusive of assertions in the fields

from them. It was the Reformation notion of the 'plain sense of scripture', a counter to the excesses of medieval allegory, that may have linked literalism with truth and hence inerrancy. To interpret non-literally is to question the inerrancy of scripture and hence its authority. This threat to the core beliefs of the group may make it difficult for members of fundamentalist churches to accept anything other than literal interpretations of the majority of the Bible. James Barr, who erroneously grouped conservative evangelicals with fundamentalists, was scathing of the tendency of some to shift ground on literalism, which he interpreted as a ruse to protect the authority of scripture in the face of the obvious evidence of science. In his view, fundamentalism was guilty of disingenuous use of literalism, clinging to it where it suited but abandoning it for metaphorical interpretation when there was no other way out (Barr 1981: 40). In effect, evangelicals are being accused of doing the very thing that their Reformation heroes abhorred: making scripture into a 'wax nose' that can be shaped to prevailing fashion. Barr's answer is the opposite of Luther's, releasing scripture from the tyranny of 'plain sense' and ignoring the issue of literalism.

Others might see this 'fundamentalist fudge' as a genuine attempt to define a line between the literal and figurative, the sort of exercise that is required by all interpreters. What is certainly true is that for some believers literalism is taken as the norm, and that it is not conceded lightly. Asked if something in the Bible actually happened, they will say yes without really needing to know what the event was. Fundamentalism is not the same as conservative evangelicalism (though Barr used the terms interchangeably), and such automatic literalism might be unusual among evangelical Anglicans. Nonetheless, there might be some who would assert the literalism of biblical events, even if they are explicitly referred to as stories within the biblical narrative (e.g. parables).

Previous Empirical Studies on Literalism

Although a great deal has been written on literalism, there are few empirical studies. In the USA, most quantitative work has been part of attempts to use Bible belief as an alternative measure to religious affiliation (see Chapter 3). Although this was not wholly successful, a by-product of these studies was evidence that literalism was related to conservatism as well as to some socio-demographic variables such as education, age and gender (Dixon et al. 1992). In Britain, one of the largest recent surveys of religious attitudes and beliefs was the 2001 survey of over 7,500 readers of the *Church Times* (Francis, Robbins and Astley 2005). The survey included 5,762 lay people in the Church of England, who were asked about a wide range of subjects, including some items on belief in biblical events such as the virgin birth and the bodily resurrection. These items provide a useful comparison with some of the results discussed later in this chapter.

Although not directly about biblical literalism, the work of Richard Hunt (1972) on the LAM scale (see Chapter 3) raised the issue of literalist interpretations of

---

of history and science. We further deny that scientific hypotheses about earth history may properly be used to overturn the teaching of Scripture on creation and the flood'.

Christianity in general. Most of the then current measures of religiosity tended to equate literal belief with religious belief, and everything else with unbelief. Hunt developed scales based on the assumption that there were three sorts of 'meaning-commitment possibilities': literal belief, anti-literal belief and mythological belief. This allowed a distinction between a rejection of religion ('anti-literal' belief) and a symbolic reinterpretatoin that assimilated both the 'intention of religious orthodoxy and the realities of the contemporary world'. This distinction seems close to the idea that biblical interpretation might be literalist or non-literalist, but not necessarily unbelieving. Unfortunately, Hunt's scales, though widely quoted, have not been applied in any sustained fashion, and biblical literalism has not received much attention from sociologists or psychologists of religion. The time seemed right to investigate literalism more thoroughly, so I incorporated measures of literal belief in the Bible and Lay People questionnaire.

Biblical Literalism in the Bible and Lay People Study

Biblical literalism was assessed in two ways.[4] The main approach was to produce a list of biblical events and ask people if they thought they had happened or if they were fictional stories. They could rate their answer on a five-point scale, with one representing 'definitely a fictional story' and five representing 'definitely happened'. The items had to be carefully selected to allow a range of answers when given to Anglican churchgoers. Using the crucifixion or resurrection was not very helpful because nearly everyone tested in pilot studies scored five for these items. The final scale (see Table 4.1) consisted of ten items from the Old and New Testaments designed to span the range of literal belief in my final sample. Those who believed all the events were fictional stories would score 10; those who believed all definitely happened would score 50. The scale had a high reliability (Cronbach's $\alpha = .92$) and was used as a measure of general biblical literalism (Village 2005d).

The order in which the items were presented was important in one respect: in the first pilot study I (rather naturally) put the item about Adam and Eve first. A number of participants commented that this first item tended to preoccupy them and shaped the way that they answered the rest of the items. The item was relocated down the list and the problem disappeared, but it was a reminder that the creation story occupies a distinct position with some churchgoers and, by itself, is not a good measure of biblical literalism.

Alongside the items in the events scale were six items that were based on the parables of Jesus. The idea was to see if passages that were 'flagged' in the Bible as stories might nonetheless be considered by some actually to have happened. A difficulty in assessing this objectively is to ensure that the question does not influence the response. There is an inherent ambiguity in asking if a parable 'actually happened or was a fictional story'. Does this mean that the parable is an account of an event that happened (a sower sowing or a prodigal son leaving home) or that Jesus actually

---

4   Some of this work is based on material published in Village (2005d).

Table 4.1   Items in the literalism and parables scales

Items	M	AC %	BC %	EV %	All %
Jesus' mother was a virgin when she conceived Jesus	4.4	68	73	93	81
Jesus raised Lazarus from the dead	4.3	72	76	93	83
Jesus turned water into wine	4.2	65	72	92	80
David killed a giant called Goliath	4.1	73	76	92	83
Moses went to Pharaoh and threatened terrible plagues	4.1	62	67	93	79
Jesus fed 5,000 people with two fish and five loaves	4.0	52	62	90	74
Joshua destroyed the walls of Jericho	3.9	58	66	83	73
Noah built an ark and filled it with animals	3.5	32	49	74	57
Adam and Eve lived in a garden called Eden	3.2	21	45	61	47
Jonah was in the belly of a fish (or whale) for three days	3.1	16	34	57	41
The story of the prodigal son who left home and later returned	2.9	51	56	37	45
The story of the Samaritan who helped a man attacked by robbers	2.9	46	62	38	46
The story of the farmer who scattered seed as he sowed	2.6	43	44	26	35
The story of the unforgiving servant who was released from his debt	2.4	36	38	23	30
The story of the enemies who sowed weeds in a farmer's field	2.4	28	32	18	24
The story of the ten virgins who waited for the bridegroom	2.3	21	28	17	21
N =	404	94	109	201	404

Note. Average score is based on responses to each item from all participants (minimum score 1, maximum 5). Percentages are based on participants who indicated the event definitely or probably happened. M = Mean score; AC = Anglo-Catholic; BC = Broad church; EV = Evangelical.

told this story? The aim was to try to identify those who could discriminate parable stories from other biblical events, so the solution was to embed the six items in the literalism scale and prefix each with 'The story of ...'. The items in the parable scale were answered differently from the others around them, and formed a distinct subset. It seemed that most, but not all, participants understood that they were different from the biblical events of the literalism scale.

The second way of examining literalism was to look in more detail at responses to the test passage in Mark 9:14–29. The aim here was to show that a 'general' belief in biblical literalism was related to the more detailed interpretation of a particular passage. Items were produced that related to whether or not the passage was an event or a story and how literally it was understood. The passage refers to a boy possessed by an evil spirit, but describes symptoms that seem to resemble epilepsy. I considered someone who believed the boy was possessed but did not have epilepsy to have a more literal interpretation than someone who thought the opposite. The nine items formed a scale measuring 'passage literalism' (see Table 4.2) that seemed to be sufficiently reliable (Cronbach's α = .88) to be taken as a measure of how literally the passage was interpreted.

Table 4.2   Items measuring literal belief in the Bible passage Mark 9:14–29

Items	AC %	BC %	EV %	All %
The boy had epilepsy*	66	68	39	53
The boy was possessed by an evil spirit	24	25	63	44
I trust what the Bible says about the boy's illness	56	58	85	71
Jesus healed the boy by casting out a spirit	42	43	83	62
Jesus' calming presence stopped the epileptic fit*	51	50	24	37
The fit stopped by coincidence when Jesus touched the boy*	14	10	3	7
This story was made up by the followers of Jesus*	4	3	1	2
This is an accurate account of what actually happened	49	59	85	70
Something like this happened, but it was not a 'miracle'*	26	25	8	17
N =	92	109	199	400

Note. The table shows the percentage of participants who agreed or strongly agreed with each item in the scale. *These items were reverse scored. AC = Anglo-Catholic; BC = Broad church; EV = Evangelical.

The biblical and passage literalism scales represent slightly different measures of biblical literalism. They were highly correlated with each other and with the Bible scale,[5] so someone who generally interpreted the Bible literally also did so for the particular test passage and was more biblically conservative. These correlations helped to give validity to the idea that the biblical literalism scale was a genuine measure of a person's general tendency to literal biblical interpretation.

---

[5]   Biblical literalism and passage literalism: $r = .73$, $df = 403$, $p < 0.01$; Bible scale and biblical literalism: $r = .74$, $df = 399$, $p < 0.01$; Bible scale and passage literalism: $r = .69$, $df = 399$, $p < 0.01$.

Scores of Individual Items

Each item in the literalism and parables scales had its own mean score, but could also be rated according to what proportion of participants believed that the event had definitely or probably happened (see above, Table 4.1). As expected, people from evangelical churches were generally more likely to believe that events in the literalism scale really happened, though, as we shall see, this was not so for items in the parable scale. Overall, the most literally believed items were miracles associated with the life of Jesus, with the virgin birth heading the list. These were believed to have happened by over 80% of the sample, and in evangelical churches the figure was over 90%. The next group were three stories from the Old Testament (David and Goliath, Moses and Pharaoh, and Joshua and the walls of Jericho), along with the Feeding of the 5,000. The Old Testament stories were ones that had historical elements but involved some sort of unusual divine intervention. The remaining items on the literalism scale (Noah, Adam and Eve, and Jonah) scored significantly lower, with only around half the participants answering 'definitely' or 'probably' happened. The parable scale items lie at the bottom of the table, with the Weeds in the Field and the Wise and Foolish Virgins coming below the Good Samaritan and the Prodigal Son.

There were a few comparable items in the *Church Times* survey. An item on the virgin birth received a positive response from 62% of lay people; 65% believed that Jesus turned water into wine and 17% believed God made the world in six days and rested on the seventh (Francis, Robbins et al. 2005, Tables 4.1 and 4.2). These figures are closest to those from Anglo-Catholics in the Bible and Lay People sample (68%, 65% and 21% respectively), which perhaps reflects the high proportion of Anglo-Catholics in the *Church Times* survey (44% Anglo-Catholic and 16% evangelical compared with 27% and 39% respectively in the Bible and Lay People Study). Given the differences in sample and items, the results are remarkably similar and give some confidence that the literalism scale reflected opinions across a broad range of Anglicans in the Church of England.

What do these rankings tell us about the way that participants deal with decisions about biblical literalism? First, it seems that there was generally a clear discrimination between parable and event. This was, perhaps surprisingly, most apparent in evangelical churches, where scores on the literalism scale were higher, and scores on the parable scale lower, than in other traditions. Evangelicals seemed to distinguish parables clearly from other events and were generally willing to accept them as stories. The results for other traditions are puzzling in that they do not show such a clear distinction between items on the literalism and parable scale. This might be because the question 'did a parable happen' was interpreted as 'was the parable told'. The variation in average parable-scale scores between the Prodigal Son and the Wise and Foolish Virgins could then reflect their familiarity to ordinary readers; people being more likely to concede that a well-known parable was told than a less well-known one. On the other hand, it might be that the figures do genuinely represent differences in people's perception of the likelihood of a parable actually having taken place. Rebellious teenagers and muggings are part of our world, but sowing weeds in a farmer's field today would make no difference in the face of modern herbicides. In this case, non-evangelicals seemed more likely to confuse event and story, even though they were less likely than evangelicals to believe that events happened.

The case of Jonah is interesting because it was the lowest item in the literalism scale and in some ways followed the response pattern of parables. Biblical scholars would probably argue that it is indeed an extended parable, but one that is not 'flagged' as such in the Bible. What is most interesting is the response of people in evangelical churches when compared with those from other traditions. Although evangelicals apparently showed greater awareness of New Testament parables as stories, 57% still rated Jonah as actually having been in the belly of the fish for three days. Parables can be treated as fictional stories if the text specifically describes that they were stories told by someone: the default position tends to assume that something happened as described.

Second, there was a distinction between events associated with the life of Jesus and those from the Old Testament. This was not necessarily because the former were more 'believable' from the standpoint of modern science. David killing Goliath with a sling would surely be more feasible to a secular mind than Jesus turning water into wine or raising Lazarus from the dead. Instead it seemed to relate to the doctrinal weight associated with an event. So the virgin birth was top of the list and, judging by pilot studies, items such as the resurrection and crucifixion would have come even higher. Miracles with less apparent doctrinal weight, such as the Feeding of the 5,000, came slightly lower.

Third, there was a clear distinction in the Old Testament material between the sagas of Genesis and other stories such as Moses and Joshua. It seemed that some decision was being made as to whether an event was feasible and perhaps whether it was intended as story or history. The story of Adam and Eve has particular significance because it has held centre stage in the creationist debates. Although the samples may not have been wholly random, it is interesting to note that 61% of evangelicals took this story literally, compared with 45% of broad-church members and only 21% of Anglo-Catholics.

These results imply that fairly sophisticated processes are at work when lay people decide on how literally they should interpret a particular biblical passage. Generally it seems that New Testament events are taken more literally than Old Testament ones, irrespective of how unlikely they may seem to secular eyes. Events that carry particular doctrinal weight are least likely to be interpreted as fictional stories. Within the Old Testament, there is some discrimination that seems to be based on the likelihood of an event being feasible, but less so in evangelical churches. Evangelicals are quick to distinguish parables as stories told by Jesus, and more inclined to rate them as fictional compared with parables such as Jonah that are not described as such in the biblical text.

Factors Shaping Literalism

Almost by definition, there were differences in literalism between church traditions, with evangelicals being generally more literalist than other Anglicans. But what might explain the variation within each tradition? To investigate this, I looked for correlations between the literalism score and a wide range of factors such as sex, age, education level, Bible-reading frequency and church attendance. These factors are themselves correlated, so multiple-regression analysis was used to identify those factors that exerted effects independently of others.

The factors that emerged as the best independent predictors of literalism in this sample were education, theological education (at university level), charismatic practice and Bible-reading frequency, though the results showed some variations between traditions (see Table 4.3).

Table 4.3   Summary of literalism score predictors by church tradition

Source of variation	AC	BC	EV
Education level	(-)**	(-)	
Theological education	(-)*	(-)*	
Charismatic score		(+)***	(+)***
Bible-reading frequency		(+)**	(+)**

Note. After Village (2005d). Signs in parentheses show the direction of the correlation. * $p < .05$; ** $p < .01$; *** $p < .001$, otherwise not significant. AC = Anglo-Catholic; BC = Broad church; EV = Evangelical.

In Anglo-Catholic and broad churches, literalism declined with increasing education, and this effect was greater among those who had specifically theological education. Evangelicals, however, showed no change in literalism with education (see Fig 4.1).

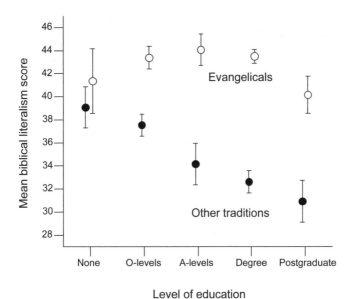

Fig 4.1   **Mean (± SE) biblical literalism score against education level**

Among evangelical and broad churches, charismatics and those who read the Bible frequently interpreted more literally, but this was not so in Anglo-Catholic churches.

A picture emerges of high literalism among those with little educational experience, and non-literal belief among educated people in Anglo-Catholic and broad churches. Educated evangelicals, however, resist this effect of education and retain high levels of literalism. This is particularly so among those who practise charismatic gifts and it is associated with frequent Bible reading. These are fairly predictable findings, and ones that could perhaps have been guessed before the results came in. Nonetheless, having empirical evidence of what was previously largely assumed is the first step on a long journey of discovery. What was more surprising was the apparently greater discernment among evangelicals between event and parable. Evangelical belief is not 'blind' literalism that stubbornly insists that everything in the Bible must have happened. It seems rather to be a principled position that is aware of differences in biblical material but generally chooses to assign a high probability of literalism to anything that is not specifically labelled as a story.

The results show the important effects of education on literalism, but also remind us not to take too simplistic a view on this. It seems that in Church of England, non-literalism is found mainly among educated people from Anglo-Catholic or broad-church congregations. Literalists include both educated evangelicals and people from all traditions who have not been educated beyond secondary school level. Literalism is not about literate liberals and ignorant conservatives. People with low levels of education seemed universally to interpret literally, but this does not mean that education would automatically change their views. This would probably happen to those in Anglo-Catholic and broad churches, but not to those who attend evangelical churches.

Literalism and Mark 9:14–29

The test passage was an account of the exorcism of a spirit from a young boy by Jesus. The symptoms described seem to be those of epilepsy,[6] but this word is not used by the writer and the passage describes the illness as due to an evil (lit. *akathartos*, 'unclean') spirit. Two items in the passage literalism scale were about the boy's illness: 'The boy had epilepsy' and 'The boy was possessed by an evil spirit'. Using answers to these two items showed that of the 404 respondents, 44% were unsure of the diagnosis, 15% believed he was possessed, 28% believed he had epilepsy, 12% believed he had both conditions and 1% believed he had neither.

Using those who made a single diagnosis (i.e. possessed or epilepsy), I investigated what factors might predict the choice using a multiple-regression model applied to binary data (that is a dependent variable that consists of two categories). Two factors emerged as significant: church tradition and charismatic score. Evangelicals were more likely to ascribe the illness to possession than were the other two traditions (23% of 201 evangelicals versus 7% of 203 from other churches) and the reverse was true for epilepsy (12% evangelicals versus 42% from other churches). In addition,

---

[6]   'a spirit that makes him unable to speak; and whenever it seizes him, it dashes him down; and he foams and grinds his teeth and becomes rigid'; Mark 9:18.

charismatics were more likely to diagnose possession than non-charismatics, irrespective of church tradition.

Most churchgoers were either unsure as to what was wrong with the boy, or believed he had epilepsy and was not possessed. This suggests an unwillingness to take the biblical diagnosis at face value, and around 40% were willing to use epilepsy to interpret the symptoms. Those who stuck firmly to the biblical diagnosis were mainly evangelicals or charismatics; the former may take the biblical text at face value, the latter might also be more open to the general idea of spirit possession.

So when it comes to the interpretation of a particular passage, we can see the influences of both a general belief about the Bible and the interaction of experience with a particular text. Evangelicals might be more willing to believe the boy was possessed because that is how the Bible describes his illness; others would pay less attention to this and be more likely to make their own judgement, based on how the illness is described. Charismatics are more likely to be receptive to the whole idea of possession compared with those whose experience does not include practices such as laying hands on people and praying for healing.

Literalism and Ordinary Readers

Literalism seems to be the product of two forces that can sometimes work in opposite directions: doctrinal belief and maintaining plausibility.

Doctrinal belief seems to work in two distinct ways. First, there is the widespread belief in certain key events that are linked to fundamental tenants of the Christian faith. The almost universal belief in the resurrection and the very high levels of belief in the virgin birth are examples of literal belief in miraculous biblical events that carry a great deal of doctrinal weight. For most lay Anglicans in the Church of England these are core beliefs, held by a large majority of members. Second, there is doctrinal belief about the Bible itself, which may determine belief about other events that carry less doctrinal weight. People with a particular belief about the inerrancy or authority of Scripture will be more likely to uphold its basic literalism than people whose core faith is not so strongly linked to the Bible. Miracles that have little direct doctrinal significance (though they may be important in a more general sense) show more variability in response from lay people, and are generally interpreted less literally.

The idea of maintaining plausibility can be traced to the writings of Peter Berger (1967; 1971; 1992), who suggested that beliefs are maintained by social institutions and rituals that make belief plausible in an increasingly secular world. Strong commitment to the institution reinforces beliefs that would otherwise erode in the face of a non-religious world view that makes them seem incredible. In the case of the Bible, education can be thought of as a force eroding literal belief, and this seems to be the case for some lay people. As literalism seems increasingly implausible, it is no longer maintained unless it threatens particular and central doctrinal beliefs. High levels of literalism are therefore restricted to those who have not experienced much education and to those who have, but who also have plausibility structures that help to maintain the belief. The findings here echo similar findings for the effect of education on views about abortion in the United States (Petersen 2001). Data from the General Social Survey suggested that the liberalizing effect of education was weakest among conservative denominations and most evident among liberal Protestants and Jews. Petersen found that frequent attendance at conservative, but not liberal, churches maintained conservative views on abortion despite high levels of education. In my study, literalism was associated with frequent attendance in evangelical but not Anglo-Catholic churches. However, this effect of attendance was not statistically significant if charismatic practice and Bible-reading frequency were added to this model, showing that these latter two behaviours may be more directly important than attendance per se in maintaining literalism among evangelicals.

These forces shaped literalism into three distinct groups in the study sample that probably reflect a more general typology:

The first group were lay people with little or no experience of higher education, who tended to interpret literally whatever their church background. This does not mean that they interpreted everything literally, rather that they were generally more inclined to believe events happened than to believe they were fiction. This might be because literalism is the 'default' position of those who have a church background but little education. Traditional beliefs, which include a literal interpretation of scripture, are perceived as plausible and therefore accepted. People with little educational background may not have the tools to interpret in any other way, or might be suspicious of unfamiliar, intellectual ideas associated with a move away from traditional values.

The second group were people mainly from evangelical churches who had some experience of higher education but who retained a high degree of literalism. Presumably, education increases the perception that certain biblical events are implausible and sets up a tension with doctrinal beliefs about the nature of scripture. Choosing or retaining literalism when education might dictate otherwise represents a statement of trust in the Bible and in the God of whom it speaks. A literal belief is seen as a faithful and true belief that honours the power of God and the veracity of scripture, even if a modern Western perspective makes some events seem highly implausible. Education, and especially theological education, may offer the tools for interpreting parts of the Bible in a less literal way, but these are eschewed in order to maintain a relationship of trust and submission.

For the third group of lay people, moving to a less literal view is not understood in terms of any abandonment of faith, and they will express literalism according to what seems feasible or what is necessary to uphold particular doctrinal beliefs. Here, there is no particular belief about the Bible that would maintain literalism in the face of implausibility, apart from those particular events linked to specific doctrinal belief. So miracles such as the resurrection or virgin birth may be retained as literal because they are foundational to particular faith understandings, but other apparently implausible events such as miracles of Jesus are interpreted non-literally because their historicity carries no particular doctrinal weight. Alternatively, the move away from literalism might be a more positive response to the power of metaphorical interpretation, rather simply a negative rejection of the implausible.

Theological and Practical Implications

This empirical study of literalism has clarified and partly explained the variations in literal belief that exist within a single denomination. If this is the starting point for doing theology, then these different beliefs have to be taken seriously. They cannot be dismissed as irrelevant, or as some sort of 'mistake'. What is the theological significance of these different kinds of belief about biblical literalism? What kind of religious understanding or relationship to the divine do they represent?

Those (mainly evangelicals) who retained high levels of literalism even with high levels of education represented one distinct group in this study. It could be argued from biblical evidence that maintaining a belief in the face of implausibility is linked with the extra-ordinary action of God. Abraham's belief in a seemingly impossible promise of fatherhood (Genesis 15:6) is the prelude to the unlikely birth of a nation. In Romans 4, Paul points to this story and uses it as an example of the kind of faith that is acceptable to God. Dunn (1988: 239) sees this faith as that which God looked for and accepted as grounds for reckoning Abraham as righteous. The fact that the reference is to the original promise in Genesis 15, and not the later embellishments in chapters 17 or 22, seems to stress the nature of this faith: 'For it is here that Paul brings out most clearly the character of Abraham's faith … The strength of Abraham's faith was precisely that it was unsupported by anything else; it was not something which Abraham could do. It was trust, simple trust, nothing but trust' (p. 238). This naked trust in the face of the seemingly impossible is seen time and again in scripture and supremely, perhaps, in the trust of Jesus heading for crucifixion but predicting resurrection. Something creative happens when people deny plausible reality in the cause of Godly devotion.

This is not to say that literalism is a virtue in itself: believing the Genesis creation account because you have never considered anything else does not necessarily require any great devotion or faith. Choosing to believe it in the face of contradictory evidence might simply denote arrogant blindness. However, it might also represent a disposition to which God responds. A somewhat stubborn refusal to bow the knee to conventional wisdom or social pressure has always been the hallmark of the saintly. To *become* like little children (Matthew 18:12) implies a self-conscious decision to take on particular attitudes: a deliberate second naivety rather than one imposed by inexperience or ignorance. Understanding literalism in this way rescues it from being dismissed as a negation of reality or blind obedience to denominational oppression. Some people prefer literal interpretations of the seemingly impossible because it is their way of expressing liberating faith.

Literal belief among evangelicals seems to be maintained particularly by Bible reading and charismatic practice. These are both associated with frequent attendance, and it seemed that social forces as well as individual beliefs may have held back the erosive force of education on literalism. It could be argued that this is sectarian brain-washing: the congregation acts to reinforce its beliefs on individuals and prevent 'deviant' beliefs. As we shall see when discussing interpretative communities in Chapter 7, the evidence for that happening in these congregations is rather mixed. It is not yet clear how much literalism is the *result* of belonging to particular churches or the reason why people join in the first place. What is clear is that, in congregations with a biblically conservative tradition, the most literal interpreters are those that show high levels of activity and commitment.

How is this to be understood and interpreted? In the liberal West there is considerable suspicion and nervousness about small, sectarian groups that shape the beliefs of their members. Perhaps there are too many echoes of mass suicides or terrorist martyrs to see such forces in anything but a negative light. Yet social cohesion and the support of the community of believers seem to have been crucial elements of the first Christian groups. When Paul urges the Roman church 'not [to] be conformed to this world, but transformed by the renewing of your mind' (Romans 12:2), he surely has in mind shared activity that is reflected widely in New Testament ideas of corporate living and collective responsibility. I shall return to this issue in Chapter 7, but suffice here to point out that if empirical evidence shows that literalism is indeed shaped by group activity and expectations this would not necessarily weaken its theological legitimacy. Indeed it might strengthen it.

This way of understanding literalism is less about arguing over whether it represents a 'true' understanding of what actually happened and more about the correlates or consequences of such belief. A theological explanation might stress the virtue of upholding the power and authority of God in the face of culturally acceptable ideas that diminish those characteristics in the minds of devotees. Literal belief can be an act of adoration that expresses the obedience of will and mind that is a prerequisite for faithful discipleship. The idea that someone might choose to hold a literal interpretation, even though they have the knowledge and insight to interpret metaphorically, might seem to be abandoning the pursuit of truth in favour of fantasy. However, it could instead be a way of maintaining the power of the text in a way that has echoes of Paul Ricoeur's search for a 'second naivety' beyond the 'desert of criticism' that allows the text to have meaning once again (see Thiselton 1992: 359).

There is a parallel here to the kind of deliberate choice that Paul urges on the issue of eating meat sacrificed to idols (1 Corinthians 8:1–13). To abstain *as if* you believed that such meat was somehow 'spiritually impure', even though you know that it is not, represents a different level of truth. The truth about the status of the meat is overruled by the more significant truth that is related to care for the spiritually weak or immature. The actions of the mature and immature are apparently identical, but they are in very different places spiritually. In the Bible and Lay People study, there were two groups with very similar literalism scores who seemed to interpret in similar ways. However, the evidence of the effect of education suggests that some may have been deliberately choosing this kind of interpretation, while for others it was the only option open for them. Both can coexist in the Christian community.

What of those educated people who had a less literal interpretation of scripture? In this study it seemed that some lay people used their educational experience (theological or general) to develop a less literal interpretation of some biblical events. This should not be confused with non-belief, as many of these people were committed church attendees with very definite belief. Instead, education enabled a different perspective on biblical literature, one that accepts the possibility of truth being sometimes different from literal truth.

On the evidence from this sample, lay non-literalists are generally rather literal, so this is by no means the total abandonment of biblical or divine realism seen in some academic circles. But it is a more nuanced interpretation than that apparent in the majority of people in this sample. Such non-literal interpretations among committed churchgoers confine the realm of the miraculous to particular events such as the virgin birth or bodily resurrection. This reduces the divergence between the biblical world of miracles and an everyday world where miracles apparently do not happen. God is present and active in the everyday world of disciples in ways that correspond with, rather than contradict, the observed patterns and rules of the world in which they live.

The strength of this position is that God is more plausible within the world view of modern Western culture. Faith is trust that God acts through the ordinary, even though this might reduce the sovereignty of God in creation. Oddly, interpreting God as a God who works without the miraculous associated with biblical literalism requires as much faith as upholding a literal view of scripture. It is just a different sort of faith. To 'wager on the divine' and at the same time accept the metaphorical nature of much of scripture requires the reader to construct a plausibility structure that has to hold religious and secular world views in creative tension. To give neither total hegemony requires careful balance because both tend to be jealous masters, demanding total allegiance. This too is belief that flies in the face of secular rationalism for it requires trust in a God who is presumably omnipotent, yet who somehow presides over a world that is largely explicable without divine intervention.

To pick up the analogy with the issue of eating meat offered to idols, a largely non-literalist position might correspond to those who stuck to their beliefs and ate such meat precisely because they knew it made no difference to their spiritual state. Paul's line of argument would suggest that this is the 'proper' response in situations where the beliefs of other Christians, or the goodwill of non-believers, are not under threat from the action. In this perspective, literalism is seen as a rather naive, immature way of understanding the Bible that is symptomatic of faith that has not seen the bigger picture of God's activity in the world. Non-literalist belief would then be 'lawful', in that it represents a correct way of interpreting some events described in the Bible, but it may not always be expedient if it threatens the faith of others. This dilemma is probably most acute for ministers who have been trained in biblical scholarship, but who operate in congregations that have not. How such ministers cope with this is a separate but related topic to the concerns of this book.

It might seem strange to draw an analogy between first-century shrine offerings and twenty-first-century biblical literalism. A literalist would certainly argue that the one was a pagan cultic practice of no importance while the latter is a central issue of the veracity of the Christian faith. Literalism cannot be dismissed as a naive or immature point of view because it shapes the whole way that God is understood to be and to act. I suspect the same would have been argued by those who saw the refusal of shrine offerings as a fundamental indicator of spiritual health and maturity. Paul moves the argument on beyond this by looking at the consequences of such belief and the way that it is expressed. This does not deny the importance of the belief to those on both sides of the argument, but what it does crucially is to find a way of allowing both views to coexist within the same community of believers.

What are the practical implications of these findings on literalism for those who minister to church congregations? The key finding is the variability in literalism within a single denomination, which may also be reflected within individual congregations. In some congregations there will be a sharp contrast between those with or without experience of higher education, while in other congregations there will be greater uniformity of belief. Preaching and teaching in mixed congregations requires the ability to allow both literalists and non-literalists to coexist, which is by no means an easy task. Exposition that only treats the text literally may leave the non-literalists frustrated and unable to draw meaning from the text. On the other hand, trampling literalist belief may verge on abuse if it is unnecessarily damaging to those who may not have the intellectual tools to understand non-literalist interpretation. It would be a shame if the only solution was to alienate one group or the other and allow a selective drift from the church to homogenize the congregation. A theological position that accepts the integrity of both sorts of beliefs provides the basis for valuing differences between individuals and perhaps suggests ways in which the focus of teaching can move from the issue of literalism to the *consequences* of treating a passage in a particular way. As we shall see when looking at personality, there is an analogy in preaching that allows different personality types to find in a sermon approaches to which they can most easily relate.

The resistance of some congregations to the effects of education on literalism raises different sorts of practical issues. Literalism is part of a wider world view that is shaped and reinforced by religious behaviours such as charismatic practice and Bible reading. For some conservatives, the goal is seen as being able to maintain a 'biblical' world view in the face of pressures to secularize.[7] There is evidence that those who do not ascribe to a literalist world view may find it hard to belong to such churches because attendance falls off among non-literalists in evangelical congregations. There is a difficult balance to be struck here if churches are to gain the advantages of supportive fellowship while avoiding the dangers of a narrow sectarianism. As the frequency of higher education increases in the general population, conservative churches in particular may need to support members who might find themselves caught between two different world views. Handled insensitively, this may cause those who struggle to leave, rather than face the pressures of being marginalized for their views on literalism. Handled carefully, it may allow members the freedom to explore difficult issues and perhaps come to understand more fully the nature and purpose of biblical literalism in their lives.

Further Research

An important outcome of the Bible and Lay People study was the development of a relatively simple, reliable and valid measure of biblical literalism among church-

---

[7]   For example, the late John Wimber, leader of the Signs and Wonders movement of the 1980s, stressed the effects of world view on the ability to accept the notion of miraculous healing: 'So, many Christians caught in the web of Western Secularism ... have a formidable barrier to cross before they can pray for the sick. That barrier is the belief or suspicion that supernatural healing is impossible today' (Wimber and Springer 1986: 30).

going Christians. The scale could be adapted for use beyond churches, though biblical illiteracy might make it difficult to test literalism in the public at large in Britain. A widely held assumption is that Britain is a post-Christian, secular society, though some have consistently challenged this view (see Chapter 2). Belief about the Bible among non-Christians is likely to be nearer to liberal belief than to conservative belief, so according to the findings reported here, literalism should be lower in the general public than among committed churchgoers. Whether this creates uniformly low literalism, or whether familiar or plausible events would be taken literally, and others not, remains to be seen.

The ordering of items on the literalism and parable scales implied that lay people use a fairly sophisticated set of criteria to decide if a particular event happened or not. General beliefs about the Bible are modified by the plausibility of the event and the doctrinal weight it carries. The items in the scale were not developed specifically to test this idea, and this is something that requires more proof. Giving people a longer list of items that were pre-selected according to the relevant criteria might allow the relative importance of plausibility and doctrinal weight to be more accurately assessed.

The effects of education were more marked in some groups than in others, apparently depending on the doctrinal beliefs about the Bible. An interesting group to examine in more detail would be evangelicals with high levels of education. The findings here suggest a conflict between educational background and doctrinal beliefs that would be most apparent in this group. It would be interesting to look for evidence of this conflict and the theological, social or emotional strategies that maintain a literal belief system in the face of threat. Another group of interest might be clergy or others who minister the word to congregations and who have had exposure to theological education. How does their literalism relate to that of their congregations and how does this affect the way that they teach and preach?

Chapter 5

Biblical Interpretative Horizons

One of the reasons why two people reading the same passage of scripture can interpret it in different ways is because they use it differently. A scholar might use the text as a means of understanding the community that produced it, while a layperson might use it to understand their own community. Robert Morgan (1988) pointed out some years ago that what someone gets out of scripture largely depends on their reasons for reading it. The different foci of attention can be thought of as different 'horizons of interest': the world of the author, the world of the text and the world of the reader. The notion of such different worlds has been familiar to scholars of hermeneutics for many years and has been developed more recently by philosophers such as Paul Ricoeur. The questions addressed by this chapter are whether ordinary readers are aware of these different horizons, whether they prefer one horizon over others and, if so, why this might be.

The Concept of Horizon in the Philosophy of Hermeneutics

The idea of human 'situatedness' and its effect on our ability to know or understand has a long pedigree in philosophy.[1] Situation is a standpoint that limits vision and creates the notion of 'horizon', a term associated with the writing of the German philosopher Hans-Georg Gadamer (1979). Human beings are bound by space and time, but also by their ability to conceive or know beyond their own experience. The heart of the philosophical debate has been whether and how it is possible to understand things that lie beyond our own horizons.

    Gadamer wrote *Truth and Method* (first published in 1960) to counter both rational and romantic approaches hermeneutics. In it, he agues that both methods objectify that which is being sought, thus misunderstanding the basic hermeneutical task. Historicism, the product of Enlightenment rationalism, was based on the possibility of being able to step into an ancient culture and perceive it as it was originally understood. This assumed the ability to leave behind our pre-understandings and prejudices and observe the past from a 'neutral' space. Romantics such as Schleiermacher developed the concept of 'divination' in hermeneutics, and developed the role of understanding in more intuitive, psychological terms (see Thiselton 1992: 204–236). Both systems sought to reproduce the world of the author as if this was something separate from the world of the interpreter. This is not only impossible, argued Gadamer, but also pointless. It is impossible because of the 'distanciation'

---

[1]   Gadamer (1979: 269) traces this back to the writings of Friedrich Nietzsche and Edmund Husserl.

effect of human creations: once a text or work of art is produced, meaning no longer resides with the author. Such objects are no longer simply purveyors of the author's intent, but objects of meaning in their own right. Each reading of a text is unique because it is the creation of a reader in a particular context and that context can never be set aside. Trying to recreate the intent of the author is also pointless because understanding is not *reproduction* but creative *production* (Gadamer 1979: 263). Truth is something created by each generation as they bring their horizon to bear on the horizons of those who have tackled the same task before them. What is the purpose of understanding something as it was originally understood without reference to the interpreter? Even if this were possible, the result would have nothing to say to the present generation.

Gadamer did not, unlike some of those who followed, abandon any notion of bringing horizons together, but he reconceptualized the task. He was aware of the prejudices and pre-understandings that interpreters bring to the text but rather than set them aside he saw them as potentially helpful in the task of interpretation. The separation of horizons produced by time is valuable because it enables the interpreter to separate 'the true prejudices by which we understand from the false ones by which we misunderstand' (p. 266). Interpretative tradition is the record of different conceptions of an object and shows us the questions we might ask and the assumptions we bring to the interpretative task. Gadamer points out that horizons are not static, but move with us: 'The historical movement of human life consists in the fact that that it is never utterly bound to one standpoint, and hence can never have a truly closed horizon. The horizon is, rather, something into which we move and that moves with us' (p. 271).

So horizons for Gadamer are not so much separated boundaries but a series of overlapping spheres. Each interpreter's horizon is created by interaction with tradition, so that understanding is less about fusing horizons and more about expanding the common horizon (p. 273). This is not a naive assimilation of the past, but is based on what Gadamer terms 'effective-historical consciousness', which seems to be the ability to distinguish our own horizon in creative tension with the past (Weinsheimer 1985: 184).[2]

Gadamer's ideas, though not entirely novel, have had a profound impact on the way that hermeneutics has evolved. Thiselton (1992: 11) sees a number of different developments that can be traced to this seminal work. The stress on the fact that all understanding is context bound led some to question the social and ethical contexts which produced texts, while others moved to a more radical position of relativizing all truth, making it pragmatic and rhetorical rather than absolute.

Paul Ricoeur found this gap between author and reader liberating and stimulating rather than alienating (Simms 2003: 39). Readers can 'inhabit' the world within the text without the encumbrance of the author's intention, and this interaction is a journey of self-discovery: 'to understand is to understand oneself in front of the

---

[2]   Weinsheimer (1985: x) points out that even Gadamer admitted the term he used, *wirkungsgeschichtliches Bewusstsein,* was 'overly ambiguous'. Although difficult to define, the concept has spurred the study of the 'reception history' of texts as a distinct discipline within literary and biblical studies.

text' (Ricoeur 1991: 88). Ricoeur's work on hermeneutics has drawn attention to the different 'worlds' involved when a text is read (Ricoeur 1981: 142–4; Thiselton 1992: 57) and this is now a widely understood way of conceptualizing the nature of texts and their interpretation. The world 'behind' the text is a way of referring to the complex weave of culture, conventions, intentions, history and chance that leads to the creation of texts. This world leaves its imprint on texts, but texts are not simply a product of this world, they are also a creator of other worlds. The world or worlds 'within' the text refers to attitudes, conventions and possibilities projected by texts. This is most obvious in narrative, but it is true of all writing. The Levitical laws of the Pentateuch project a world that is ordered in space and time with respect to the sacred. The Pauline epistles project a world centred on the apostle and his oversight of the early church. These projections are not unambiguous, and different readers will create different worlds as texts interact with human imagination. When readers inhabit a world in a text the process becomes transforming as this world interacts with the world 'in front of' the text, that is, the world of the reader. This latter world is shaped by the culture, conventions and understanding of the society in which reading takes place, as well as the unique world of particular readers formed by their origins, history and experience. Understanding the text is in effect a self-understanding in relation to the text.

The Concept of Horizon in Biblical Studies

The notions of horizons and text worlds have become a familiar part of the discourse of academic hermeneutics, and they have had profound effects on biblical studies. These effects are not always recognized for what they are: the notion of interpretative horizons in biblical study is one that is widely understood, but rarely discussed explicitly. It is most immediately associated with Anthony Thiselton, who used the word in the titles of his two important works on philosophy and biblical hermeneutics: *The Two Horizons* (1980) and *New Horizons in Hermeneutics* (1992). Thiselton sums up well the enterprise of biblical hermeneutics and its possibilities in the introduction to *The Two Horizons:*

> The goal of biblical hermeneutics is to bring about an active and meaningful engagement between the interpreter and text, in such a way that the interpreter's own horizon is re-shaped and enlarged. In one sense it is possible to speak, with Gadamer, of the goal of hermeneutics as a 'fusion' of horizons. In practice, because the interpreter cannot leap out of the historical tradition to which he belongs, the two horizons can never become totally identical: at best they remain separate but close. (Thiselton 1980: xix)

Horizon, then, represents a fundamental aspect of any interpretative task. While most interpretative traditions are aware of the existence of horizons, they differ in how they react to them. Those that accept the possibility of understanding the original meaning or intention of the author will look to enter the world behind the text and perhaps bring it into some relationship with world of the reader. Thiselton's words arise from someone who is generally optimistic about the possibility of linking horizons, and this shapes the way he goes about the interpretative task. If, on the other hand, it is assumed that there is no possibility of bringing horizons together, then the task itself becomes something quite different. It could be argued that the general trend in biblical studies described in Chapter 2 has been to move from historical methods, which confidently accepted their created images of the world of the author, to postmodern methods that have abandoned even trying to enter that world. This is grossly simplified, but does perhaps serve as a way of categorizing different ways of understanding the 'otherness' of the biblical text. How, then, do different approaches to academic biblical scholarship understand interpretative horizons?

Segovia (1995a) characterized historical criticism as based heavily on positivism, leading to the idea of the text having an objective and univocal meaning that can be retrieved by applying the correct methods of analysis. The enterprise of interpretation is perceived as one of constantly refining understanding in the light of new findings, and thereby bringing the reader ever closer to the original meaning of the text and the 'horizon' of the author. The very existence of such a huge body of historical scholarly work on the Bible highlights the complexity and difficulty of the task, but it does not necessarily question the possibility of success. In horizon terms, this represents strong awareness of the separation of horizons, but an assumption that they can be brought together. Historical criticism arose in a period of some naivety regarding hermeneutical method: although there was recognition that all interpreters approach texts with some pre-understanding that might lead to bias, it was assumed that this could be laid aside in order to allow objective analysis of the evidence. In this sense, little attention was paid to the horizon of the reader. The aim was less to fuse horizons than to move the scholar behind the text and understand the world through the author's eyes. The reader's horizon was an unfortunate distraction that had to be dealt with by trying to make scholarship as objective as possible.

Literary criticism marked a move away from the preoccupation with recapturing the horizon of the author. Meaning was something that arose from an interaction of text and reader, with the text as the controlling horizon. Segovia (1995a) highlights the strong similarities of literary criticism to its predecessor, at least in its early manifestations. Both relied heavily on textual analysis and both were based on a positivist and empiricist assumption that application of method would reveal meaning. For literary critics the focus was originally on the text, which was assumed to contain the conventions and codes that could be properly understood by 'competent' readers. Historical research might be needed to uncover the codes of various genres of writing, but this was not an end in itself. The focus was on the view of the world embedded in the text, which could be objectively understood by scholars. Again, the aim was less to fuse horizons than to move the scholar into the horizon of the text by understanding the competency required of an implied reader. Segovia argues that even when the focus of literary criticism expanded to include the reader, this was still an exercise in understanding the response of idealized readers to the text. The possibility of different readings was accepted, but only to a limited extent and as circumscribed by limits within the text (1995a: 17).

Segovia's own interest is to promote 'cultural studies', a much more thoroughgoing interest in readers and their particular cultural and social location. This reflects a growing interest in the horizon of present-day readers, which stems partly from literary studies and partly from ideological struggles against poverty, sexism and racism. In cultural studies, texts are seen as a construction of the reader, rather than as separate containers of objective meaning. The horizon of the reader is dominant, and bridges are made to the text with a strong self-conscious awareness of cultural or social location. This move to cultural studies is heavily influenced by postmodern perspectives on scholarly enterprise in general and on the notion of objectivity in particular. Traditional scholarship is perceived to be authoritarian in its attempt to impose objective truth on the rest of the community of Bible readers. In horizon terms, the reader's world has become totally dominant. There is little attempt to fuse or bridge between horizons by linking the reader to the separate world view of an author or a text. Instead, these things are assumed to be idealized entities that are unattainable and irrelevant. Cultural studies have become a paradigm for scholars sharing interpretations in a way that deliberately avoids any claims to universality. For many this means explicitly defining the characteristics of their own horizon and reminding readers that this situatedness is a given for the interpretation that follows.[3] Such scholars are not only aware of the separation of horizons between the original author and current readers, they are also aware of the separation of the horizons of present-day readers.

It seems fair to say that academic interests embrace all three worlds of author, text and reader. Perhaps what unites and defines scholarly biblical study is the avoidance of any real application of interpretation to the life of the reader. To a large extent, academic exploration of the Bible remains wary of the notion that the text might speak with an authority to readers that lies beyond the text or its human author.

Horizon and Ordinary Readers[4]

The concept of horizon is an important marker for defining academic approaches to scripture. To be aware of different horizons is to show the kind of perception that is the starting point for the vast majority of scholarly approaches. To read scripture solely as if it were written for you, and for this moment of your life, is to enter into a relationship with it that most scholars would find hard to understand. This does not mean that lay people cannot do both. They may know that this is an ancient text that arose in a very different time and culture, but nonetheless believe that it contains a message that speaks to people in any culture at any point in history.

There are several slightly different aspects of horizon that could describe the approach of ordinary readers. The first is the extent to which someone is aware of the existence of horizons: do they perceive this text as something written for another culture in another age? Do they notice the gap, or are they unaware of it? Is this a strange, bewildering piece of writing that speaks of the unfamiliar and unknown, or is it something that seems to relate directly to their culture, society or life? These questions arise when a particular reader encounters a particular text and tries to make sense of it in relation to their experience. We can refer to the degree of strangeness or 'otherness' perceived by someone reading scripture as a measure of *horizon*

---

[3]   The collections of essays in Kitzberger (1999) and Segovia and Tolbert (1995a; 1995b) are good examples of this approach.

[4]   Some of this section is based on work published in Village (2006).

separation. A high degree of separation implies a sense that a text is referring to something that belongs to another world, a sense that things were different then and that some things referred to are opaque to modern readers. Low separation implies a text that is translucent, referring to things that seem to be part of the everyday life of the reader.

A second parameter, related to horizon separation, is *applicability*, the extent to which the text has a message for readers that is relevant to their lives. The two are not entirely the same because it is possible for someone to perceive a text as being entirely transparent and with an obvious meaning, but that meaning has no particular bearing on their life. However, it seems unlikely that people who perceive a passage as entirely strange, obscure and opaque will find in it something that applies to their particular situation. High horizon separation might therefore be associated with low applicability, even if the opposite is not always true. Applying passages in this way is not part of the academic discourse of biblical studies, but it is a central reason why most lay Christians read scripture. Although a scholar might be content to read, understand and move on, most ordinary readers will look for what the passage teaches them to believe or about how they should behave.

This leads to the third aspect surrounding horizons and ordinary readers, namely *horizon preference*. Scholarship is interested in the worlds of the author, text and reader, but what about ordinary readers? When they read scripture, do they see it as pointing mainly back to the world of the original human author, do they remain within the world created by the text, or do they bring the text into their own world and relate it in some way to what they do or believe? They may, of course, do two or three of these things in any combination, but if they were forced to attend to just one of these three horizons of interest, which would it be? Again, this might well be related to horizon separation and applicability, because readers who perceive little distance between horizons should find it easier to interpret it within their own world, whereas those who are aware of separation are likely to understand the passage as relating mainly to the world of the author.

These three aspects, horizon separation, applicability and horizon preference, seem to be important parameters to measure when it comes to ordinary readers. They relate to some key aspects of biblical hermeneutical theory, and they could point to some crucial differences between ordinary and scholarly readers. Until relatively recently, the difference could be described in fairly straightforward terms: scholars perceive the text as a window to the original author; lay readers are largely unaware of the world behind the text and use the text to guide their everyday life. These assumptions have not been tested in any systematic or empirical manner, perhaps because it was taken as axiomatic that scholars separated horizons and lay people did not. If this bland assumption ever held sway, there are good reasons for thinking that things may be changing. First, as we have seen, there is no longer any simple definition of what constitutes a scholarly approach to scripture. Second, the growing availability of education and scholarship could mean that even those lay readers who are not formally trained in biblical scholarship might approach scripture in ways that show an awareness of different horizons. The best way to investigate this is to find ways of quantifying horizon separation, applicability and horizon preference among ordinary readers.

Measuring Horizons in the Bible and Lay People Study

Two possible ways of assessing horizon variables are either to ask general questions about the way people use scripture or to ask questions in relation to particular passages. The former requires less effort, but answers might depend heavily on what parts of scripture were being referred to, so general questions may result in vague and uncertain answers. Using test passages seems a better approach, though it means conclusions may not hold for other types of scripture.

The measures of horizon used here are based on the test passage in the Bible and Lay People questionnaire, Mark 9:14–29 (see the Appendix). This story of a miraculous healing through exorcism seemed to contain the right mixture of distance and familiarity. The boy's symptoms appear to be those of epilepsy, but they are ascribed in the text to demon possession. The story has clear links to common human reactions (the father's cry of 'I believe, help my unbelief!', and the concern expressed by the disciples about their failure to heal), but it also has puzzling aspects, such as the nature of the healing event, Jesus' rather harsh reaction to the father's honest request for help and the way that Jesus seems to offer help only when he sees the crowd approaching.

After testing a wide range of items, the horizon separation scale in the final questionnaire was reduced to seven Likert-type items (see Table 5.1). These formed a scale that had an acceptable reliability (Cronbach's $\alpha = .72$), though the inter-correlation of items was rather low. Around a quarter of participants found the story hard to relate to their lives or could not imagine it happening today. Around two-thirds found the story to be self-explanatory or a straightforward account. This implies a general tendency to fuse, rather than separate horizons. However, around half also thought the story had some aspects that were difficult to understand or that it showed how differently people thought in those days. This suggests that the story was not wholly transparent to everyone and that the overall perception of the story was somewhat mixed.

Table 5.1   Items in the horizon separation scale

Item	IRC	%
This story is self-explanatory*	.34	59
I find this story hard to relate to my life	.45	28
I cannot imagine this happening today	.55	27
This is a straightforward account of a miraculous healing*	.40	69
We can never know what was wrong with the boy	.43	52
This story has several aspects that are very hard to understand	.47	45
This story shows how differently people thought in those days	.42	58

Note. The table shows the percentage of 404 participants who agreed or strongly agreed with each item in the scale. IRC = Item–rest correlation. * These items were reverse scored.

Applicability deals with what the passage can teach and whether it contains some message from God. The scale measuring applicability consisted of six items and had a good degree of reliability (Cronbach's α = .84; see Table 5.2). Nearly everyone sampled thought this was a story from which they could learn something, and very few thought it had no relevance. Around three-quarters understood the passage in terms of God speaking to them or teaching them to pray and act in faith, pointing to a high degree of applicability for most people in this sample. As expected, there was a strong negative association between horizon separation and application (r = -.57, df = 319, p < 0.001), so people who perceived a separation of horizons tended to be less likely to see the story as having anything to say about their lives.

Table 5.2   Items in the applicability scale

Item	IRC	%
A story that has no relevance to my life*	.64	5
A story that has no direct application in today's society*	.66	3
An event from which we can learn something	.61	95
A story from the life of Jesus that shows who he was	.58	91
God speaking to me through the Bible	.63	73
God teaching me to pray and act with faith	.62	82

Note. The table shows the percentage of 404 participants who agreed or strongly agreed with each item in the scale, IRC = Item–rest correlation. * These items were reverse scored.

Measuring preference for horizon was slightly more complicated because the pilot studies revealed a tendency for people to select all horizons if given the opportunity. In other words, ordinary readers can see the story as pointing to the intentions of the author, having value as a story in itself, and as having relevance to their own lives all at the same time. Using forced-choice questions is rather artificial, but it was a better way of revealing underlying predispositions. The eight items developed from the test passage had three possible answers, each of which related to the author, text or reader horizons (see Table 5.3). The items were introduced by the phrase 'This story shows …' and participants were asked to choose one answer for each item. Author answers always mentioned 'the writer', text items referred to the story as such, while reader items applied the story to 'today'.

Adding up the number of author, text and reader choices gave scores for each horizon. The maximum possible score for each horizon would be 8, if one horizon was consistently selected in each item, and the minimum was 0, if a particular horizon was never chosen. The scores for each horizon were not completely independent because a high score in one horizon necessarily implied a low score in at least one of the other two horizons. Nonetheless, it was possible to use the scores to investigate the factors that might shape horizon preference. Where participants answered all eight questions, text-horizon items were chosen most often, closely followed by

Table 5.3   Items in the horizon preference scales

		This story shows …	A	IRC T	R
1	A	The writer's fellow Christians could not always heal people	.26		
	T	Why the disciples were not always able to heal people		.28	
	R	Why people are not always healed when we pray for them today			.32
2	A	The writer believed that Jesus was able to perform miracles	.30		
	T	Jesus was renowned in his lifetime as a powerful worker of miracles		.17	
	R	Jesus performs miracles today			.48
3	A	The writer encouraged his readers to have faith in Jesus	.38		
	T	Jesus encouraged the father's weak faith		.36	
	R	God encourages us today when our faith is weak			.43
4	A	The writer was trying to dispel the fear of evil in the early church	.47		
	T	Jesus overcame the people's fear of evil		.41	
	R	Through Jesus, we need not fear evil today			.48
5	A	The writer wanted to denounce his faithless generation	.34		
	T	Jesus was sometimes angry with the faithless people he met		.41	
	R	God is sometimes angry at our lack of faith today			.49
6	A	The writer believed that prayer could exorcize demons	.41		
	T	Jesus believed that his disciples must pray if they were to heal		.39	
	R	Prayer is vital for a successful healing ministry today			.50
7	A	The mind of the original writer	.37		
	T	The attitude of Jesus to his generation		.36	
	R	What it means to be a faithful disciple today			.52
8	A	The writer had compassion for the sick and demon-possessed	.13		
	T	The compassion Jesus had for the sick and demon-possessed		.40	
	R	That we should have compassion for the needy people we meet			.38

Note. From Village 2006. IRC = Item–rest correlation for items in the same horizon, A = Author; T = Text; R = Reader.

reader-horizon items, with author-horizon items being chosen much less frequently.[5] This avoidance of the author horizon in favour of the text or reader horizons is in line with the idea that lay people are less interested in the historical background or origins of biblical texts and more interested in the meaning of the text or its application.

---

[5]   The average numbers of choices among 400 participants were 3.6 (SD = 2.1) for text-horizon items, 3.2 (SD = 2.3) for reader-horizon items and 1.3 (SD = 1.5) for author-horizon items.

These preliminary analyses paint the sort of picture we might expect for lay people. What biblical scholars would score in this exercise is difficult to tell. Presumably, there would be a greater sense of horizon separation, less application and greater choice of the author horizon, though the latter might depend on the sort of biblical scholar being examined. It would be interesting to compare the results here with similar exercises on different parts of scripture. Would parts of the Old Testament have greater horizon separation and lower applicability? Would epistles score higher on the author horizon? Such comparative work would require participants to read several different passages, and so there may need to be fewer questions on each. Given the size and scope of the Bible and Lay People questionnaire, it was not possible to do this sort of work in this study.

Factors Determining Horizon Separation and Preference

Although the general picture that emerged from the study of horizon was much as expected, there was some variation in both the extent of horizon separation and in horizon preferences. Investigating the factors that predict this variation might shed light on what shaped ordinary readers' response to passages in terms of horizon. What sorts of people were likely to perceive the gap in horizons, or to show the strongest preference for or avoidance of a particular horizon?

Horizon separation was related to a wide range of factors, but multivariate analysis identified four important independent predictors of horizon separation: biblical literalism, belief in supernatural healing, membership of a church healing team and whether or not the person had heard the passage before (see Table 5.4).

Table 5.4   Analysis of variance of horizon separation

Source of variation	df	F
Heard story before	1	4.4*
Member of a healing group	1	7.2**
Supernatural healing score	1	52.9***
Literalism score	1	26.7***
Error	358	(11.1)

Note. Heard story before (1 = yes, 0 = no) and member of a healing team (1 = yes, 0 = no) were entered as factors, supernatural-healing and literalism scales were entered as covariates in a general linear model. The value in parenthesis is the mean square error. $^{*}p < .05$; $^{**}p < .01$; $^{***}p < .001$.

People who showed strong literal belief in the Bible perceived little separation of horizons in the test passage. Presumably those who find it difficult or unnecessary to believe that an event happened as described will be likely to perceive it as a strange, mythological tale rather than as something that might happen today. Belief in supernatural healing was assessed through a twelve-item scale (see Village 2005c and Chapter 9) and this was a strong predictor of low horizon separation in this biblical passage. Belief that miraculous healing can happen today was likely to be important in determining how familiar a biblical healing story seemed to the reader, and such a belief had an effect over and above a general belief in biblical literalism. Interestingly, the effect of belief was heightened in this case by religious practice, because, all other factors being equal, readers who also belonged to a healing team showed a stronger merging of horizons than those who did not. Religious belief and religious practice in this case seemed to reinforce each other.

Familiarity with the idea of miraculous healing or exorcism seemed to help to bring the two horizons together. A familiarity with this specific passage also seemed to reduce separation. Although only 11% of people who answered the question indicated that they had not heard the story before, they had significantly higher horizon separation scores, even after allowing for the effects of other independent variables. Perhaps biblical passages are always a bit strange when we first encounter them, and become less so simply by virtue of repetition. This might be a case of familiarity breeding 'contempt' for the strangeness of the text, something that biblical exegetes often warn against. On the other hand, it might be the case that only when readers have encountered a text a few times can they begin to make sense of it, and begin to see its relevance to their own life.

Although it is usually assumed that education helps readers to discern the separation of horizons, education (general or specifically theological) did not exert much influence in this case. As we saw in Chapter 4, literalism is partially influenced by education, but only in some church traditions. When it comes to horizon separation, the difference appears to be related to prior beliefs about biblical literalism and supernaturalism, and to particular religious practice related to the passage in question. Education does not seem to override or influence this perception, at least for the sort of education experienced by people in this sample. It might require a more thoroughgoing immersion in historical criticism to change a sense of immediacy. Given the moves in biblical scholarship to accommodate a broader range of approaches to scripture, such a programme might seem misplaced or unwarranted.

The predictors of preference for author, text or reader were identified by analyses of variance, using the scores for each horizon as dependent variables (see Table 5.5). These analyses were not entirely independent of one another because a factor associated with an increase in preference for one horizon was likely to be associated with a decrease in preference for at least one of the other horizons. The significant predictors of horizon preference were: general education level, theological education, belief in supernatural healing and biblical literalism. Some predictors were associated with shifts between the author and text horizon and some with shifts from author to reader or text to reader horizon.

General education and theological education had similar but independent effects on horizon preference. Although the author horizon was not chosen often, it was more likely to be chosen by those who had experience of higher education. Interest in the text horizon also increased with levels of education, whereas interest in the reader horizon declined. Plotting horizon scores against education level (see Fig 5.1) showed that the author- and reader-horizon scores formed a mirror image, suggesting that the main effect of education was to shift interest away from the

Table 5.5   Analyses of variance of horizon preference scales

Source of variation	df	Author F	Text F	Reader F
Education	1	10.9**	12.4**	27.1***
Theological education	1	14.1***	0.8	8.7**
Member of a healing group	1	3.7*	1.6	0.0
Supernatural healing score	1	17.2**	1.0	10.6*
Literalism score	1	25.7***	8.1**	0.0
Error	381	(1.5)	(4.3)	(4.7)

Note. Theological education and membership of a healing group entered as factors (1 = yes, 0 = no), and education, supernatural healing and literalism entered as covariates in a separate general linear model for each horizon. Values in parentheses are mean square errors. $^*p < .05$; $^{**}p < .01$; $^{***}p < .001$.

reader horizon towards the author horizon. This effect was heightened among those who had theological education to at least higher education certificate level. Such education tends to stress the historical background to biblical texts, so an increased awareness of the intentions or world of the author is not surprising. This does not exclude other ways of understanding the text, and even those who had the highest author-horizon scores were likely to choose that horizon only two or three times out of eight. Nonetheless, people with high levels of education were less likely to apply the passage to their own life and times.

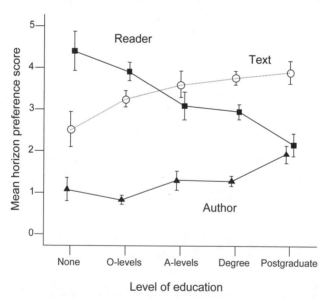

Fig 5.1   Mean (± SE) horizon preference scores against education level

Belief in supernatural healing was negatively correlated with preference for the author horizon, positively correlated with preference for the reader horizon, but not correlated with preference for the text horizon. It seemed that those who believed that miraculous healing was possible today perceived the story as showing less about the human author and more about how disciples should behave today. Although literalism was negatively related to education and positively to belief in supernatural healing, it exerted an independent effect on horizon preference that was associated with a move from the author to the text horizon. The effect was independent of education and it seemed that interest in the text was not simply an interest in the passage as a story, but an interest that stemmed from a belief that this event happened as recorded. There were thus two slightly different effects of literalism and belief in supernatural healing on horizon preference, even though these two are closely correlated. Supernatural belief influenced the extent to which the passage was interpreted in the world of the reader rather than the world of the author, whereas literal belief influenced the extent to which the passage was interpreted in the world of the text rather than the world of the author.

Theological and Practical Implications

In some ways these findings confirm the widely perceived separation of academic and lay interest in the Bible. Lay people tended to avoid the author horizon and were likely to apply the story to their own life or society. Those that did show interest in the author horizon were often people who had some theological education and who may not, therefore, have been strictly 'lay' interpreters. Having acknowledged this general trend, it would be unwise to categorize ordinary Bible readers too simplistically. There was considerable variation in the extent of horizon separation and horizon preference, and it is clear that different subgroups existed within the sample. These groups were defined mainly by individual differences in belief and educational experience.

As with literalism, education emerged as an important influence, though not always as expected. In theory, education should increase the sense of horizon separation by inculcating a critical detachment that makes the reader aware that the Bible arose in a very different culture from our own. Theological education might fairly be assumed to do this in a more focused and effective manner. However, there was no evidence of any such effect. Instead, beliefs about biblical literalism and supernatural healing were more directly important, as was the religious practice of belonging to a church healing prayer group. Education did, however, have a strong influence on preference for the author horizon and avoidance of the reader horizon. It seems that education may not make a text like Mark 9:14–29 seem more distant, but might make readers more reluctant to apply it to their own lives.

Application (at least as indicated by preference of the reader horizon) is not a simple matter of believing that it happened as written and then transferring that event to the here and now. Indeed, literal belief was not, ultimately, associated with application. Instead, literal belief tended to lead to an interest in the text horizon. The people most likely to apply the story were those who believed that supernatural events like the one described in the passage happen today, that is, what Jesus did is a direct paradigm for the actions of his followers today and this is possible because, in effect, disciples can do what their master did. This certainly seems to be the logic of the story because it contrasts the disciples' inability with Jesus' ability. The implication is that true belief and persistent prayer would enable the disciples to succeed in the task of exorcism and healing. Applying that sort of story is easier if the reader believes that it is possible for present-day disciples to perform miracles. Notice that although literal or conservative beliefs about the Bible are strongly related to belief in supernatural healing, they were not as important as belief in healing for creating interest in the reader horizon. It is belief specifically associated with the text as a healing story that engendered application in this case.

Insofar as they support widely held views on the differences between scholarly and lay readings of the Bible, these findings raise familiar questions about the role and purpose of theological education. Here I want to explore the notion of whether lay readers of the Bible should be encouraged to foster a sense of distance from biblical texts, or whether should they be left in 'blissful ignorance'. Church-based theological education often involves some attempt to help students appreciate the difficulty of fully understanding an ancient text in its own terms. The reasons for encouraging this sort of study are not hard to discern because critical distance is an important check to religious communities that too easily seek to appropriate texts entirely on their own terms. Forcing present-day realities and personal agendas onto biblical texts and passing them off as 'what the text has always meant' does not honour the sacredness of those texts, or those who wrote them. The first task of theological education must be to cause readers to pause before they too easily fuse their horizon with that of the text. In Ricoeur's terms, this means losing our 'first naivety', and it is the inevitable consequence of scholarly activity. But is this something that would benefit all lay readers? After all, once the genie is out of the bottle it cannot return.

Many would argue that gaining critical distance does not mean that readers are for ever captive to the rather dry world of critical scholars, endlessly speculating on the past but never changing the present. Ricoeur talks of a 'second naivety', which allows the text to transform, even while acknowledging its separateness from our own lives. I suspect that while many have tried to develop this insight and to work out what this second naivety might look like, rather fewer have succeeded. Theological education by churches is partly an attempt to enable readers to apply texts to their own world in a way that is not wholly dominated by that world or by the assumptions that they bring to the text. This empirical study seems to highlight the difficulties of that task. Education, especially theological education, seemed to move readers to the author horizon and perhaps left them there. This might be drawing too much from what was admittedly a rather crude study, but the evidence is there to be refuted or confirmed. Perhaps the options for the reader horizon were too simplistic for genuine second naivety, so that the theologically literate preferred the safer ground of the author's world. But it might also suggest that the task of education is sometimes left unfinished, destroying the first naivety without allowing the second.

The perceived gap between reader and text was reduced if readers came to the text with certain presuppositions about the Bible and about the supernatural. For the scholar, this confirms that presuppositions make us blind to the 'otherness' of the text and explains why lay people fail to truly understand it. For lay people this confirms that scholars lose that crucial childlike faith that enables the text to be properly understood as a message for them and their lives today. Who is reading 'correctly' here? If correct reading is about understanding the text in the terms in which it was written, it could be argued that the objective, analytical approach of the scholar saves readers from blind prejudice and allows the text to be understood now as it would have been then. Certainly this was how a generation of historical critical scholars understood their task, though few scholars would make such bold claims today. We have seen how the attack on modernity has questioned the very idea that it is possible to approach a text from an objective stance. It is no longer credible to claim that a detached, critical stance to scripture is a better way of reading, even if such a stance were possible in the first place. That being so, it is equally possible to argue that someone who takes a generally literalist interpretation of scripture, and who believes that miracles can happen as described in the Bible, is more truly approaching the text in its own terms than someone whose beliefs are at odds with those of the original authors.

This could be seen as an argument for not letting the scholarly genie out of the bottle in the first place. Why impose on lay people the necessity of losing a naivety that is required for 'true' understanding of the message of scripture? There is some scriptural warrant for a healthy scepticism towards scholarship. Jesus thanks the Father that 'these things' are revealed to naive children and not to the wise and intelligent of the world (Luke 10:21). Paul specifically argues that worldly wisdom cannot conceive the fundamental truth of the Christian Gospel (1 Corinthians 1:18–30). Do the virtues of innocence outweigh the dangers of ignorance? As I argued in the last chapter, a decision to hold to a literal view in the face of conflicting evidence is not necessarily about stubborn ignorance. So too an ability to relate directly to a text because it accords with our beliefs and experience is not necessarily a sign of blinkered reading. It could equally be that a presupposition that a text is recalling something that actually happened, and that this sort of thing can and does happen in our world today, is precisely the kind of presupposition required to read this sort of text 'correctly'. It is reading with the grain of the text that allows the text to have some meaningful engagement with the reader. Empirically, this seems to be the case, and education does not seem to threaten this relationship. The question remains as to what is to be gained by challenging or changing this status quo.

The danger that scholars perceive in this naive approach to scripture is that the biblical text is moulded to fit the existing world view and prejudices of the reader. The text cannot then challenge or transform, but only confirm and conform. Without awareness of the separation of the text from the reader, the text simply becomes an extension of the reader, with the likelihood that readers will project their own sinful practices through the text (Fowl 1998: 74). The Bible becomes a stick with which to beat others and fend off the truth. This charge is often laid by scholars to conservative or fundamentalist approaches to scripture, though it could equally apply to any church-based interpretations. To be fair, this danger is also inherent in some scholarly approaches: Thiselton (1992: 549–50) argues that strongly socio-pragmatic methods of reading, such as that championed by Stanley Fish, fail to separate the text from the reader and thereby prevent a real challenge to readers from beyond their own world. Others such as Francis Watson (1994) have also questioned the critical objectivity of scholars, arguing that progress in biblical studies is not so much a growth in objective knowledge as the ebb and flow of arbitrary fashion. So can and should scholarship help ordinary readers avoid the dangers of pre-critical use of scripture?

The sort of people who read a healing story in the New Testament and see it as a paradigm for their own ministry are not necessarily doomed to bigotry and spiritual stasis. To be sure, some who take a literal view of the test passage in Mark 9 may see this as justifying cruel and foolish attempts to cast out demons from innocent children, but is the fault with the basic perception of the story? A world view that conceives the possibility of demon possession is not one that sits easily with Western secularism, but some might see that as pointing to its value rather than its danger. The issue is not so much how the horizons are understood, but the consequences of that understanding. Many who merge the horizons of author, text and reader might use the passage to ends that few could criticize. Jesus' condemnation of a faithless generation in Mark 9:19 may be taken as a direct challenge to readers to be faithful and true to the God that they serve. This story might spur deeper efforts to help the poor and vulnerable in the world precisely because it shows that Jesus helped someone who came to him in desperation. The counter might be that this is actually a rather un-literal and symbolic interpretation of the passage that transfers the particular event of exorcism to a more acceptable general concern for the needy. Such interpretations are possible with or without literal belief and with or without belief in supernatural healing today. The key point here is that such beliefs do not automatically create self-serving interpretations, just as lack of such beliefs does not guarantee the absence of self-serving interpretations either.

What, then, of readers who might exploit this story by using it as a justification for mistreating those they deem to be possessed by evil spirits? This is not a hypothetical question: recent events in Britain among some congregations suggest that children have been seriously abused in the name of 'spiritual liberation'.[6] Surely, it could be argued, a healthy distanciation would allow this biblical story to be seen as a primitive response to a misunderstood ailment. It may have been an appropriate diagnosis and treatment in the first century, but not in the twenty-first. There is certainly no biblical warrant for abuse, whatever the cause of illness. But is it ever appropriate to exorcize demons rather than consult a doctor? Can this story ever be used to guide the response of disciples to those who, for whatever reason, appear to be under an extraordinary influence of evil? There is no easy answer to this question because to rule out exorcism altogether risks giving unwarranted power to a Western secular world view. Christian faith for many believers is, by definition, an acknowledgement of the reality of spiritual forces. It may be wrong to demonize

---

6   Growing fears for the safety of children in some churches in Britain led to a conference in July 2006 hosted by AFRUCA (Africans Unite Against Child Abuse) entitled *The Role of Faith Organisations in Safeguarding African Children*. In the same year, a government-sponsored report identified 74 possible cases of abuse linked to churches performing exorcisms on children (Stobart 2006).

epilepsy or mental illnesses, but it may also be wrong to assume an entirely physical root-cause for all malaise. Nonetheless, those who hold a biblical world view and thereby ignore the insights of modernity, and especially in this case the insights of modern medicine, have no place to hide if this leads to harm that could have been avoided. Jesus himself reminded us that good intentions are no substitute for proper action (Mathew 7:21, 21:28–31).

This line of argument points again to the *consequences* of reading, rather than the way of reading, as the main locus for judging whether a naive merging of horizons is suitable interpretative practice for lay people. Stephen Fowl has made this point more generally in his book *Engaging Scripture*, especially in his chapter on 'Vigilant Communities and Virtuous Readers' (1998: 62–96). In his view, the test of reading practices lies less in their particular method than in the outcomes they have for the life of the reading community. Readings that promote the sorts of virtues generally associated with Christian discipleship are to be encouraged, almost irrespective of how they relate to any notion of truth. Fowl promotes 'underdetermined interpretation' as a way of removing issues of meaning from the interpretation of the Bible. This returns to Robert Morgan's point, mentioned at the beginning of this chapter, that meaning depends mainly on the aims of the interpreter. Fowl draws on the work of Jeffery Stout (1982) to argue for the sort of Bible reading that is self-consciously aware of the aims, interests and practices of the interpreters.

Applying that argument to the notion of 'first naivety' suggests that theological education in churches may be less about breaking down inherent naivety and more about the ethics of reading. The immediacy of being able to connect a text to your own world, rather than viewing it as the strange product of some distant culture, is something precious that should not be destroyed lightly in the pursuit of some sort of objectivity. What matters is whether reading the text leads to the sorts of beliefs, practices and behaviours that are in line with the overall tenor of the Gospel message. This is not a full answer to the question, however, because it leaves open the issue of what yardstick is used to judge 'ethical' readings, a subject beyond the scope of this discussion. The point here is that naive perceptions of horizons are not necessarily wrong in themselves, and may indeed be a virtuous way of approaching scripture.

Difficulties may arise for lay readers who do perceive the 'otherness' of the text and who cannot relate it to their own world. If a narrative is one that cannot be conceived of as having literally happened because such things do not appear to happen today, then it is likely to be seen as being strange, distant and perhaps irrelevant. According to the findings here, this leads to a tendency to interpret the story as telling us about the author, but not necessarily as having much to teach us today. This conclusion exaggerates the effects to make a point: in practice very few participants showed a really marked preference for the author horizon. Nonetheless, it raises the question of how someone who does not believe in the realism of such a New Testament miracle story can appropriate it as having something to say to them. One solution, advocated by some popular writers, is for readers to realign their world view with that of the biblical authors.[7] However, literal belief in the Bible and

---

belief in miraculous healing are not things that can necessarily be summoned up by an act of will or by peer pressure. Something more creative is required for people who cannot, or will not, relinquish a world view that is at odds with that portrayed in biblical texts.

Non-literalists tended more often to choose the author horizon over the text horizon, suggesting that it was difficult for them to 'suspend disbelief' and interpret the text as a narrative. Perhaps what might help would be a better acquaintance with the power of narrative worlds to convey religious information. In scholarly circles, narrative theology has a growing following, and there are numerous discussions on how God is revealed in the stories of scripture. In the case of the test passage, the story may seem odd for some Western Christians, but perhaps the characters and their motivations, emotions and volitions are more familiar. The ability to interpret characters within a narrative may depend on innate abilities linked to personality (see Chapter 6) or might be something that can be taught. Participants in this study with high educational experience were more likely to choose the text horizon and it would be interesting to see if this was related to education in the art of reading narrative. There is a great deal written about different ways of appropriating biblical texts other than by literal interpretation, but how much these are available to ordinary readers requires further investigation.

The practical implications of these findings stem from the issues I have just discussed. A central question is the aim and effect of education, and particularly theological education, in terms of how it shapes the horizon of interest of ordinary readers. Given that this largely revolves around the world of the text and the reader, it may be better to shape courses that impart a more sophisticated way of appreciating the importance of narrative and ways of creatively engaging with the world of the text. Education that becomes mired in controversies about the world of the author may be less useful, and there is a risk of leaving people unable to use scripture as a sacred text. Courses that stress the consequences of reading, rather than simply the meaning of the text, might enable some self-critical evaluation by those who otherwise would apply texts to their own lives as an unconsidered reflex.

A second practical implication arises from the finding that those who had not heard the text before tended to perceive it as more distant and opaque. This effect was independent of church tradition or beliefs about the Bible, and may refer to the simple process of familiarity by repetition. It serves as a reminder that people hearing a story for the first time need some space in which to orientate themselves towards it. It also reminds those for whom biblical stories are the stuff of everyday life that not everyone will relate to them quite so easily. This may be especially important when preaching to congregations that contain infrequent worshippers. The simple act of reiterating and expanding the text may help to shrink the distance between the world of the text and the world of the listener.

Further Research

The findings of the Bible and Lay People study show that the concepts of horizon and interpretative worlds are ones that are amenable to empirical study among ordinary readers. There is work to do in refining the scales used to measure horizon separation, most obviously in finding out if separation is really distinct from applicability. The measures were specific to the test passage and not generally applicable to the whole Bible, but there could be further work using the same text on a wider variety of church denominations.

A key question is whether horizon separation is a general attribute for a given reader, or whether it is passage specific. In this study, people who believed in miraculous healing, or who practised healing prayer, were likely to perceive this passage as a familiar narrative. This may not be so for other sorts of texts, where other beliefs and experiences may be more important. A more focused study of horizon separation could employ a variety of biblical genres and record other predictors that might be relevant. One general predictor might be familiarity with the text. In this study of churchgoers, familiarity with the test passage was high and the number of people who had not read it before was too low to permit further analysis. Working with a variety of passages, and working in and beyond churches, might help to explicate the effect of familiarity on horizon separation. Does familiarity break down perceived horizon separation irrespective of how similar the contents of the text are to the life of the reader? Or are there some texts that remain for ever strange and distant?

Making deductions by observing churchgoers is dogged by the difficulties caused by the non-random segregation of people between congregations. Beliefs are not randomly distributed among churches because people with certain beliefs tend to congregate in certain types of churches. These beliefs are associated with particular practices, including practices related to the Bible. So it is hard to isolate the effects of particular variables on horizon separation and preference. Longitudinal studies may be of some help, but are hard to conduct. In the case of familiarity, it might be possible to measure the perception of horizon separation in congregations before and after exposure to unusual texts.

Chapter 6

Personality and Scripture

The idea that biblical meaning arises in the interaction of text and reader raises the question of the nature of those things that readers bring to texts that might influence how they interpret. Readers bring their individuality and uniqueness, which is why different people reading the same passage may produce several different interpretations. But just what is the individuality that readers bring, and is it something that can be understood in empirical terms? If a hundred people read a passage there might be several interpretations, but probably not a hundred. Some people will share the same views, others will not. Is this because, despite their individuality, they share some common characteristics?

One of the ways that we understand differences between people is to talk about different personalities. This chapter examines the relationship between personality and Bible reading among lay people. The topic falls under the general interaction of psychology and religion and the specific relationship of psychology and the Bible. Before looking in detail at personality, I shall outline the nature and development of these wider fields of study. These outlines are necessarily brief, but should help to locate the Bible and Lay People study of personality within a broader context.

Psychology and Religion

The interaction of psychology and religion has a long and somewhat troubled history that at various times has involved psychologists trying to interpret and 'explain' religion, theologians rejecting psychology outright, and a more balanced dialogue between the two fields (Parsons and Jonte-Pace 2001). The earliest interaction, which fell under the general heading of 'Psychology of Religion', began during the development of modern psychology in the late nineteenth and early twentieth centuries. David Wulff (2001) argues that this interaction was typified by the application of psychological theories and methodologies in an attempt to reinterpret or reform religion from a secular, scientific perspective. Perhaps the classic example of someone seeking to reinterpret religion is Sigmund Freud, who argued that religion was an expression of an infantile wish projection and a sublimated cultural expression of the libido: in effect a universal human neurosis (Palmer 1997: 14). Not all psychologists were so resolutely dismissive. Within the field of psychoanalysis, Carl Jung did much to counter Freud's reductionist view of religion, stressing the fundamental significance of archetypes, symbols and myths (Palmer 1997). In a different tradition, William James (1902) was a pioneer in establishing the notion of careful empirical observation of religious phenomena through the lens of psychology.

Wulff argues that the initial close engagement of psychology and religion faltered after the First World War, partly due to changes in the field of theology and partly due to changes in the field of psychology. Although in the early years some liberal theologians were drawn to psychological explanations that reduced religion to a purely human phenomenon, this humanist approach was eclipsed by the rejection of secularism associated with post-liberal theologians such as Karl Barth. At the same time, psychology came to be dominated by behavioural approaches that tried to model human behaviour using objective data. Not surprisingly, religion was perceived as rather woolly and intractable, and an already marginal field of psychology came to a virtual standstill. Indeed, the relationship between psychology and religion was nothing short of poisonous (Ellens and Rollins 2004: 1), and remained so for decades.

Interest in religion among psychologists was gradually revived from the 1950s as behaviourism lost its dominance and a new generation of humanist, cognitive and developmental psychologists used empirical methods to examine the phenomenon of religion. A key early figure was Gordon Allport (1950), whose notion of intrinsic and extrinsic religiousness became one of the dominant ways of describing religiosity over the next several decades. His attempts to measure these variables (or, to use the jargon of the field, 'operationalize the construct') were not wholly successful, but they nonetheless set a paradigm for a wide range of studies in the psychology of religion. The fields of social and cognitive psychology have provided a rich methodology that explores the correlation between religious expression and social or individual psychological variables, including studies that have investigated the correlation between personality and religious expression.

Wulff argues that alongside the rise in empirical studies has been the continuing development of the psychological interpretation of religious content. These studies are based on the sort of 'depth psychologies' associated with the work of Freud and Jung, which stand in sharp contrast to the basic aims of empirical approaches:

> Whereas the empirical approach is inherently a psychology of religious *persons* and is therefore focused on individual differences in piety, the interpretative perspective is foremost a psychology of religious *contents* and thus seeks out the *meaning* of the objects, stories and rituals that together compose the religious traditions. Even when this content is idiosyncratically appropriated or transformed in individual lives, the accent remains on its meanings, not on the range of its variations. (Wulff 2001: 22, author's italics)

This area of psychology and religion has developed the ideas of Freud and Jung, using a variety of concepts to explore the role of religion in shaping the human psyche. Religious beliefs, experiences and practices are assumed to arise from the operation of unconscious psychological operations. It is this legacy, more than the empirical studies of social psychologists, that has so far had the strongest influence on the field of biblical psychology.

Psychology and the Bible

The specific interaction of psychology and biblical studies reflects the wider trends described above. Wayne Rollins (1999) has given a comprehensive review of the historical roots of psychological interest in the Bible. Although this can be traced back to the sixteenth century and beyond, a seminal work was Franz Delitzsch's *A System of Biblical Psychology*, published in 1855. This was an attempt to use the Bible to identify the essential human condition and what it means to be regenerated in the image of God. He used terms such as conscious, unconscious, ego and archetype well before they were taken up and developed by later writers such as Freud and Jung. This approach of using the Bible as data to describe and prescribe the human condition was developed by M. Scott Fletcher (1912) in *The Psychology of the New Testament*, which represented a fusion of the historical-critical and scientific-psychological ideas of the period.

This early infatuation was ended abruptly by the same forces that led to a general separation of psychologists and theologians. In the field of biblical studies, Ellen and Rollins (2004: 2) point to a particular spat arising from an early study of the gospels by four psychoanalysts, which concluded that Jesus was mentally diseased. Albert Schweitzer's repudiation of this work as being worth 'exactly zero' seems to have set the tone for what followed. The idea that psychology and biblical studies had anything to say to each other remained out of fashion in both disciplines until the 1970s.

The extraordinary growth of interest in linking psychology and biblical studies since then can be traced to developments in both fields in the latter half of the twentieth century (Kille 2004). The changes in fashion in psychology have already been mentioned, and these paved the way for psychologists to take an interest in the Bible and its readers. From the other direction, the link has been promoted by the change in biblical studies from an endeavour dominated by historical approaches to one that embraced a wider range of methods. It is this latter change that has largely shaped the interaction of Bible and psychology to date.

The main arena of interaction is the field of psychological biblical criticism. Rollins (1999: 65) traces the resurgence of this discipline to an essay by F. C. Grant in 1968, which pointed to the potential value of depth psychology and psychoanalysis for biblical studies. There followed a number of publications from 1970 onwards, which reflected Freudian or Jungian interpretations of scripture as well as the influence of a wide range of psychological theories. The growth of interest among biblical scholars eventually led to the formation, in 1991, of the Psychology and Biblical Studies programme by the Society of Biblical Literature in the United States. Since then, the number of publications has burgeoned, and there are now a number of reviews and major contributions to this academic discourse.[1]

---

[1]   Introductory monographs include Rollins (1999) and Kille (2001). The journal *Pastoral Sciences* dedicated volume 45 (1997) to articles on this subject, while the four volumes of articles edited by Ellens and Rollins (2004) give a comprehensive overview and detailed picture of the discipline.

The nature of this discourse owes much to the fact that it is driven by biblical scholars rather than by psychologists. The methods are similar to other biblical criticisms (historical, narrative, rhetorical, etc.), but in this case the lens through which the text is viewed is that of psychological theory. Volume 1 of *Psychology and the Bible* (Ellens and Rollins 2004) gives a good indication of the scope of the enterprise, with titles such as: 'Sexuality in the Hebrew Bible: Freud's lens'; 'Jung, analytical psychology and the Bible'; 'Developmental psychology in biblical studies'; 'The psychosymbolic approach to biblical interpretation' and so on. Such studies investigate the nature of symbols and myths in the Bible, the psychodynamics of biblical stories, the psychology of biblical personalities and the biblical view of human nature.

This method of biblical interpretation clearly has some links with the way readers read, but it has not penetrated the field of lay reading to any great extent. Rollins (1999) devotes most of his overview of the subject to the history and future prospects of the field of psychological biblical criticism and its exegetical agenda. His last chapter deals with the hermeneutical agenda, and it is here that he deals rather briefly with psychology and the reader, including the way that readers approach texts. It is this rather neglected area of study to which the rest of this chapter is devoted. Before looking at this, it is worth pausing to reflect on the history of the relationship of psychology and the Bible, and why it has developed the way it has.

There may be strong parallels between the development of literary and psychological criticism in biblical studies. Early literary analysis explored the world of the text at the expense of the world of the author, and psychological biblical criticism has done the same. Although there have been some attempts to recreate the psychological world of the biblical authors (Berger 2003), the bulk of studies have combed the Bible for patterns and ciphers that point to the underlying psychological world implied by the text. In many ways the field is concentrated on the world 'within' the text, in a way that is analogous to literary criticism. The 'implied psyche' is a construction of critics who analyse the text with a particular psychological lens. Literary critics took some time to discover influence of 'real readers', and psychological biblical critics are likewise taking some time to discover the influence of 'real psyches'. As yet, the guild of biblical psychologists has not really grasped the importance of the psychological makeup of ordinary readers for the interpretative process. Perhaps in both disciplines this is because academics find the conceptual world of implied readers and their psyches so much easier to handle and understand than the rather messy, intractable world of their real counterparts.

Psychology and Readers

As I have sought to demonstrate, the rise in popularity of biblical psychology has not been as important in shaping an interest in psychology and readers as it might have been. Although most psychological biblical critics are aware of the implications of psychology for real readers, the field has developed mainly through the interaction of theoretical psychology with biblical exegesis. An interest in psychology and readers, rather than psychology and texts, must look elsewhere for its roots and parallel methodologies. As I discuss later in this chapter, such roots include the application of empirical methods to the psychology of religion, and particularly the relationship of personality and religion. Parallel methodologies are also found to some extent in empirical studies of reading, especially those with a psychological focus.

Interest in the empirical study of literature in general is growing rapidly and can be traced to several different sources (Hakemulder 2006). One direction stems from literary critics who realized that the reception of texts by readers could shape meaning as much as the texts themselves. The other direction has been from psychologists studying perception and wanting to know how the reception of simple texts in the laboratory relates to the more complex process of reading full literary texts.

Literary critics became interested in the process of reading when they tried to understand how textual meaning was transferred to readers. The German school of reception aesthetics concentrated on the way that readers identify pattern and meaning in a text. Wolfgang Iser (1978) argued that readers 'actualize' meanings that are latent in the text: as a text is read, the reader is offered different possibilities for resolving meaning, and will eventually choose one 'path' through the text rather than another. Iser stopped short of showing how this worked in practice, though others have tried to suggest how it might work on specific biblical texts.[2]

Iser's approach was influenced by the notion of gestalt, which was a key paradigm in cognitive psychology for much of the twentieth century. Gestalt psychology focused on the way that the brain shapes reality and distinguishes familiar patterns, and this gave a psychological framework for interpreting the act of reading. Iser's work thus raised the issue of what readers bring to texts in a way that was more psychologically orientated than the concepts of prejudice and pre-understanding that had dominated earlier generations of biblical hermeneutists such as Rudolf Bultmann (1985: 145–53). Nonetheless, this was still a theoretical speculation that was not very well supported by empirical observations.

One secular critic who tried a more empirical approach was Norman Holland (1975) in his book *Five Readers Reading*. Holland used Freudian theory to interpret the way in which five subjects sought meaning in short stories such as William Faulkner's *A Rose for Emily*. The data consisted of in-depth interviews with five people who were asked to read the stories and then talk about them with the researcher. On the basis of this evidence, Holland suggested that reading was strongly shaped by readers trying to express their own identities through the stories they read. Holland drew heavily on Freudian notions of the self and how identity is formed, projected and protected. Such analyses were difficult, time consuming and invariably subjective, which highlighted the problems inherent in analysing the act of reading in detailed psychological terms.

This has not stopped people trying, and empirical approaches to reading are becoming increasingly common in the fields of linguistics, poetics and literary studies.[3] Many of these empirical studies are attempts to test literary theories derived

---

2. For example, W. Randolph Tate's (1994) exposition of the Gospel of Mark consciously draws on Iser's theory.

3. The analysis of specific texts or acts of communication comes under the general term 'Discourse Analysis', which covers a wide range of approaches (Johnstone 2002; van Dijk

from linguistics or poetics, but there is a growing number of psychologically based studies (see Kreuz and MacNealy 1996; Schram and Steen 2001). For example, the theory of 'structural affect' (Brewer 1996) postulates that narrative structure determines how emotional states and knowledge about characters are created in the reader, and there is some empirical evidence to support this (e.g. Graesser and Klettke 2001). Others have tried to test psychoanalytical theories of the effects of reading (e.g. van Peer and Stoeger 2001), while yet others have taken a more social-psychological approach (e.g. Hakemulder 2001). A detailed account of such research is unnecessary here because, to date, there has been little or no connection between these empirical literary studies and studies of Bible reading. What they do represent, however, is a growing expertise and methodology that may yet be applied to the reading of the Bible. Empirical studies of 'secular' literature might make an interesting contrast with similar studies on sacred texts. Reading sacred texts may share many features with the reading of ordinary texts, but it is also likely to be influenced by particular religious commitments to the nature of the text and the significance of the content.

Psychological analysis of the process of Bible reading is rare. An early contribution was that of Cedric Johnson (1983), which arose from collaboration between the Fuller Graduate School of Psychology and the Rosemead Graduate School in the United States. This book is aimed at a popular, rather than academic, market and there is relatively little empirical evidence to support the theory. What makes this book interesting, however, is that Johnson comes from a conservative evangelical position, and is therefore wrestling with why interpretations differ and what this means for biblical truth. Johnson looks at a number of psychological theories and how they might influence the way the Bible is read. The chapter on personality is partly based on Freud, with suggestions on how the unconscious might influence the way readers interpret. Thus the notion of biblical authority might be shaped unconsciously in a given reader by the authority figures that they experienced in the past. This is the classic Freudian theory of 'transference', which, like most of Freud's theories, is virtually impossible to test empirically. Johnson also mentions cognitive style (including dogmatism) as possible influences on the way that scripture is understood or interpreted. Unfortunately, the chapter dedicated to personality does not actually mention any of the mainstream psychological theories of personality, so we cannot tell what Johnson might have made of their effect on interpretation.

Another link between psychology and Bible reading is in the field of Christian psychoanalysis and counselling. Rollins (1999: 198) points to the innately therapeutic purpose of the Bible and mentions some writers who have used biblical texts in pastoral counselling, notably Donald Capps (1981; 1984). This sort of practical encounter draws on the transforming nature of biblical texts for the human psyche, as well as confronting the way that clients might shape texts to their own ends.

1997). Empirical studies make up a small but increasingly important aspect of this field (see Kreuz and MacNealy 1996). Scholars working in this field formed their own association, the IGEL (Internationale Gesellschaft für Empirische Literaturwissenschaft) in 1987. Since then there has been a steady growth in publications, though the discipline is still in its infancy.

The interaction of psychology and the Bible has to date generated rather little in the way of empirical evidence. There is certainly scope for more study, as Rollins (1999) points out. The most profitable links between psychology and ordinary Bible readers so far have been in the area of personality, and I shall devote the rest of this chapter to this subject.

Personality and Religion

Personality is about the way that people think, behave and interact with the world around them, including other human beings. It points to characteristics that are fairly stable and that shape the way people behave generally, rather than in any particular instance. We often use words that describe peoples' general nature: 'outgoing', 'hard-nosed', 'affable', 'shy', 'warm', 'easy-going' and so on. When we do this, we understand that people cannot be fully described in a single phrase, nor does the use of such phrases mean that a person is always like that. Affable people sometimes get angry, easy-going people sometimes get anxious and outgoing people sometimes prefer to be alone. This does not invalidate the descriptions, which we understand to be meaningful even if not accurate all the time.

Personality is something that most of us understand, even if we might struggle to give it an exact definition. Leslie Francis (2005: 7) argues that personality describes our deep-seated nature, 'the heart of who we are', and that it refers to individual differences over which we have little control. This, he suggests, makes personality value-neutral and distinguishes it from 'character'. He cites the notion of introversion and extraversion as personality traits that are neither good nor bad and qualities such as love, joy, gentleness, anger or hate as aspects of character that have moral direction. Psychologists may sometimes talk of 'normality' and 'pathology' when referring to personality, but they tend to avoid morally loaded terms. There may not be good or bad personalities, but there may be unusual, abnormal or pathological ones, and some of these can lead to socially undesirable behaviours.

Psychologists have invested a lot of energy in trying to define and understand personality, and part of this understanding has involved categorization. No two people are exactly alike and it is obvious that there are many different kinds of people. The variety of personalities is bewildering, but it is not an infinite variety. It is not true that there are as many personalities as people because, if that were so, we could not talk of people in the way that we do. Rather, we observe that people have characteristics that they share with others. Psychologists use models to try to explain both the variety and the commonality of human personalities.

Before looking more closely at models of personality, it may be useful to pause for some reflection on the whole enterprise of assessing personality. Some people reject any use of personality theory in Christian circles, arguing that it undermines the uniqueness and integrity of individuals. Personality theories seem to label people, and labels are thought to be disabling and demeaning. Perhaps because personality relates closely to the very essence of what makes people who they are, some people have a particular reluctance to accept any part of trying to model personalities. This is unfortunate, and confuses the empirical act of pattern recognition with the moral act of judgement. For example, we all have a character of height, which for adults falls within a range of 0.57 m (the shortest adult recorded) and 2.72 m (the tallest). Our height is an intrinsic part of who we are as individuals, though many people share the same height. That height might fall below, near or above the average height for a given group of people: in my case white males born in England in the 1950s. I can hardly be devalued if other males of my age share my height, nor should I feel demeaned or superior because some people are shorter or taller than I am. My height is a fact of my life, shaped by genes and upbringing. Similarly, if I am categorized as 'average height', it is a way of simplifying my exact height by relating it to the distribution of heights in the population. People of average height are not necessarily all *exactly* the same height, nor are they necessarily similar in any other respect.

This does not mean that the categorization of height cannot be abused. We can identify people as unusually tall or unusually short but then go on to use that in a demeaning way. We might attach stereotypes or completely erroneous ideas to unusual height and as a consequence devalue a person's uniqueness. But this is not a consequence of observing a person's height; it is a consequence of how we use that information. To argue that we cannot categorize people is to confuse the simple description of people with some value-laden prejudice. The two are not the same, and there is no reason why they should be inextricably linked. Although this applies to personality as it does to any other attribute, particular care is needed because of the complexity of human personalities. If psychologists do not always stress this complexity, it is usually because it is accepted as a given. Simplification is a necessary part of trying to order and understand.

Developing a descriptive model is only part of understanding personality. To understand it fully we need to know what forces shape personality and the consequences of personality. We need to know not just *how* people differ, but *why* they differ and what that difference means in terms of attitudes, behaviours and social interactions. Most models of personality have some theoretical basis that explains why people differ. In many cases it is assumed that personality is largely an inherited characteristic, though it can sometimes be affected by what happens to us in life.[4] Looking at what personality does is usually about comparing attitudes or behaviours between people of different personalities. Such correlations are generally the best that can be done to test for the effects of personality because personality is generally stable. We cannot change an individual's personality and compare behaviour before and after such change, so empiricists rely on correlation rather than experimentation.

There are several models of personality that have been used in research into personality and religion (see Francis 2001 and 2005 for more details). Most of these are based on the idea of personality traits, and have not been used to any great extent in work related to biblical interpretation, so I shall not describe them here. Models of personality based on traits assume that there are a number of fundamental aspects of human nature that vary along a continuum, which allows for a great deal of variation. A different kind of model is that based on the ideas of psychological

---

4   For example, in extreme cases some people seem to change personality as a result of brain damage caused by accidents.

type, first put forward by Carl Jung (1921; 1971). Jung based his theory on the way that he assumed humans related to the world around them, the way that they perceived information and the way that they processed information in making decisions. In each case, he argued, people have a preference for a particular mode of operating, and these preferences give rise to psychological type, the basis for human personality. This model of personality makes predictions about the way that people might attend to, or interpret, the Bible, so I will outline the theory and measurement of psychological type in some detail.

Psychological Type

Jung developed his idea after reviewing the writings of poets and philosophers. The foundations of his theory were the two basic types of introversion and extraversion. He termed these 'attitude types' and contrasted them with the 'function types' related to the two processes of perceiving and judging, which roughly correspond to acquiring information and evaluating it. Jung argued that the attitude types reflected the way that individuals relate to objects: extraversion refers to the tendency to perform in the external world through interaction with others; introversion refers to the tendency to perform in the interior, individual world of contemplation. These correspond roughly to the notions of 'thinking aloud' versus 'thinking to yourself'.

Jung analysed the way in which the attitude functions affected the function types of sensing, intuition, thinking and feeling. The former two he termed 'irrational' because they were connected with the non-evaluative process of perceiving. The latter two he termed 'rational' or 'judging' types because they were connected with the process of discrimination or evaluation.

The perceiving process is concerned with the way that people acquire information, and it functions by sensing and intuition. Sensing, as the name implies, is primarily concerned with gathering information from the senses. The emphasis is on discrete information, carefully observed and recorded. The intuitive function is concerned with relating bits of information and projecting possibilities by novel combinations of ideas. Information is not treated in isolation but perceived in relation to existing knowledge and ideas.

The judging process is concerned with the way that people evaluate information, and it functions by feeling and thinking. The feeling function relates evaluation to values and rational feelings, whereas the thinking function relates evaluation to logic and rational thinking (cognition). In common parlance, we talk of making decisions 'from the heart' or 'from the head', and this corresponds to the two functions of the judging process.

Jung's theory has been developed by a number of different psychologists who have tried to find ways of measuring these aspects of personality. The most influential of these has been the mother-and daughter-team of Katherine Cook Briggs and Isabel Briggs Myers. They developed Jung's ideas through a process of observation shaped by theory. If Jung was right, people should show characteristics related to each dimension: introversion or extraversion, sensing or intuition, thinking or feeling. Their observations led them to conclude that there was something else that differed between people that might be termed their 'attitude to the outer world'.

Some people seemed to stress the importance of judging and evaluation, while others were more content to observe the world around them. This, they assumed, was related to whether people used their preferred judging or perceiving process in dealing with the world around them, so they used these terms to define this fourth polarity of 'judging' versus 'perceiving'.

The instrument they developed to assess psychological type, the Myers–Briggs Type Inventory (MBTI), therefore measures personality on four dimensions (Myers and McCaulley 1985). These are: preferred location of processing (extraversion, E, versus introversion, I); preferred mode of perceiving (sensing, S, versus intuition, N);[5] preferred mode of judging (feeling, F, versus thinking, T) and preferred attitude to the outer world (judging, J, versus perceiving, P).

The theory of psychological type developed by Briggs and Myers relies heavily on the notion of preference (Myers and Myers 1980). People are capable of operating in different ways, but they tend to prefer some ways over others. A key analogy is right- or left-handedness because this encapsulates the way in which people *can* do things with the 'wrong' hand, but they do them more comfortably and proficiently with their preferred hand. The same is true for psychological type preferences. For example, a person may prefer to make decisions objectively and logically, but this does not mean that they cannot make them by taking into account other people's feelings. This point is crucial to understanding type, and those people who dismiss it as 'type casting' have probably not grasped the nature of this personality model. Although it arose from theoretical speculation, it is also based on observations of the way people are. Its utility lies not so much in being able to assign people to pigeonholes from which they cannot escape, but in its ability to explain the sorts of individual differences that are readily apparent when people are observed with care. According to this model of personality, characteristic attitudes and behaviours stem from various psychological functions, and these indicate underlying preferences. These characteristics are therefore used to identify a person's likely psychological type.

Extraverts show their preference by the way that they are energized by interaction with other people. They may enjoy opportunities to interact with others at parties, over the telephone or in groups. They form ideas through this interaction and may discover what they believe or think about something by exploring it in dialogue with others. Introverts, on the other hand, are comfortable with solitude and can more easily deal with ideas on their own. They are energized by spending time in contemplation and are often exhausted by interacting with other people.

Sensing people are generally good at observing through sight, sound, taste, touch or smell. They pay attention to detail and avoid speculating too far beyond what they observe. They value discussions that are 'down to earth' or practical, and respond well to the routines of life. Intuitives, on the other hand, find it difficult to stick with routine. They enjoy change or the imagined possibilities of the future. The information they receive sparks the imagination and may lead them to 'flights of fancy' or to questioning received wisdom. Intuitives prefer the wide picture to the

---

[5]   Intuition is symbolized with N to distinguish it from introversion, and is often written as iNtuition.

narrow focus, so will often want to set out basic principles, objectives and goals before they deal with details and practicalities.

Those who judge by feeling are sensitive to other people's emotions or ideas. They seek harmony and unity of purpose in a group and dislike upsetting people. They are good at judging how others are reacting, and may back away from making divisive decisions if these are strongly opposed. Those who prefer to judge by thinking, on the other hand, are more comfortable with objective arguments and logic. They can appreciate and respond to issues of principle, and generally rate holding on to these more highly than avoiding upsetting people. Thinking types can be scrupulous about fairness and are disinclined to bend the rules.

Those who orientate to the outer world through judging tend to prefer an orderly life. They value organization and schedules, will try to work to deadlines and like completing tasks. They are happy within the ordered confines or rules of organizations such as clubs and societies. Those who orientate to the outer world through perceiving, on the other hand, prefer a less ordered approach to life. Calendars are guidelines not tramlines, deadlines are provisional and time keeping is not a top priority. They may find the restrictions of belonging rather irksome and prefer not to be confined by a rules-based organization.

These four dimensions and their associated preferences give rise to 16 different psychological types that are abbreviated as ESFJ, ISTP and so on. The characteristics of each preference are assumed to build up complex patterns of personality that relate to the different sorts of people we may encounter (for examples, see Bayne 1997; Francis 2005; Goldsmith and Wharton 1993; Myers 1993; Myers and McCaulley 1985; Myers and Myers 1980). One advantage of this model is that fairly simple, opposite preferences in four independent dimensions can build into a wide range of personalities. Types are not rigid categories, and the richness of descriptions in each function means that the 16 types cannot be defined precisely. Nonetheless, proponents of psychological type argue that the model offers a useful pragmatic tool for exploring personality.

There have been a number of refinements of the psychological type model (see Bayne 1997). Perhaps the most widely used is the notion of 'type dynamics', whereby one of the functions in the perceiving or judging processes (i.e. S, N, F or T) is assumed to be the dominant mode of psychological function. The idea behind this is that people have a preferred locus of operation (the inner or outer world) and a preferred way of operating (judging or perceiving), and they will revert to this way of operating as their 'default' mode. Type theory argues that the J or P preference indicates which process is normally used in dealing with the outer world. For Js this will be the judging process (F or T); for Ps this will be the perceiving process (S or N). For extraverts, this external function will be the dominant one because the outside world is their preferred locus of operation. Introverts, however, tend to use their dominant function internally, so for them the dominant function will be in the opposite process to the one used in the outer world. So, for example, judgers (J) who prefer extraversion (E) will default to using their preferred judging function (F or T) in interaction with the outer world and this will be the dominant function. In contrast, judgers (J) who prefer introversion (I) will use their judging function in the outer world so their dominant function will be in the perceiving process (S or N).

So, the dominant function for ESTJs is T, because this is the preferred function in the outer world, while the dominant function for ISTJs is S because this is the preferred function for the inner world. Using this idea, it is possible to define dominant functions for each of the 16 psychological types (for example, see Goldsmith and Wharton 1993: 35). Type dynamics are based more on theory than on observation, and the evidence supporting dominance is not wholly convincing (Bayne 1997: 49–59). Nonetheless, it is a widely used concept and at least worth bearing in mind when empirically testing the value of type theory for biblical interpretation.

This model of personality works in a typological rather than trait-based way. In other words, the difference between functions is assumed to be a difference in *kind* rather than a difference in *degree*. Jung himself was somewhat ambiguous on the issue of whether people fall mostly into one category or the other. He uses the term 'differentiation' to suggest that types are more apparent in some people than in others. When writing about extraverted and introvert types, for example, he speaks about a third group where it is 'hard to say whether the motivation comes chiefly from within or without. This group is the most numerous and includes the less differentiated normal man' (Jung 1971: 515–16). This seems to imply that he is using types to define the extremes of traits in which most people fall somewhere near the middle. Yet when he comes to explain his use of the term 'attitude' he describes a disposition that 'will either determine action in this or that definite direction' (ibid. 414). The analogy seems to be reaching a fork in the road, with just two possible directions, rather than having to decide to go in any direction from where you stand. This suggests that types are categorical rather than continuous, and this ambiguity has led to an ongoing debate as to the nature of psychological types.

Although those who shaped psychological type theory after Jung argued strongly that preference is typological, the evidence for this is ambiguous, and there are several studies that suggest types could be treated as traits (Arnau et al. 2003; Bess and Harvey 2002; Loomis and Singer 1980). Preferences may be more sharply defined in some people than in others, so that some people find it much more difficult to function outside their preferences. The analogy with handedness is useful here because people can be ambidextrous to varying degrees. There is a good case for suggesting that assigning people to one type or another using some quantitative cut-off point is merely a way of simplifying the construct, rather like comparing taller than average people with shorter than average people. Such artificial categorization loses valuable information,[6] and several people have tried assess Jungian types without assuming a dichotomous classification in each dimension (Singer et al. 1996; Thompson 1996). The jury is still out on the exact nature of Jungian types, but there is some justification for treating the model in either way.

---

[6]   For example, some type measures cannot use information from people who score equally in both categories of a dimension. This can be overcome by treating tied scores in a consistent way, but this will always carry a degree of arbitrariness.

Psychological Type and Religion

There is growing evidence that psychological type can predict various aspects of religious behaviour. The two main sorts of studies that have demonstrated this are those that compare the distribution of types in various religious or secular groups, and those that correlate type preferences with various attributes of religiosity. Studies of type distributions across religious groups have included churchgoers and ministers (Francis 2001). A growing number of studies across a wide range of Western Christian churches indicate that churchgoers tend to prefer introversion over extraversion and judging over perceiving (Francis 2005: 110–21). Francis suggests that this reflects an emphasis on the inner spiritual journey that appeals to introverts, and worship services that value structure, pattern or discipline and therefore appeal to judging types. Congregational trends for preferences in the perceiving process seem to vary between different types of church styles. Sensing types tend to predominate in Anglican and evangelical Protestant churches, but other studies have found a more even balance, or a preponderance of intuitive types (Francis 2005: 115–16). Different church traditions seem to attract different proportions of S and N types, and in the Bible and Lay People sample there was a higher proportion of preferred intuitives in Anglo-Catholic churches than in evangelical ones (Village et al. 2007). Churchgoers also generally demonstrate a strong preference for feeling over thinking. This is partly linked to the fact that preferred feeling is more frequent among women than among men (Bayne 1997: 37–9; Kendall 1998), and the fact that women are also more likely to attend church. However, the preponderance of F types is not wholly explained by sex ratios, and some churches do seem to project a faith that is likely to be more attractive to feeling types than to thinking types (Francis 2005: 117).

Psychological type is also related to religious expression, particularly in the perceiving and judging processes. Conservative or traditionalist Christians seem to prefer sensing to intuition, whereas the opposite is true of those with a more liberal, pluralistic or mystical approach (Francis and Jones 1998; Francis and Louden 2000; Francis and Ross 1997; Village 2005b). The relationship of the judging process to religion is more difficult to define and empirical studies have given varied results. There is some evidence that a preference for thinking is linked to both conservatism (Francis and Jones 1998) and charismatic belief (Francis and Jones 1997), though in the Bible and Lay People sample charismatic expression was associated with a preference for feeling rather than thinking (Village 2005b).

Studies relating psychological type to religious affiliation or religious expression are relatively new, and our understanding is likely to increase over the next few years with the deployment of more sophisticated instruments on a wider range of people. The key point here is that there is growing evidence to suggest that psychological type is a useful model for exploring the links between personality and religion. The purpose of the rest of this chapter is to see if this link extends to the reading and interpretation of scripture.

Measuring Psychological Type Preferences

The MBTI is the most widely used way of assessing psychological type. It uses a battery of items delivered in workshops by trained practitioners. This makes it suitable for using type theory to help people understand themselves, but less suitable for empirical research where type preferences have to be assessed more quickly and easily. The Keirsey Temperament Sorter, KTS (Keirsey and Bates 1978), measures the same dimensions of type, though its authors used the typology to define certain basic temperaments, rather than psychological types. Nonetheless, its 70 items are a quicker way of assessing type and it seems to give similar results to the MBTI (Francis, Craig and Robbins 2005; Quinn et al. 1992; Tucker and Gillespie 1993).

The Bible and Lay People questionnaire included a version of the KTS (© Keirsey 1995) that was used to assess psychological type preferences of participants. The sorter consists of forced-choice items (choose a or b), with 10 measuring E-I and 20 for each of S-N, F-T and J-P. The number of items chosen in each case is used to assign type, assuming that preferred type in each dimension is indicated by a person choosing more responses of one type than its opposite. The authors of the KTS used even numbers of items for each dimension, which leaves the possibility of ties. Psychological type practitioners conventionally deal with these by assigning ties to I, N, F or P, though the KTS assumes that type cannot be assessed if there are ties in any dimension.

An alternative way of using the information from the KTS is to interpret the number of items chosen for each type as a score of preference. This assumes that someone who chooses all 20 S items (and therefore no N items) has a stronger preference for sensing than someone who chooses 10 S and 10 N, who in turn has a stronger preference than someone who chooses all 20 N items and no S items. Although this way of using the sorter runs against the grain of a theory based on typology, in practice it may be a more useful and powerful way of analysing the results (see Village 2005b for a fuller discussion of this). In what follows, I have used scores to analyse correlations in the various dimensions, and categories where I am investigating dominant function. Using scores is preferable from a statistical point of view, but categories are more familiar to those who use psychological type theory in churches.

Personality, Scripture and Ordinary Readers[7]

Preferred Interpretations

Psychological type theory predicts that people may have different preferences for how they relate to scripture. The most developed application of this idea has been by Leslie Francis, who proposed that people may attend to different parts of an expository sermon, depending on their type preferences in the judging and perceiving processes (Francis 1997). Preferred sensors will attend to descriptions of sense information

---

[7]   Some of this section is based on work published in Village and Francis (2005).

and pay attention to the details in the text. They may value an expanded reiteration of the text more than an exposition that uses the text as a starting point for apparently unrelated ideas. Preferred intuitives, on the other hand, will tend to become bored unless the expositor draws wider inferences, raises fundamental questions or makes speculative analogies based on underlying ideas in the text. Preferred feeling types will pay special attention to issues in the text that relate to human values and to what it says about the way that we should relate to other people. In contrast, preferred thinkers will want to analyse the text for its coherence; they will look for logical inferences and extract issues of principle.

Francis developed this idea in a series of co-authored books based on the lectionary readings of the synoptic gospels (Francis and Atkins 2000, 2001, 2002) and in what he calls the SIFT method of preaching (Francis 2003). This is based on the notion that a sermon will be most effective if it contains elements of all four preferred ways of relating to the text. The preacher's first task is to 'establish the text' by recalling the content, expanding on facts and details and highlighting what can be seen, heard, touched, smelt or tasted. Sensors are encouraged to employ their senses as they pay particular attention to experiencing the text. Next, the preacher may help intuitives by offering connections to bigger ideas and possibilities Questions may be asked and left unanswered as a way of firing the intuitive imagination. To engage preferred feelers, the sermon needs to highlight the inter-personal and human side of the text. The stance or attitudes of the characters or writer are expressed and used to suggest ways in which listeners can live harmonious and compassionate lives. Preferred thinkers will attend especially to the underlying principles suggested by the text, the moral ideals and how they might shape the way we order our decision making.

Francis argues that psychological type shapes the way that listeners interpret or attend to spoken interpretations of a biblical text. By implication this should also apply to people reading texts. This seems a reasonable suggestion, but is it true? There is some empirical evidence from a study of biblical interpretation in the United States (Bassett et al. 1993). The researchers did not test the idea as such, but developed interpretations of four biblical texts that were shaped by different learning styles and by the psychological type perspectives of thinking or feeling. These items were given to 74 students who also completed the MBTI and a questionnaire measuring learning styles. The conflating of leaning style with feeling and thinking makes the results difficult to interpret, but there was some evidence to suggest that preferred feelers tended to choose feeling-type items, but the same was not true for preferred thinkers. Leslie Francis and I decided to use the opportunity afforded by the Bible and Lay People study to test the theory more explicitly.

The method involved producing short interpretations of the test passage (Mark 9:14–29) and asking participants to choose between them. There were five pairs for sensing versus intuition interpretations, and five pairs for feeling versus thinking (see Table 6.1). To test the influence of dominant type, we presented four slightly longer interpretations and asked people to choose the one they preferred (see Table 6.2).

The interpretations were produced using the known characteristics of each function and were tested blind on 20 psychological-type practitioners to ensure that they did

Table 6.1   Short interpretative items based on Mark 9:14–29

Type	Items
	Interpretative choices by perceiving personality function
N	Perhaps religious faith is often a mixture of belief and doubt.
S	I can picture the scene clearly as the father cries out 'I believe; help my unbelief!'
S	I can picture the boy writhing on the ground, dust and foam sticking to his face.
N	Why does the boy start to writhe on the ground when he is brought to Jesus?
N	Jesus takes the boy by the hand and brings him to life: a metaphor for resurrection?
S	With simple authority, Jesus commands the deaf and mute spirit to leave and never enter the boy again.
S	The disciples were inspired to pray with faith: the pathway to future success.
N	The disciples learnt through the down-to-earth experience of failure.
S	This story is a vivid account of a healing that speaks for itself.
N	This story raises questions about the nature of sickness and the power of prayer.
	Interpretative choices by judging personality function
T	This is evidence that the disciples were already trying to heal the sick.
F	The disciples felt ashamed that they couldn't meet the father's cry for help.
T	It seems unfair to blame the father for doubting when the disciples had just failed to heal his son.
F	I can feel the deep love of the father for his son.
F	You can feel the awe that struck those who witnessed this miracle.
T	There is no direct evidence to show how the onlookers reacted to these events.
T	The evidence suggests that the boy had epilepsy; though what matters is how it was perceived at the time.
F	I feel sympathy for the boy, who must have been very frightened.
F	This is a story about people who feel hope, doubt, fear and love.
T	This story is evidence that unbelief and lack of prayer can lead to a failure to heal.

Note. S = Sensing, N = Intuition, F = Feeling, T = Thinking. Items were presented randomly in pairs (SN or FT) and participants were given the following instructions: 'These statements are comments on the story, given in pairs. In each case please circle the ONE statement (a) or (b) that you prefer'.

indeed reflect the sort of things that might have been said by someone with a given preference (Village and Francis 2005). To test the hypothesis that readers prefer interpretations that match their preferences in the perceiving and judging process, the relevant KTS scores were correlated against the number choices of each type. Because both KTS and interpretations were presented as forced-choice questions, it

Table 6.2   Longer interpretative items based on Mark 9:14–29

Type	Items
S	Imagine you are watching this scene. There is a noisy, heated argument that the disciples seem to be losing. When Jesus arrives everything is suddenly quiet. When the boy is brought to Jesus, the spirit makes him writhe on the ground, foaming at the mouth and sending up clouds of dust. The crowd is running to see what is happening but Jesus remains calm as he addresses the unclean spirit: 'Come out of him and never enter again'. A scream fills the air, then the boy lies so still that he seems dead. For a moment the silence is penetrating. Then gasps fill the air as Jesus lifts him up and shows that he is healed. Learn through the experience of the disciples: pray and have faith, even if you fail at first.
N	This story raises all sorts of intriguing questions and possibilities. The failure of the disciples is swept aside by the awesome presence of Jesus. Did he really expect them to succeed, or was their failure part of God's plan? Can we understand *our* failures as possibly being part of God's plan? The father wants to believe in Jesus, but the failure of the disciples makes him doubt. Or perhaps faith is always a mixture of belief and doubt. Something makes Jesus respond to the desperate child before him: was it the father's mustard-seed of faith or the need to demonstrate what *real* faith can do? Even if we believe in Jesus, do we have faith to overcome evil through prayer?
F	It's easy to identify with the characters in this story. You can sense the anxiety and frustration of the disciples when they can't help the desperate father by healing his son. Jesus is understandably angry at their lack of faith, yet he wants to encourage them to succeed. In private his anger subsides as he helps them to understand why they failed. We all share the agonized cry of the father: 'I believe, help my unbelief.' As we sympathize with father, we learn not to be critical of those whose faith is weak. Jesus has a deep compassion for the plight of the boy, and liberates him to new life though his supernatural power.
T	This story appears to be straightforward, though a closer look shows that scripture must be read carefully and thoughtfully: (a) Jesus seems to heal the boy immediately, without prayer, yet tells his disciples that only prayer can drive out such spirits. This seems illogical, but Jesus' whole life was prayerful, so perhaps he did not need a *special* prayer. (b) Jesus' anger at the father seems a bit unfair when the father has good reason to doubt. Perhaps he was trying to goad the father into expressing what faith he had. (c) Jesus' last remark seems to imply there are different kinds of evil spirit. This story is evidence that Jesus had an extraordinary and deep understanding of people and the spiritual world.

was necessary to use only one score for each process (S to test the perceiving process and F to test the judging process).

I mentioned earlier that psychological type preferences are linked with other factors such as sex differences and religious conservatism. If items were chosen according to their degree of conservatism, there might be a link to type that was entirely spurious. To rule this out it was necessary to use a multiple regression model that allowed the effect of type preference to be tested after allowing for other factors that might have affected the choice of items. Alongside the relevant psychological type score, the analysis also included the Bible score (as a measure of a person's conservatism), sex and education.

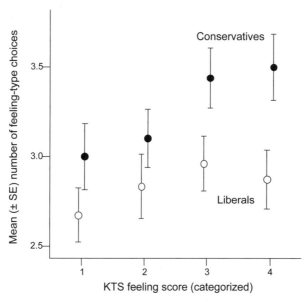

In the event, it was biblical conservatism and psychological type that were the main predictors of preferred interpretations (see Table 6.3).

Table 6.3 Analysis of variance for the number of sensing-type and feeling-type interpretative items chosen

Source of variation	*df*	*F*
Sensing items		
KTS sensing score	1	4.1*
Bible score	1	57.6***
Error	390	(1.2)
Feeling items		
KTS feeling score	1	8.5**
Bible score	1	14.9***
Error	390	(1.2)

Note: KTS scores and Bible score were entered into a general linear model. Values in parentheses are mean square errors. * $p < .05$; ** $p < .01$; *** $p < .001$.

Sensing items were more likely to be chosen by conservatives than liberals,[8] and by those with a high KTS sensing score (see Fig 6.1). Feeling items were also more likely to be chosen by conservatives, and by those with a high KTS feeling score (see Fig 6.2).

Fig 6.1 Preference for sensing-type passages in relation to KTS score

[8] In this context, conservatives were classed as those with average or above bible scores, and liberals as those with below average bible scores.

Fig 6.2 Preference for feeling-type passages in relation to KTS score

Dominant function was compared with interpretative choice of the four longer items by examining the proportion of people with a particular dominant function that chose the four items listed in Table 6.2. In this sample of 395, 41% of participants were dominant S, 39% dominant F and around 10% dominant N or T. If there was such a relationship, percentages along the diagonal in Table 6.4 should be higher than the rest. However, the four items were chosen in roughly equal frequencies in each dominant type and there was no evidence of preference for the predicted interpretation. Since all the experts who blind-classified these longer items put them in the appropriate category, it seems unlikely that this lack of correlation was due to the items not reflecting the likely preferences of each type. Instead it may be that either the notion of dominant type is itself is rather suspect or, if it is a genuine facet of personality, it is not employed in the process of choosing preferred interpretations.

Table 6.4 Choice of interpretative items by dominant psychological function

| Dominant type | N | Percentage choosing item of type | | | |
		Sensing %	Intuition %	Feeling %	Thinking %
Sensing	161	**25**	26	24	25
Intuition	42	12	**29**	19	40
Feeling	153	30	23	**24**	23
Thinking	39	31	33	23	**13**
All	395	26	26	23	25

This is the first clear empirical evidence that psychological type preferences within the judging and perceiving processes may indeed shape the interpretative preferences of ordinary readers. Treating the two processes of perceiving and judging separately showed a stronger effect than using the four dominant types together. This suggests that readers might keep the two things separate when they encounter a text. Thus one process is concerned with assessing what the passage is about, and this is done in a more sensing or more intuitive fashion, while the other process is concerned with evaluating the passage, and this is done in a more feeling or more thinking fashion. The test items used here were not created in order to test specifically perception versus judging, and this is something that needs more careful investigation. Rather than speaking of four dominant ways of approaching a passage, we might instead speak of two preferences, sensing or intuition and feeling or thinking.

Reader Imagination and Biblical Narrative

Psychological type theory also suggests that some people may find it easier to relate imaginatively to a text than others. There are several different ways in which a narrative text might engage readers. Sensing types might be aware of the different sensing information, but intuitives may find it easier to create an imaginary scene in which they become part of the story. Preferred feelers may find it easier than preferred thinkers to relate to the characters in a story.

The notion of imagining oneself into a biblical text has roots that go back a long way in the Christian tradition. Most obviously it relates to the legacy of Saint Ignatius, who developed a series of *Spiritual Exercises* for his followers (Corbishley 1963; Lonsdale 2000). Over a period of up to forty days, exercitants were helped to discern the will of God by a mixture of reading, prayer and meditation. The meditations included periods of actively imagining oneself in a biblical or religious narrative. The fifth contemplation of the nativity, for example, relies on imagining with the senses:

> *Look* in imagination at the persons, meditating and studying in detail the situation in which they find themselves, drawing some profit from the sight ... *Listen* to what they are saying or might say. Turning to myself I will derive some benefit ... *Smell* the indescribable fragrance and *taste* the boundless sweetness of divinity ... *Touch* by kissing and clinging to the places where these persons walk or sit, always trying to profit thereby. (Corbishley 1963: 49, translator's italics)

The Ignatian exercises have undergone something of a revival in the last few decades, and even writers from an evangelical tradition have suggested using this sort of approach to reading scripture (e.g. Huggett 1986, 1989). These days it is not unusual for people in a wide range of church traditions to be asked to imagine themselves in a Bible story as onlooker or character. This raises the question of whether particular psychological types might find such activity easier or more appealing than other types. The stress on seeing, hearing, smelling and touching in the Ignatian nativity exercise might suggest that sensing types would warm to this approach. On the other hand, this is *imagined* rather than actual sensing, so it might be easier for intuitive types. If the narrative includes people, it should be easier for preferred feeling types than preferred thinking types to empathize with someone in the story.

In the Bible and Lay People questionnaire, participants read the passage from Mark 9:14–29 and were then asked if they could imagine themselves in the story as one of the characters. The aim was to see if imagining into the story was linked to psychological type preferences. Of 398 participants who gave valid replies, 65% could identify with a character in the story and 35% could not: I have termed these 'imaginers' and 'non-imaginers' respectively. Can membership of these two groups be predicted, and is psychological type important in shaping the ability to interact with a narrative in this way?

To test this it was necessary to find out which factors were related to imagining and then use multivariate analysis to identify the key predictors. The results showed that women were much more likely to be imaginers than were men, as were those who preferred feeling to thinking in the judging process. Intuitives were also more likely to be imaginers than sensors, but the difference was not statistically significant.[9] Although there was a higher proportion of feeling types among women than among men, the relationship of psychological type and imagining was apparent in both, and preference for feeling remained a significant predictor of being an imaginer even after allowing for sex differences (see Fig 6.3).

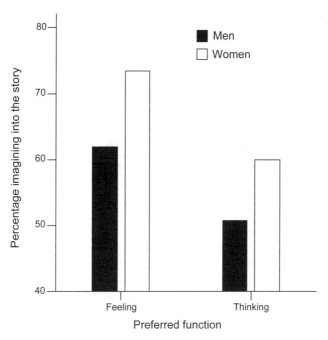

Fig 6.3   Percentage of imaginers by preferred judging function

---

[9]   Of 248 women, 70% were imaginers compared with 56% of 146 men ($\chi^2 = 7.9$, $df = 1$, $p < 0.01$). Of 265 preferred feelers 70% were imaginers compared with 55% of 104 preferred thinkers ($\chi^2 = 7.9$, $df = 1$, $p < 0.01$). Of 67 preferred intuitives 73% were imaginers compared with 64% of 312 preferred sensors ($\chi^2 = 2.1$, $df = 1$, Not Significant).

The psychological type preferences most likely to influence imagining were thus a preference for feeling over thinking and, to a lesser extent, a preference for intuition over sensing. Although the latter was not statistically significant in the initial analyses, the two psychological processes are thought to operate independently, and so there might be additive effects. If so, the proportion of imaginers should be highest in preferred NFs and lowest in STs, which was indeed the case.[10] The importance of intuition for imagining also emerged from an examination of dominant type. The frequency of imaginers was highest among dominant intuitives, intermediate among dominant sensors and feelers and lowest among dominant thinkers. These trends were apparent in both sexes, though statistically significant only in the combined data (see Table 6.5).

Table 6.5   Percentage of imaginers by dominant psychological function

		Dominant function			
		Intuition %	Feeling %	Sensing %	Thinking %
Men	Imaginers	63	57	53	43
	Non-imaginers	37	43	47	57
	$N=$	8	42	40	23
Women	Imaginers	93	71	72	46
	Non-imaginers	7	29	28	54
	$N=$	14	91	75	13
Both sexes	Imaginers	83	67	65	44
	Non-imaginers	17	33	35	56
	$N=$	23	135	115	36

Note. For both sexes: $\chi^2 = 9.9$, $df = 3$, $p < 0.01$.

There is thus some empirical evidence to suggest that psychological type might influence the way that readers engage with biblical narrative. Participants in the Bible and Lay People study were not asked to meditate actively on the passage, so this was not a full test of the relationship of type to this way of reading scripture. If they had been asked to meditate on the passage, introverts might have been more able to do so than extraverts. Instead they were asked specifically to identify with a person in the narrative and, as predicted, preferred feeling types found this easier than preferred thinking types, probably because of their more developed sense of empathy. The greater imaginative faculties of intuitives were less important in this exercise, though it did seem intuition would aid the ability to imagine oneself as a character in the story.

[10]   Imaginers comprised 78% of 54 NFs; 68% of 203 SFs; 58% of 12 NTs and 54% of 90 STs.

The results might have been different had the test passage been something more akin to the Ignatian exercise quoted earlier. Here the very strong directive to use the senses may have meant that sensors would engage more easily with this passage than would any other type. Different functions might be important in different kinds of passage, though I suspect that those who are comfortable with intuition are always likely to find the general process of imaginative engagement more to their liking.

Theological and Practical Implications

The empirical evidence is that at least one model of personality can predict both the way that someone engages with scripture and their preferred style of interpretation. This evidence must be tempered with caution: in both cases there were other factors that also predicted the interaction. Preference in interpretation is strongly linked to general biblical conservatism or liberalism, and imagining oneself as a character in a story is also linked to being female or male. The findings argue against the notion that lay people interpret *solely* according to their personality type, but they do show that personality might be part of the complex process that determines how people read the Bible. How does this relate to notions of God speaking to people through scripture?

It should be said at the outset that the investigation did not engage with issues about the truth or otherwise of particular types of interpretation. Indeed the whole thrust of the SIFT method of preaching is about preferred ways of *attending to* scripture rather than the content as such. The theory transcends content by arguing that, whatever the doctrinal content of a passage, different people will engage with it in different ways. In this sense, the link of personality to scripture might be seen as a secondary affair, related to individual taste rather than to life-transforming power. I think there are good grounds for suggesting that it is much more important than that. Ignoring our innate preferences may prevent us from perceiving the Word of God, even when we hear it.

Mark's account of the Parable of the Sower includes words from the lips of Jesus that have longed puzzled biblical scholars: 'To you has been given the secret of the kingdom of God, but for those outside, everything comes in parables; in order that "they may indeed look, but not perceive, and may indeed listen, but not understand; so that they may not turn again and be forgiven"' (Mark 4:11–12). The quote is from Isaiah, perhaps the product of a frustrated preacher who finds his words falling on deaf ears:

> And [God] said, 'Go and say to this people: "Keep listening, but do not comprehend; keep looking, but do not understand". Make the mind of this people dull, and stop their ears, and shut their eyes, so that they may not look with their eyes, and listen with their ears, and comprehend with their minds, and turn and be healed'. (Isaiah 6:9b–10)

Jesus is aware that the same words spoken can evoke very different reactions. Seed falls on a variety of soils and its fate is very different. This might be because the message is heard and understood, but treated differently, or it might be because it is never really 'heard' in the first place. This could be a scriptural reference to 'selective attention', a phenomenon that is apparent in everyday life and of interest to psychologists. The difference between looking and perceiving, or between listening and understanding, is familiar to cognitive psychologists, who have long understood that complex processes in the nervous system determine how we attend to, or ignore, the mass of information that constantly assaults the senses.[11] The process of 'getting used' to sensory input so that we no longer respond to it is called 'habituation' and is a vital process that prevents sensory overload. This may work at simple level, for example when we adjust to wearing woollen underwear or to living next to a busy railway line. Or it may work at a more complex level driven by our prior knowledge, beliefs and expectations.[12] Jesus implies that some people do not so much reject the message of the Kingdom as never really hear it in the first place. The parables are heard (or read), but they invoke neither recognition of the truth nor understanding of the message. Seed falls on the path and never even sprouts.

The implication is that humans must be predisposed to receive the challenge of God. For some, the message is never comprehended because they selectively reject it at an early stage in the process of perception. Unconscious forces 'switch off' the processes that would allow the mind to identify, and respond to, that which the senses are receiving. In theological terms, the Word encounters unreceptive hearts and is never acknowledged for what it is. 'He was in the world, and the world came into being through him; yet the world did not know him' (John 1:10). The corollary of this is that there are minds that are predisposed to hearing and responding. The logic of the Parable of the Sower is that those who are open to hearing God will 'comprehend' the parable and respond to its message.

Are there parallels here with the way that readers seemed to choose interpretations according preferred psychological type? To argue the case it might be necessary to go beyond the available data and ask what would happen if someone always interpreted entirely within the confines implied by their preferred psychological type.

Sensors might find themselves so preoccupied with the immediate text that they are unable to connect it with other related passages of scripture and unable to see how it adds to broader biblical themes or principles. The temptation to take historically-rooted passages and apply them directly to the lives of readers, without a wider overview, could lead to actions that are far from those implied by the Bible as a whole. Intuitives, on the other hand, may spin and weave truths that are largely of their own making. The simple and obvious cannot satisfy their desire to imagine new possibilities and raise new questions. So a message that should be received as

---

[11]   For an introduction to the field of attention in cognitive psychology, see Slack (1990) or Eysenck and Keane (2000).

[12]   Early studies of attention by cognitive psychologists (e.g. Broadbent 1958) assumed that information that was not attended to was filtered out at an early stage, before it could be processed. Such 'bottom-up' models had to be modified in the light of evidence that even information we apparently ignore is nonetheless received and processed by the brain. Increasingly, psychologists are realizing that attention is also controlled by 'top-down' processing that allows previous knowledge and expectations to actively filter sensory input. Several theories have been suggested to explain such 'high order processing' (reviewed by Wells and Matthews 1994), but no one theory has gained general acceptance.

simple enough for a child may become a complex flight of fantasy that successfully prevents any real change in the life of the reader.

Those who prefer feeling may find the judgements of scripture hard to reconcile with their essentially empathic nature. Passages that clearly speak of the judgement that awaits those who violate God's rules may be quietly ignored or explained away. The desire to harmonize and avoid painful truths may lead to a bland Bible that lacks any cutting edge, and a God who always accepts everything and everyone. Preferred thinkers might find in scripture a rational God who always abides by the rules that he himself created. They may perceive a God who judges fairly and justly, yet who is immune to the cries of those who have no logical defence for their actions. The rational mind might find God's apparent 'lapses' of unjustified grace difficult to explain, and may ignore passages of scripture that do not fit in with a reasoned understanding of the divine economy.

These are caricatures, of course, but they make the point that the influence of personality on the reading of scripture can be more than a matter of preference and taste. It shows that the kinds of predispositions that we bring to scripture can be much more damaging and pervasive that a simple matter of what we believe about the Bible or about God. What this points to is the oldest and most besetting sin of all: idolatry. Idolatry is, at heart, a reversal of the creative process referred to in Genesis 1:26. Created in the image of God, we recreate God in our own image. Empirical theology exposes a route whereby scripture reading might reinforce this idolatry. If we allow our innate psychological preferences too much sway in guiding our reading, we may hear only words that reinforce the notion of a God that is like us in every way. It is not that we reject other notions; we simply do not perceive them.

This is not a new idea; indeed, as I have argued, it is present in scripture itself. Neither is it unfamiliar in academic circles: scholars have long warned that readers may shape scripture in their own image. What a personality approach can do is to give substance to that shaping, and shed light on the particular ways people might perceive scripture. What is more, the various tendencies can be predicted and to some extent quantified, offering a tool for better self-understanding.

Another way of looking at personality preferences is to see them as strengths rather than weaknesses. If the different ways of attending to scripture are seen as complementary, then they become ways in which the potential pitfalls of each can be overcome. The focused, down-to-earth approach of the sensor balances the hopeful imagination of the intuitive. The ability of sensors to focus and apply detail allows scripture to speak to this world now. The ability of intuitives to see the bigger picture brings a wider perspective that allows scripture to interpret and judge itself. The harmonizing, accepting approach of the feeler balances the fairness and principles of the thinker. The ability of feelers to understand others prevents us from cold-hearted judgement. The ability of thinkers to understand the importance of principle prevents us from soft-headed capitulation to evil.

Creating a balance works at individual and corporate levels. Psychological type practitioners not only help people to identify and affirm their preferences, they also help people to be aware of their corresponding weaknesses, and use their non-preferred functions. At the individual level, each reader can be encouraged to understand his or her own psychological type preferences along with the associated strengths and weaknesses. Familiarity with the opposite type enables people to see different ways of attending to scripture. Being able to say 'This is not what I prefer but I can do it if I choose' seems to be a mature and helpful way of approaching the reading of scripture.

At a corporate level, personality theory might help with scripture reading by encouraging the church to accept and use individual differences. Although type practitioners encourage individuals to work in non-preferred ways, this does not alter the basic fact that different types exist. Using the innate skills of different types is as important as encouraging the development of skills associated with non-preferred type. Allowing individuals to be what they are is not the same as sanctifying their failures. Rather it points to the essentially corporate nature of the church, which is no less true when it comes to reading and understanding scripture. If personality is God-given, then there ought to be a God-given way of using it to good effect. Corporate engagement with scripture is more than just the sharing of opinions. It is a chance to benefit from the gifting of other people, to have our own preferences acknowledged and valued and to have our particular blind spots exposed and questioned. The implication here is that congregations or Bible study groups need to be heterogeneous gatherings when it comes to psychological types. Separating sensors from intuitives, or feelers from thinkers, is likely to lead to a false sense of harmony that looks suspiciously like a hermeneutical apartheid whereby readers associate with similar psychological types in huddles that are incapable of interpreting beyond the group norm. Whether this actually happens is related to the issue of interpretative communities, which I deal with in the next chapter.

Another important implication of the findings of the Bible and Lay People study is the way that innate preference or ability might affect the manner in which ordinary readers engage with scripture. The evidence here is that ability in one particular way of approaching scripture, reading oneself into the story, is related to psychological type preference. It seems likely that this might apply to a range of methods and psychological types, though the evidence is yet to be established. If it is, it will raise the issue of whether method, by limiting what can be gained from reading, also limits the scope of scripture to transform the reader. Here it is sufficient to note that while personality might positively predispose readers to particular ways of relating to scripture, it might by the same token prevent them relating in other important ways. As with preferred interpretations, preferred method of reading may be something that both helps and hinders a rounded appropriation of scripture. Healthy reading may be that which allows a variety of interaction so as to maximize the benefit of scripture for the reader.

Further Research

It is clear that empirical studies of scripture reading are a minority interest in the field of biblical psychology. Nonetheless there is a general growth in empirical studies of reading and psychology and a great deal of scope to apply empirical methods to observe the process of Bible reading. The particular area of psychological type and scripture would benefit from more studies of the type reported here. Different types of scripture could be used and a wider range of church traditions needs to be sampled. Studies could be extensive, as here, or intensive, by using small groups in MBTI workshops and the like. The former would give larger and more representative samples; the latter would be able to use longer test passages and test items.

The advantage of using a test passage is that it directly relates to the act of reading, rather than asking indirect questions about how people might prefer to interpret. The difficulty is in creating test items, because technically there is no way of being certain that a given item truly reflects its associated type. The most stringent approach would be to blind test all items a priori on psychological type practitioners, and use only items that they all identify correctly. This is time consuming and would need to be done for each test passage and its associated items.

A key question is whether the effect of type operates through dominant type, or through the two processes of perceiving and judging. Is interpretation a two-stage process of attending to the information and then assessing its meaning? If so, instruments could deliberately divide the process into two parts, shaping S/N items around issues of perception and F/T items around issues of judgement or evaluation. If the process is two-stage, items placed in the 'wrong' section might be less predictive than those in the 'right' section.

Another aspect that needs further work is to uncover the relative effects of personality when compared with other factors that influence interpretative choices. Theological content in particular might have an overriding effect in many passages. A controlled study could produce the same content in different styles and the same style with different content (e.g. conservative versus liberal) in an attempt to vary the two independently. Again, this would require careful testing of items for both aspects.

The work on imaginative reading and type could be expanded in several directions. The investigation of people on Ignatian retreats might be one way of exploring this sort of reading in more detail. There are also many other different ways of engaging with scripture, and enough variation in psychological types to generate a range of hypotheses. Do extraverts really prefer group Bible study to personal reading? Do sensors prefer a Bible study that involves a verse-by-verse exposition of a passage while intuitives look for theme-based studies that draw on a range of texts? A useful approach might be to measure both willingness to use, and ability in, a particular method and relate this to psychological type. This would help readers and Bible study leaders to match readers and reading.

Beyond personality there is a host of questions relating psychology to Bible reading. The approach here has been to generate questions from psychological theory and see how they might apply to the particular act of reading scripture. There are signs that a more rigorous empirical approach might emerge from those using the Bible in clinical practice, and from those biblical psychologists who are starting to move from psyches implied in the text to the psyches of real readers. The dominance of Freudian and Jungian theory (or their successors) in the field of psychological biblical studies is both a help and hindrance here. On the one hand, there is a wealth of ideas such as object-relations theory and individuation that provide theoretical bases for understanding the way that Bible reading affects readers (for example, see some of the articles in Ellens and Rollins 2004). On the other hand, Freud's ideas are notoriously difficult to verify or falsify by empirical observation.[13] Perhaps more fruitful ground for empirical approaches to scripture reading would be to draw on theories from cognitive psychology, along the lines of some of the empirical studies in other branches of literary study and discourse analysis.

---

[13]   See Kline (1972), Eysenck and Wilson (1973) and Fisher and Greenberg (1985) among others for an insight into this intense and long-running debate.

Chapter 7

Interpretative Communities and Scripture

The preceding chapters have examined how individual differences shape the way that ordinary readers interpret the Bible. There remains another possible influence on interpretation that has been widely discussed in literary circles, and this is the effect of interpretative communities. This idea stems from the suggestion that reading is not always an isolated, individual process, but one that can be linked to a community of like-minded readers. This is especially true for sacred texts because these are the products of faith communities and their reproduction and interpretation is often guarded by those same communities. In the history of the Christian church, errant interpretations of scripture have earned the wrath of the community, with sometimes dire consequences for those bold enough to go against the majority understanding. Indeed, one of the signs of this displeasure was excommunication: expulsion from the community.[1]

The Reformation is sometimes described as an attempt to free scriptural interpretation from the tight control of the community, represented by the Roman Catholic Church. In fact, corporate interpretation remained important for the early Reformers, who understood the dangers of allowing individuals to interpret the Bible as they wished.[2] What had changed was the locus of the community rather than its control over interpretation. Thus different ideas of the place and role of scripture emerged in various Protestant schools, which developed their own communities with their own particular interpretations. Thiselton argues that it was the advent of the Enlightenment that truly shifted the locus of interpretation to individuals by stressing the autonomy of the independent, rational self as the true basis of knowledge (1992: 143). This way of viewing knowledge tended to reduce the influence of factors external to the individual, including the role of the church, in deciding what the Bible meant. Furthermore, the translation of Bibles into the vernacular and the

---

[1]   The Papal Bull *Exsurge Domine,* issued by Pope Leo X on 15 June 1520 prior to the excommunication of Martin Luther, includes the following: 'Finally, let the whole church of the saints and the rest of the universal church arise. Some, putting aside her true interpretation of Sacred Scripture, are blinded in mind by the father of lies. Wise in their own eyes, according to the ancient practice of heretics, they interpret these same Scriptures otherwise than the Holy Spirit demands, inspired only by their own sense of ambition, and for the sake of popular acclaim, as the Apostle declares. In fact, they twist and adulterate the Scriptures. As a result, according to Jerome, "It is no longer the Gospel of Christ, but a man's, or what is worse, the devil's"'. <www.papalencyclicals.net/Leo10/l10exdom.htm>, accessed 26 April 2007.

[2]   Thiselton (1992: 182) writes: 'Luther's position … is sometimes misunderstood. He attacked authoritarian and self-serving appeal to tradition as a means of forcing scripture to speak with a certain voice. But he did not seek to substitute individual opinion for tradition in a way akin to the mood of post-Enlightenment rationalism'.

growth of literacy enabled more and more ordinary believers to search the scriptures for themselves. Given this trend towards individualism in biblical interpretation, it is worth enquiring into the role of church communities in influencing the way that lay people interpret their scriptures today. Does each reader engage with scripture in isolation, or does the church community to which they belong shape the way that they interpret it?

This is not simple a question. For a start, it is not easy to tell what constitutes a reading community because community influences may operate at different levels. At a basic level, Christians are part of a broad community whose reading of the Bible will be different from that of people of other faiths or no faith. Reading with the belief that the Bible is sacred scripture is bound to be different from reading with the belief that this text has no particular religious significance. Yet even within the Christian community there are wide variations in how scripture is understood. I have already demonstrated differences between liberal and conservative Bible belief among Anglicans, and this wide divergence of opinion is likely to be stretched to even greater extremes across the full range of Christian denominations.

Different Christian denominations or traditions could be said to represent different reading communities that shape the way that their members read scripture. But traditions are sometimes broad and rather nebulous constructs. In the Church of England it is debatable how many lay people either understand or react to the ecclesiastical structures that constitute the hierarchy of community influence. Ask the average lay person to explain the role and nature of policy-making in their denomination and they are likely to look at you with a mixture of ignorance and indifference. For many people, it is their local congregation that is the main, and perhaps only, manifestation of the church community. Congregations might be better candidates for reading communities than either denominations or traditions within denominations.

Another reason why assessing the importance of any community effect on reading is difficult is because worshippers tend to segregate into different kinds of congregations. Congregations belong to particular traditions within denominations (e.g. Anglo-Catholics within Anglicanism) or denominations within wider traditions (e.g. Anglicanism within mainstream denominations), and people may join congregations because they are inherently drawn a particular way of reading scripture. In this model of community, congregational similarities of reading practice are a by-product of the gathering of like-minded people, rather than the influence of a community style on individuals. Theoretically, it should be possible for an empiricist to test the importance of individual versus community effects: all that is required is to measure the interpretation of individuals and then redistribute them at random into established congregations of different reading practices. If they continue unchanged, the community has little effect. If they adjust to match the community in which they are placed, there is evidence of a 'community' effect. In practice, researchers suggesting such an elegant experiment are likely to be given short shrift by those who for some reason do not share their passion for empirical evidence. Faced with such a lamentable lack of enthusiasm, the best that can be done is to observe people in different congregations and to try to parcel out the relative effects of individual and community. Observations of those who, for various reasons, change congregations might be useful, but are difficult to interpret without detailed knowledge of interpretation before and after the move, or some insight into the reason for the change. People who change because they are looking for a church that handles scripture in a particular way may show a different response from those who, for example, change because they move house and join the nearest Anglican church irrespective of its tradition.

There are other problems that arise even before tackling the difficult task of assessing a community effect on interpretation. These stem from the theoretical basis of the term 'interpretative communities', which has a particular origin and usage in literary circles that needs to be explained and understood before any attention is given to empirical testing.

The Concept of Interpretative Communities

The idea of different schools of biblical interpretation is not new and stems from the early days of Judaism and Christianity. For example, Patristic interpretation is usually characterized by contrasting the more allegorical bent of the Alexandrian school with the more literalist approach at Antioch (Young 2003). Different understandings of the Bible and different hermeneutical methods have grown, flourished, withered and sometimes re-sprouted in the long history of the church. Allegorical interpretation is an example of a method that has waxed and waned in its popularity over the centuries: having been unfashionable for many years, it has recently undergone something of a revival in academic circles (Madsen 1994; Snodgrass 2000; Whitman 1987; Young 1993). These different schools might be thought of as different interpretative communities that shaped the way that the sacred text was read and understood. Particular beliefs about the Bible and particular ways of handling the text were passed from experts to novices, thereby perpetuating an interpretative community.

Schools of interpretation, explicit or otherwise, are still very much in evidence. Recently, John Webster (2003) commended the idea of the 'theology school', using as his example the writings of the Reformation theologian Zacharius Ursinus. Ursinus argued that the chief role of the then new schools of theology was to search scriptures and rightly divine the Word of God. Webster analyses the reasons why this close link between the academic study of scripture and the practical requirements of the church has been broken. His own approach argues for the restoration of a thoroughly dogmatic understanding of scripture that consciously shapes the reading of scripture according to a particular view of the nature of God. While some may criticize this theological approach, it is simply making explicit the ground rules for a particular reading community. Other communities may have different rules that are based mainly on method rather than theology, but they nonetheless shape reading according to particular fashions or assumptions. In this sense they are interpretative communities.

This relatively simple and intuitive understanding of community has been given a more nuanced understanding in literary critical circles, notably by the writings of

Stanley Fish (1980; 1989; 1994). His use of 'interpretive communities'[3] has led to a widespread debate in literary circles that has also drawn attention from biblical scholars and theologians (Adam 1990; Fulkerson 1998; Kolbrener 1996; Lieb 2002; Moore 1986; Noble 1996; Saye 1996; Vanhoozer 1998). Although Fish was not the first to suggest the idea,[4] he has been its most prominent and thoroughgoing advocate, and uses the term in a radically postmodern way. No discussion of community effects on Bible reading can avoid engaging in some way with Fish's notion of interpretative community, even though, as I shall attempt to demonstrate, his notion of community is not open to empirical testing and has been rejected by some on hermeneutical and theological grounds (Noble 1994, 1995, 1996; Thiselton 1992: 549–50).

To understand Fish, it is useful to explore how and why he arrived at the notion of interpretative communities. Fish is a literary critic and professor of law whose interests have included poetics (especially the poetry of Milton), literary analysis, and hermeneutics. His seminal work was a collection of essays published in 1980 under the title *Is There a Text in This Class?* Fish questioned the then dominant paradigm of literary formalism, which assumed that meaning was encoded in the text by the choice of words, arrangement of sentences and the wider structuring of ideas. Formalism leads to the sort of structural analysis of poems and narrative that is the bedrock of literary discourse. Interpretation in this paradigm is about deciphering the codes inherent in the text that are aimed at the implied reader. Fish challenges the assumption that meaning resides in the text (that is, in the writing on the page) by arguing that readers create meaning in the act of reading. This act is so strongly governed by the reader that, for Fish, the text does not exist as an independent entity until it is read. Readers *create* texts by shaping the written word to conform to their expectation of what they are reading. Different readers create different texts and so interpret what they read in different (and sometimes very different) ways.

In 'How to recognize a poem when you see one', Fish (1980: 322) cites an 'experiment' that proves his point. After teaching a class on linguistics and literary criticism in the university, he wrote a list of names on the board as suggested reading. They were the names of writers who had published in that particular field. The next class that arrived had been studying religious poetry, and Fish asked them to interpret the 'poem' on the board. This they did, with great enthusiasm and creativity. This creativity is Fish's point: the students took a more or less random list of names and, within the context of their class, created a new text. Fish argues that this activity is all-controlling and leaves no room for locating meaning in the text: 'there are no stops on the anti-formalism road' (Fish 1989: 25). Fish is renowned for his uncompromising rejection of the idea of a text that exists independently of the reader. So when another professor on the campus, who was delivering a course of lectures in the English department, was asked by a former student of Fish 'Is there a text in this class?', he was momentarily unsure if this was a request for a core textbook or a question about his views on the independence of the text (1980: 305).

---

[3]   Fish uses the American spelling; I shall use 'interpretative'.
[4]   Michaels (1977; and reprinted in Tompkins 1980: 185–200) traces this thinking in the American context to the ideas of C.S. Peirce in the nineteenth century.

Fish has elaborated this anti-formalist idea by arguing that all writing is inherently ambiguous: thus there is no limit to the interpretations that can be put upon it. Control lies not in the written word but in the persuasive powers of those who create and propagate particular interpretations. Fish subsequently expanded this notion to a wider 'anti-foundationalist' position that undermines the objectivity of all knowledge, including the interpretation of law and the justification for political action (Fish 1989, 1994, 1995). Meaning is rhetorical because things mean what we can persuade others they mean. If we are sufficiently persuasive, virtually any meaning can be attached to anything.

If this is so, why are there not an infinite number of interpretations? How can meanings remain stable over time or between individuals if individuals alone shape meaning? This is where Fish turns to the notion of interpretative communities. Meanings are stable because they arise from communities, not from individuals. Interpretations are shaped by community perceptions and expectations that limit how a piece of writing can be understood. In Fish's world, communities create texts, and the texts that they create are highly restricted: 'since the thoughts an individual can think and the mental operations he can perform have their source in some or other interpretive community, he is as much a product of that community (acting as an extension of it) as the meanings it enables him to produce' (1980: 14).

It is worth noting at this juncture how Fish arrived at interpretative communities. His assumption that readers and readers alone create texts left him with a need to explain the stability and persistence of interpretations in a way that did not concede any control by texts. He achieves this by talking of community because this seems to allow meaning to be shared, yet not locatable in the written word. Community here is a rhetorical creation, designed to persuade us of his original proposition in the face of apparently contrary evidence. This makes it difficult to pin down these interpretative communities. At various times Fish seems to refer to the community of the academy, the community of literary critics, the community of his university department or different communities within the same department. It is hard to connect any interpretative community to a specific social community, and Fish is loath to do so.

The difficulty in relating interpretative communities to actual communities comes about largely because Fish in his early writing uses the term as a shorthand way of referring to people who share the same interpretative strategies. 'members of the same community will necessarily agree because they will see (and by seeing make) everything in relation to that community's assumed purposes and goals' (1980: 15). This circularity makes it difficult to evaluate the importance of communities in the real world. If interpretative community means a collection of people who interpret the same way, then by definition they will always be homogenous. Groups of people with mixed interpretations of the same text are not a heterogeneous interpretative community; they are several intermingled communities.

Fish has been criticized on several fronts, not least because his original ideas seemed to make it impossible for new interpretations to emerge in a community, or for individuals to change their interpretations. As he originally defined community, members necessarily agreed, and were unable to create the texts of other communities. This implies either that change must be arbitrary or, more likely, that communities are self-perpetuating and impervious to new interpretations. The reality is that interpretations do change, and change is often developmental rather than disruptive. When pushed on this, Fish argued for more diversity in interpretative communities than his early writing had implied: 'The answer lies in the nature of an interpretive community which is at once homogenous with respect to some general sense of purpose or purview, and heterogeneous with respect to the variety of practices it can accommodate' (1989: 149). This difference between general purpose and particular practice allowed Fish to argue that interpretative communities, far from being homogeneous and static, are actually 'engines of change'. Communities, and the minds of community members, are not stable or fixed but assimilate new ideas and are self-transforming. Presumably this is because members are open to persuasion to a different point of view.

Allowing diversity within communities suggests that Fish intended the term to be more than just a shorthand way of saying 'people who interpret the same way'. Real communities exert real influence on readers that persuades them to interpret in a particular way. Fish is convinced by the overarching force of rhetoric, and the ability of the powerful to persuade and inculcate novices into the mores of the community. If this is so, it ought to be possible to identify this force at work and to demonstrate that belonging to the community is the best (if not only) predictor of interpretative practice. The idea should be disprovable if individual variation is more important in predicting interpretation than membership of the community. However, Fish has made it difficult to test this idea in relation to particular social communities by, on the one hand, defining communities as readers who agree; and on the other by allowing for variety of practice. If a social community is shown to have a range of interpretations, this could, according to Fish's ideas, be because there are different interpretative communities within it, or because these diverse interpretations represent varied practice within a single interpretative community. Either way, the notion of interpretative community, as defined by Stanley Fish, will resist being proved or disproved since he has argued for both unity and diversity.

This has not stopped empiricists trying to identify interpretative communities. Several people claim to have done so by contrasting the different ways that experts and lay people handle literature (see, for example Dorfman 1996; Hanauer 1995). Such studies have shown that readers with different expertise handle literature in different ways, but this is not the same as demonstrating some kind of community effect. It could equally be an individual effect of education or experience. Defining interpretative communities according to expert or lay readers risks the sort of circularity inherent in Fish's definition in the first place. What is needed is a social community that may influence reading but is not defined solely by the way it reads.

Churches are an obvious example of such communities, and there are a number of theologians who have stressed the importance of reading and interpreting scripture within a faith context.[5] Rather fewer people have tried to apply Fish's

---

[5]   The idea is widespread in various forms including those such as Brevard Childs (1993) who advocate a canonical approach to scripture, those like Francis Watson (1994: 4–6) who stress that the church is the primary reading community of the Bible, and those such as George Lindbeck (1984; 1989: 99) who argue more generally that doctrine arises as Christian communities interpret their narrative history.

ideas to Christian congregations interpreting scripture, and those who have (e.g. Forstorp 1990; Fulkerson 1998; Svensson 1990) have not always considered the prior question of just how important the community effect is for ordinary readers. Is it an all-powerful and pervasive force that brings uniformity to diverse readers; or is it a minor influence compared to the power of individual preference? The Bible and Lay People study offered a chance to compare the explanatory power of individual differences with the power of belonging to a particular congregation. The different congregations sampled belonged to different traditions that would be expected to 'pull' interpretations in different directions. Looking for a community effect in this situation is not an unfair test, which it might be if all the congregations were identical. Similarly, people within congregations were sufficiently varied to enable meaningful comparison of the relative effects of individual differences and community membership on interpretation.

Are Congregations Interpretative Communities?

Community and Individual Predictors of Interpretation

The most direct measures of interpretative strategies in the Bible and Lay People study were the degree of literalism and the measures of horizon separation and horizon preference. These indicated the ways in which a passage was likely to have been understood and perceived, and the focus of attention in terms of author, text or reader. A first step in investigating congregations as interpretative communities was to examine the variability of interpretation within and between congregations. Strong community influence predicts that interpretation will vary much more between congregations than within them. Indeed, a Fish-type argument is that there is little or no variation within congregations but very marked variation between them. This extreme position was clearly not the case in the Bible and Lay People sample. Comparing literalism scores between traditions, for example, shows that although average scores varied significantly, there was a high degree of overlap between the individual scores of people in different traditions (see Fig 7.1). The same sort of spread was apparent within congregations in any given tradition.

To examine variation within and between congregations, I selected two from each of the three traditions, Anglo-Catholic, broad church and evangelical, that had reasonable numbers of participants. A simple initial analysis was to test variation between traditions and between congregations within traditions for each of the five measures of interpretation (see Table 7.1).

If congregation alone was included in the analysis it was a significant predictor of all interpretative variables apart from the reader-horizon score. However, including church tradition showed that the majority of this variation was between congregations that belonged to different traditions, rather than between congregations within the same tradition. There was some congregational variation in the literalism scale because although the two evangelical congregations were much more literal than the

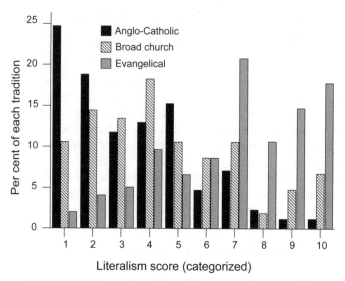

Fig 7.1   Histograms of literalism scores by tradition

Table 7.1   Analysis of variance of various measures of biblical interpretation

Source of variation	df	Literalism F	Horizon separation F	Horizon preference Author F	Text F	Reader F
Church tradition	2	64.0***	11.4***	10.2***	3.5*	0.9
Congregation	1	0.9	1.9	0.6	3.6	4.8*
Tradition–Congregation	2	6.2**	1.5	2.8	0.4	2.5
Error	367	(55.7)	(18.1)	(2.1)	(4.3)	(5.3)

Note. The interaction term Tradition–Congregation tests if the variation between congregations within traditions differed between traditions. Values in parentheses are mean square errors. *$p < .05$; **$p < .01$; ***$p < .001$.

rest, one was also significantly more literal than the other.[6] The only other variable to show a clear congregational effect was preference for the reader horizon, where there were differences between some congregations, but no clear overall difference between traditions. For the other variables, differences between congregations arose because they came from different traditions.

Although the variation between congregations was largely explained by the traditions to which they belonged, this would still seem to be *prima facie* evidence for the influence of congregations on biblical interpretation. Congregations might be

---

[6]   This is indicated by the significance of the 'Tradition–Congregation' source of variation in Table 7.1. Overall, there was no difference between congregations within traditions, but there was a difference in the two evangelical congregations.

the prime reading communities, though they are clearly linked to wider interpretative communities related to different traditions within Anglicanism. However, it is possible that the reason why congregations differ is because the individuals within them differ. For example, literalism is related to educational experience (Chapter 4) so the difference might be because particular congregations happen to have people of different educational backgrounds, rather than the congregation acting as an interpretative community. To test this, various measures of individual difference were added to the model, to see if they explained differences without recourse to a congregational or tradition effect. The measures of individual difference available were: sex, age, education, theological education, Bible score, charismatic score, supernatural healing score and the various psychological type (KTS) scores. All of these variables might have had some influence on biblical interpretation generally and some were known to influence the particular measures of literalism and horizon separation or horizon preference used in the Bible and Lay People study. When these were added to the analysis of variance model, the effect of tradition and congregation disappeared in all but the literalism scale (see Table 7.2). In other words, for horizon separation and horizon preferences any differences between congregations seemed to be better explained by individual differences between congregation members rather than by any effect of congregation on interpretation as such. In the case of literalism, there was a highly significant effect of tradition even after allowing for the effects of individual differences. This implies that belonging to a particular tradition (rather

Table 7.2   Summary of analyses of variance of interpretation measures with individual difference variables added to model

Source of variation	Literalism	Horizon separation	Author	Text	Reader
Church tradition	***	-	-	-	-
Congregation	-	-	-	-	-
Sex	-	-	-	-	-
Theological education	-	-	**	-	*
Education	**	-	*	**	***
Age	-	-	-	-	-
Bible score	***	***	-	-	*
Charismatic score	-	-	-	-	-
Supernatural healing score	***	***	***	-	-
KTS extravert score	-	-	-	-	-
KTS sensing score	-	-	-	*	-
KTS feeling score	-	-	-	-	*
KTS judging score	-	-	-	*	*

Note. Church tradition (1 = Anglo-Catholic, 2 = Broad church, 3 = Evangelical), congregation, sex and theological education were entered as factors and the remaining variables entered as covariates separate general linear model for each independent variable. $^*p < .05$; $^{**}p < .01$; $^{***}p < .001$, otherwise not significant.

than a particular congregation within that tradition) might shape a person's degree of literalism, irrespective of their personal beliefs about the Bible or educational experience. The difference between congregations with a given tradition is small compared with the differences between traditions.

There was thus some evidence that membership of a congregation within a particular Church of England tradition might shape the way that members interpret the Bible in terms of literalism. The evidence is circumstantial, because it remains possible that people joined congregations that interpreted the Bible in a similar way to themselves. The net result would be the same: congregations or traditions in which lay people had a broadly similar interpretative strategy that could not wholly be explained by individual characteristics.

Interpretation and Marginalization in Congregations

One way of checking the importance of biblical interpretation as a factor shaping, or shaped by, congregational membership, is to see if it is related to a general sense of belonging to a congregation or agreeing with the teaching in a church. If the way people interpret individually is influenced by community norms, then those who interpret differently from their fellow congregational members might feel less at home, and be more likely to disagree with what they are taught, than those who interpret with the majority. To test for this, I included two questions in the study. The first was a forced-choice question related to a sense of belonging: *Which one of these statements is most true of you?*

1. I feel entirely at home in my church
2. I occasionally feel out of place in my church
3. I feel I don't really belong in my church.

Overall, most participants felt entirely at home (64% of 400 respondents), and only 5% felt they did not really belong in their church (Village 2007). For the analysis that follows, respondents were categorized as those who felt entirely at home and those who did not.

The second was a forced-choice question related to disagreement: *Which one of these statements best describes your reaction to the teaching (sermons, mid-week study groups, etc.) that you receive from your church?*

1. I never disagree with the teaching I get at my church
2. I occasionally disagree with the teaching I get at my church
3. I often disagree with the teaching I get at my church.

Occasional or frequent disagreement was fairly common among respondents (70% answered choice 2 and 2% answered choice 3). For the purpose of this analysis, respondents were divided into those who never disagreed and those who did at least occasionally.

The next step was to identify people whose interpretation was marginal relative to the rest of their congregation. For the six congregations for which I had sufficient responses, I calculated the standardized residuals for the literalism and horizon-separation scores. Residuals were a measure of how far a person's score deviated from the congregational average, and standardized residuals are expressed in terms of standard deviations.[7] This allows people to be categorized according to how marginal (that is deviant from the average) their interpretation is, relative to their particular congregation, and for these scores to be combined across congregations. For each of the two measures those more than 1.5 SD above or below the average score were classed as 'marginal interpreters'. This was an arbitrary figure, but one that cast around 10–12% of each congregation as marginal compared with the rest. Marginal might be because they interpreted more or less literally, or with greater or less horizon separation. The direction of disagreement was less important in this context than the extent of disagreement.

Over the six congregations there were 386 people of whom 31 were classed as marginal in literalism, 31 as marginal in horizon separation and 16 as marginal in both. For each measure of interpretation, the normal and marginal interpreters were tested for their sense of belonging and frequency of disagreement. For both literalism and horizon separation, marginal interpreters were less likely to feel entirely at home than were majority interpreters, and more likely to disagree with what they were taught.[8] It seems, then, that marginalization in interpretation is indeed linked to a more general sense of marginalization within a congregation. Having said that, it should be noted that a large majority of people felt entirely at home and an even larger majority sometimes disagreed with what they were taught. Nonetheless, there was a link between a general sense of belonging and interpretation of the Bible in these congregations, which offers further support that they were, to some extent, interpretative communities.

Changing Congregation and Interpretation

A third line of evidence comes from looking at biblical interpretation in relation to movements from one interpretative community to another. Fish's notion of interpretative community suggests that when people move to a new community their interpretation should become indistinguishable from those who have always been in that community. This would be the case if congregations exerted an overriding influence on interpretative practice. If, on the other hand, interpretation is governed by

---

7   Standard deviation (SD) is a widely used measure of the extent of spread around a mean value. In a normally distributed population around 68% of people will lie within ±1 SD of the mean and around 95% will lie within ±2 SD of the mean.

8   For literalism, 48% of 46 marginal interpreters felt entirely at home compared with 66% of 336 majority interpreters ($\chi^2 = 5.6$, $df = 1$, $p < 0.02$); 87% of these marginal interpreters sometimes disagreed with what they were taught compared with 73% of the majority interpreters ($\chi^2 = 4.0$, $df = 1$, $p < 0.05$). For horizon separation, 45% of marginal interpreters felt entirely at home compared with 66% of majority interpreters ($\chi^2 = 8.3$, $df = 1$, $p < 0.01$); 87% of marginal interpreters sometimes disagreed with what they were taught compared with 73% of majority interpreters ($\chi^2 = 4.0$, $df = 1$, $p < 0.05$).

individual differences, people might continue to interpret in their new congregation as they had in their old.

It was not possible to examine this in detail in the Bible and Lay People Study, but the questionnaire did ask if people had previously worshipped at a different church and, if so, what sort of church. Using this information, combined with the tradition of their current church, it was at least possible to say if they had always been in the same tradition, or if they had moved to a more conservative (i.e. evangelical) or more liberal (i.e. Anglo-Catholic) tradition. A few people who had worshipped in other churches had come from more than one tradition, and they were excluded from this analysis. The best single measure of interpretation to use in this context was the degree of literalism, since this was lowest in Anglo-Catholic churches, intermediate in broad churches and highest in evangelical churches, which meant there were clear predictions for the direction of change for those moving between traditions.

Participants were divided according to their past and current experience of traditions:

1. *Always Anglo-Catholic*: those who had always been in their current Anglo-Catholic church or who had moved from another Anglo-Catholic church.
2. *New Anglo-Catholic*: those in an Anglo-Catholic church who had come from a broad or evangelical church.
3. *Former Anglo-Catholic*: those in a broad church who had moved from an Anglo-Catholic church.
4. *Always broad church*: those who had always been in their current broad church or who had moved from another broad church.
5. *Former evangelical*: those in a broad church who had moved from an evangelical church.
6. *New evangelical*: those in an evangelical church who had moved from an Anglo-Catholic or broad church.
7. *Always evangelical*: those who had always been in their current evangelical church or who had moved from another evangelical church.

The average literalism scores for these different groups showed that those who moved mostly had scores intermediate between those who had always been in their tradition (see Fig 7.2). Thus, for example, evangelicals who had always been evangelical had significantly higher literalism scores than evangelicals who had come from less conservative traditions. In broad churches, former evangelicals tended to be more literal, and former Anglo-Catholics less literal, than those who had always been in broad churches. The only exception to the sequence were Anglo-Catholics who had always been so, who were more literal than new Anglo-Catholics.

These results are intriguing, though it is difficult to be certain exactly what caused these trends. I had no way of knowing how individuals interpreted in their previous church and I could not tell if people moved because they already interpreted differently or if they changed as a result of the move. One possibility is that there is a time lag between arriving in a new church and moving towards the community norm, though there was no difference in these small samples between those who had been in their present church for one year or less and those who had been present

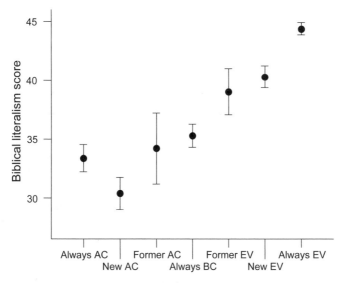

Fig 7.2   Mean (± SE) literalism score by previous tradition category

Note. See text for explanation of categories.

for up to five years. What Fig 7.2 does show is that traditions are not homogenous with respect to literal interpretation, and that part of the variation is related to the previous church communities to which individuals belonged. In statistical terms, replacing present tradition with a variable that assesses present *and* previous tradition significantly improved the prediction of literalism scores. This suggests that when it comes to biblical interpretation, people carry with them some influence of their previous experience of other traditions, and that their present congregation has partly, but not fully, shaped their interpretative practice. The results are consistent with the idea that interpretation is partly shaped by individual differences and partly by some community effect.

Interpretative Communities in the Church of England

What can be concluded from these different lines of evidence regarding the role of biblical interpretative communities in the Church of England?

First, there is some evidence of a 'community effect' that goes beyond the effects of individual difference, but this effect is by no means overarching. It is apparent through belonging to congregations of a particular tradition, and in some measures of interpretation but not others.

Second, people who interpret differently from the majority of their congregation report a lower sense of belonging, and are more likely to disagree with what they are taught. Again, the effect is small but significant, suggesting that biblical interpretation does play a minor part in community belonging. Other factors such as psychological type, age and frequency of attendance are probably more important for creating a sense of belonging in these Anglican churches (Village 2007).

Thirdly, those who move between traditions seem to change their interpretation partly, but not wholly, towards the norm of their new tradition. This is further evidence that if there is a community effect it is partial rather than absolute. People seem to retain a trace of their past history, suggesting some resistance to community pressure.

This is the first study, to my knowledge, that has attempted to quantify the influence of community on biblical interpretation relative to other possible effects. The picture that emerged is consistent with Fish's later ideas on interpretative communities, rather than his earlier notions. That is, congregations are communities that have a common purview or purpose with respect to biblical interpretation, but within that overall purview there is some variety. None of the congregations I studied were closed, uniform communities where everyone interpreted in a similar fashion. There were distinct and predictable patterns, but always room for different interpreters. These 'marginal' interpreters to some extent felt outsiders and it is possible that this sense of isolation from the norm would lead people to leave. However, in this study such people were unlikely to be picked up in the sample.

The literalism scale revealed quite subtle variations between people in the same tradition, partially reflecting their past history of church membership. A large proportion of people in this study had moved between churches of different traditions, and this mixing partly explains why variation of interpretation within the congregations I studied was as large as it was. Far from conforming to the pattern of long-standing members, incomers seemed to retain traces of their previous history. This transfer of interpreters between congregations may be preventing the Church of England from polarizing completely into separate interpretative communities.

These were Anglicans in England, where the role of the Bible in church life is mixed and not always central. In other traditions there may be much tighter control of individual interpretations and the 'community effect' could be much stronger relative to individual difference.

Theological and Practical Implications

The radical ideas of Stanley Fish have attracted criticism on both philosophical and theological grounds, and few would go as far as he does in making texts the slaves of reading communities. Theologically, some of the resistance to assigning too great a role to community in determining the meaning of the Bible comes from those who wish to affirm the ability of the Word to challenge and transform individuals and communities of readers.[9] If readers alone determine meaning, they are likely to resist biblical messages that threaten the status quo. Communities become self-regulated and self-perpetuating institutions that find in the Bible only support for what they already believe. The possibilities of the prophetic, transforming Word are lost.

---

[9]   Thus Thiselton (1992: 550) writes: 'the notion that biblical texts do not transform readers "from beyond", or that they merely evoke "constructions" drawn from the hitherto undiscovered inner resources of the reading community does not cohere readily with Christian theology'.

Another weakness of the kind of interpretative communities proposed by Stanley Fish is epistemological. Thiselton (1992: 545) criticizes Fish for suggesting that texts cannot resist the rhetorical power of the interpretative community, drawing on the work of Ludwig Wittgenstein to argue that language is not always as ambiguous as Fish makes out. In a similar way, Paul Noble (1994) shows how Fish's examples of the ambiguity of texts are highly selective and not representative of language in general. Noble (1995) has also shown that Fish's anti-foundationalism undermines realism and leads inexorably to solipsism.

These arguments do not necessarily negate the importance of some sort of community role in shaping how scripture is understood. Indeed, the idea that readers extract truths from the Bible in isolation from their religious community is both unlikely and unappealing. Unlikely because the evidence shown here is that readers are influenced to some extent by interpretative practices within their congregation or church tradition. Unappealing because Christianity is essentially a corporate religion where individuality is expressed within a framework of shared responsibility for the care of each other and the mission of the church.

The evidence from the Bible and Lay People study indicates that interpretation for most people is shaped both by their individual experiences and by the congregations or traditions to which they belong. The nature of the community influence was not examined in detail in this study, and remains something that requires further exploration. It might come through what is preached and taught by clergy, how interpretation is modelled in the pulpit and in Bible studies, the influence of fellow worshippers or through engagement with the writings or teaching of particular traditions. Lay people seem to be partly aware of what is 'normal' in their congregation insofar as those who are not 'normal' seem to sense that they do not fully belong. Whatever the nature of this community effect, it is clearly going to influence the interpretation of particular scriptural content. Even if we reject Fish's notion that the text is not even created until it is read, it remains true that a given text may lead a reader in several directions, and those directions are influenced by the community in which the text is being read. The community is an extra-textual effect (though it may itself be the product of interaction with the text) that influences the possible outcome of reading. As such, it lies in the same category as individual differences that shape interpretation, and has to be subject to the same theological scrutiny.

There are both virtues and vices associated with a community effect on lay readers. At its worst, it represents the power of the self-serving and self-perpetuating sect. In such sects, those who challenge the narrow norms of biblical truth are either forced to recant and conform or are driven out. This may be a well-meaning attempt to be faithful servants of God, or an unthinking slavery to tradition. Either way it is a dangerous assumption for a religion based on the life and teachings of Jesus of Nazareth. There is ample evidence that Jesus challenged the norms of reading communities that had lost sight of the God they sought in the minutiae of their interpretative strategies.[10] One way of understanding the ministry of Jesus is that he offered new interpretations of scripture that the established interpretative community

---

[10]   Examples include the 'woes' against the scribes and Pharisees in Matthew 23 and the dispute over legalities in Mark 7:1–13.

The Bible and Lay People

was unable or unwilling to hear. Congregations that are so sure of their interpretations that they will allow no other are in danger of falling into the same trap.

At its best, the community effect represents the way in which the written word becomes the transforming Word of God in the lives of particular individuals and congregations. It is a counter to the self-seeking individualism that makes readers shape scripture in their own image. Without some interaction with the reading community, individual readers simply interpret as they will, and churches are no more than convenient associations of like-minded people. Individuals who resist hearing or responding to community mores and interpretative wisdom may ultimately miss the authentic voice of God. Community reading at its best implies a corporate act of discernment, perhaps through long and painful experience. It implies a willingness to lay aside individual fancy in order to seek the common mind and the common good. It implies the ability of truths to be nurtured and passed on, so that the valuable insights of previous generations are not lost. In short, it represents the life of the Gospel community interacting with its sacred scriptures.

Stephen Fowl (1998: 75–83) speaks of 'vigilant communities' of readers that are able to 'attend to the faculties by which they come to perceive Jesus and make judgments about him' (p. 77). Fowl draws attention to the phrase in Luke 11:34–35 which calls followers to have a 'single eye', and treats this as a call for Christians to be focused on God in a singled-minded way. Such a focus should enable the sort of self-critical reflection by individuals that prevents them from underwriting their sinful practices by recourse to scripture. In short it requires an awareness of sinfulness, and the community act of forgiveness. Community here functions to create the right sort of reading, which for Fowl involves 'charity in interpretation': the ability to understand why someone might hold a different interpretation, without minimizing the disparity of views.

A New Testament example of a congregation wrestling with unity and diversity is Corinth, as revealed by the Pauline correspondence. Much has been written about the nature and cause of the clash between the church leaders at Corinth and their founding father (see, for example, Burke and Elliott 2003; Hurd 1965; Thiselton 2000; Witherington III 1995). What is of interest here is the way that Paul balances the need for unity against the obvious fact of diversity. Some might argue that Paul leaves no room for opposite opinions to his own, and that he is essentially the arbiter of interpreting the new faith. But this is far from the case. He recognizes both the legitimacy of different views in some areas and the difference between his own views and those ideas that are not open to negotiation.[11] In one intriguing passage, he addresses the fact of diversity and dispute, and appears to interpret it as a necessary means of reaching consensus: 'For, to begin with, when you come together as a church, I hear that there are divisions among you; and to some extent I believe it. Indeed, there have to be factions among you, for only so will it become clear who among you are genuine' (1 Corinthians 11:18–19). Although this verse is not

---

[11]   In 1 Corinthians 7, when dealing with marriage, Paul is careful to identify what seems to be his teaching ('I and not the Lord') from what he sees as the unequivocal command of God ('not I but the Lord').

usually taken to suggest that Paul viewed factions in a positive or even neutral way,[12] this is the most obvious meaning and might have something useful to say about interpretative communities. Even if factions are viewed in a positive light, they are by no means a way of legitimizing everyone's point of view: they are instead a means of achieving a common mind. Paul retains a sense that some are 'genuine' and others are not, with the implication that there is a single or limited range of acceptable lifestyles or beliefs within the community. Diversity on important issues is inevitable, and allows different perspectives to be aired and tested. The end goal, however, must be consensus on the 'correct' position. Paul is uncompromising when the issues seem to be so clear-cut that diversity is simply a measure of sinful indulgence, as with the case of incest in 1 Corinthians 5. With issues that seem less important, however, he is willing to allow diversity of views, as with the eating of meat offered to idols in 1 Corinthians 8. The model seems to be summed up by the image of the body in 1 Corinthians 12: different people may do different things but all must work for the common good.

How does this relate to diversity of interpretation in present-day congregations, and to the notion of the 'interpretative community'? It would seem to suggest that diversity is inevitable and, within limits, is helpful and necessary. Helpful because it is an expression of individuality that reminds the church of the value of each person. Necessary because it allows ideas to be tested and challenged. A congregation that permits only a single or limited interpretative strategy is unable to discern truth from falsehood because there is nothing with which to test the status quo. Paul's picture of a healthy congregation is one in which ideas wrestle with each other in the public arena, so that the correct idea (which for Paul would surely amount to the true voice of God) can be understood and followed. This might sound like the sort of rhetorical battle that Stanley Fish would define as the role of the interpretative community. However, the difference lies in epistemology: whereas Fish would argue that the winner has no legitimacy other than winning the argument, others (including Paul, I am sure) would see different grounds for deciding truth.

---

[12]   This passage, and particularly verse 19, has puzzled commentators for some time (see Thiselton 2000: 855–6). The English translation here uses 'divisions' for *schisma* and 'factions' for *hairesis*. The latter did not originally have the negative connotations of heresy, referring instead to a doctrine, party or sect (Arndt and Gingrich 1979), though it could also refer to dissension and faction. Most commentators see the divisions referred to as different from those dealt with earlier in the letter, but still in an entirely negative context. Gordon Fee (1987: 538), for example, suggests the idea that 'there must be factions among you' is either ironical or more likely an eschatological reference to the supposed divisions at the end times. Thiselton puts the idea of the necessity of division into the mouths of Paul's opponents by translating verse 19: 'For "dissentions are unavoidable" it is claimed among you'. However, it is difficult to keep an entirely negative view of 'factions' without resorting to translations that rely on unusual word usage or rather tenuous historical background on supper etiquette (for example, Campbell 1991). The idea that factions might have a positive side, as I suggest, does not seem to have been raised in the literature, though some of the Patristic commentators use this verse to argue for the value of dissention and even heresy in helping the truth to emerge (Kovacs 2005: 185–6).

This model of congregational life has no place for the monolithic interpretative community. Such a thing is an idealized myth, and it is dangerous to equate unity with uniformity. Rather, it points to diversity of views being shaped and moulded by community life, so that there is a sense of unified purpose and commitment. This is not the same as excluding someone who disagrees, though this remains a necessary option in some extreme cases. Rather it is about being able to bring ideas to the forum of debate and being willing to change others or be changed ourselves in the light of lived-out experience.

The empirical approach to interpretative communities followed here allows the unity and diversity of real congregations to be better understood and appreciated. It highlights the importance of individual experience in creating diversity, as well as the importance of fluid exchange between congregations. Incomers are not just a boost for membership numbers; they can bring with them a healthy new insight that keeps the community open. The evidence is that they may change their views as well as changing the overall range of opinion within the congregation. Congregations do seem to transform people to some extent and they are not simply collections of like-minded individuals. But how and why this happens, and over what time scale, remains to be seen.

In practical terms, being able to discern and quantify any community effect on Bible reading may help churches to evaluate their ability to teach and guide their members. If individual differences largely explain how the Bible is understood, it raises the question of how far the congregation is functioning as a corporate entity discerning the will of God. If community effects are overwhelming, it raises the question of whether the congregation has a strong but narrow teaching ministry, and how it deals with people who interpret differently from the rest. Does it allow them a place in the community, or does it deliberately or unconsciously expel them?

A related practical issue that emerges from this study is the importance of incomers for congregations wishing to maintain a healthy interpretative diversity. Given the other evidence that marginal interpreters can feel out of place, there is a challenge for congregations to deal effectively with new recruits, especially those who come from another tradition or no tradition. Are their insights received and valued, or do they have to 'serve time' until they are heard? Those who come with previous experience of another tradition may need sensitive handling because otherwise helpful insights can be lost from those who too frequently tell everyone 'what we used to do in my previous church'. This sort of mantra can be counter-productive, causing long-standing members to ignore new insights and newcomers to feel ignored. Unless newcomers receive some encouragement they may leave, perhaps depriving a closed community of an opportunity to hear the authentic Word of God.

Further Research

Literalism probably provides the easiest and most relevant measure of biblical interpretation with which to explore congregations as interpretative communities. The literalism scale may need to be adapted for use in a wider range of congregations, but it is simple to administer and seems able to distinguish a range of interpretative positions. Employing it in congregations over a wide range of churches and traditions would allow the variance of the literalism score to be compared, provided a sufficient proportion of each congregation participated in the study. This might then indicate the extent of the 'community effect' in particular congregations on the assumption that a strong community effect is indicated by a small variance in literalism scores and vice versa. This assumption would need to be tested, but if variance does prove to be a reliable and valid index of community effect, it could be related to a wide range of predictor variables across different congregations.

There is also the question of just how any community effect is mediated, and how it might work in practice. Presumably, congregations exerting a strong community effect would be ones where there is frequent teaching on the Bible, where particular beliefs about the Bible and its interpretation are promoted at the expense of others, and where individuals are encouraged to read and interpret the Bible for themselves. Such evidence should be easy to find, though it might be difficult to quantify.

A key issue is to unravel the difference between a community effect that changes an individual's interpretative practice, and one that merely encourages self-selection of congregations according to previous predispositions. Given that a purely experimental approach is unattainable, the next best thing would be close observation of 'natural experiments' where people change church of their own volition. Longitudinal studies could measure interpretation soon after someone arrives in a congregation and then at various times thereafter. Community influence would tend to move individuals nearer to the congregational norm the longer they remain.

Chapter 8

The Holy Spirit
and Biblical Interpretation

The Bible and Lay People study began with open-ended interviews of 26 people from a range of Anglican churches in central England. These helped to identify the kinds of issues that might be important for lay people and how they might interpret and speak of scripture. One of these interviews stands out in my mind because it represented views that were radically different from the majority. The interviewee was a female nurse from a broad-church congregation. During the interview it became clear that she had been strongly influenced by the Charismatic Movement, and that she brought her faith into the realm of her work by praying (in secret) for her patients to be healed. She expected, and reported seeing, miraculous healing that she attributed to the direct action of God. This was not of itself unusual, and such prayer was not uncommon among those who took part in the study. What was unusual about this participant was that she hardly, if ever, read the Bible. When pressed on this she said that she was content to discern God's will through prayer and to rely on the direct intervention and guidance of the Holy Spirit. She had not found the Bible particularly helpful in guiding her daily life and practice. Such a thoroughgoing charismatic but 'biblically detached' faith was unusual among the Bible and Lay People sample. All the other charismatic Anglicans I spoke with read the Bible frequently and said that scripture was central to the way in which they understood their faith and discerned the will of God. They were, in effect, 'charismatic evangelicals'.

This chapter explores the relationship between biblical interpretation and charismatic beliefs, practices and experiences. My interest in this field was sparked by my own charismatic experiences and also by some of the people who participated in the Bible and Lay People study. What is the relationship between 'biblical' and 'spiritual' sources of revelation for ordinary readers of the Bible? Theologically there has been a long debate on the role of the Spirit in interpreting the Bible, but I shall touch on this only tangentially. My main interest is in the way that interpretation might be shaped by the different background experiences that readers bring to the Bible. In particular, I will use the study sample of Anglicans in the Church of England to explore the relationship between a person's interpretations of the healing story in Mark 9:14–29 and their charismatic experience, beliefs about supernatural healing and experience of such healing.

Charismatics in the Church of England

The link between charismatic and evangelical expressions of faith may be partly due to the nature of charismatic faith and partly due to accidents of history. From the early days of the Pentecostal Movement in America, biblical interpretation was pre-critical and literal, being based on the idea that the experiences of present-day believers exactly matched those described in the Bible. Scripture was taken as the inspired, reliable and authoritative Word of God, with little interest in the historical background (Karkkainen 1998). These views generally paralleled those found in evangelical and fundamentalist churches, and there was a further convergence in the mid-twentieth century as pentecostals developed ministerial training and biblical scholarship that mirrored those of evangelicals (Archer 1996; Dempster 1993; Hey 2001; Karkkainen 1998). The Charismatic Movement grew out of Pentecostalism from the 1960s, representing the spread of pentecostal worship and ideas to mainstream churches (Anderson 2004; Synan 1997, 2001). As the movement grew and expanded into new churches, it carried with it its hermeneutical roots. Charismatic belief about the Bible has therefore always tended to be conservative, reflecting its pentecostal roots and mirroring that found among evangelicals.

This innate link has been strengthened in the Church of England by the way in which the Charismatic Movement has evolved within the denomination.[1] Pentecostalism had several independent routes into mainstream churches in Britain in the twentieth century, mostly through the American Charismatic Movement (Anderson 2004; Scotland 2003; Synan 2001). Anglican churches were first influenced in the 1960s and 1970s by the 'Neo-Pentecostal' or Charismatic Movement associated with American Episcopalians such as Richard Winkler and Dennis Bennett (Synan 2001: 151–8). The key figures in Britain were Anglican clergymen such as Michael Harper, David Watson and John Perry, who all had roots in the post-war Anglican evangelical revival. Charismatics were present in other Anglican traditions but they were somewhat overshadowed by the early importance and numerical growth of charismatic evangelicals (Hocken 1997: 105; 2002; Steven 2002: 13). This dominance was strengthened by another wave of charismatic renewal in the 1980s and 1990s associated with the 'Signs and Wonders' ministry of John Wimber (Anderson 2004: 159; Gunstone 1989; Hunt 2000; Steven 2002: 25–31). This movement had a widespread influence in a variety of church traditions, but some of the key Anglican churches affected were again evangelical churches such as St Andrew's, Chorleywood and Holy Trinity, Brompton. The evangelical-charismatic nature of this movement is typified by the success of the Alpha Course developed by Holy Trinity Church Brompton (Gumbel 1994, 1999). The course text (Gumbel 1993) is based on material that would be very familiar to anyone schooled

---

[1]   James Steven (2002) has a very useful summary of the history of charismatic renewal in the Church of England in his book on charismatic worship. Peter Hocken (1997) documents a number of independent events that pre-dated the main renewal among evangelical Anglicans. Nigel Scotland (2003) also has a useful discussion of the rise of the Charismatic Movement among evangelicals in the United Kingdom.

in post-war Anglican evangelical missions, but with a new and important emphasis of the work of the Holy Spirit.

This history has led to a strong link between charismatic and evangelical belief in the Church of England. The link is not necessarily cause and effect, but reflects the dominance of evangelical expressions of charismatic belief. In the Church of England there is a large group who are neither evangelical nor charismatic. There is also a sizeable group who are both, and the numerical preponderance of these two groups alone could largely account for the overall link between conservative Bible belief and charismatic practice.

Charismatic Belief and the Bible and Lay People Study

The Bible and Lay People questionnaire contained several different measures of practice and beliefs associated with the Charismatic Movement. A five-item scale measured charismatic practice and experience, based on the frequency with which people spoke in tongues, gave words of prophecy, were guided by visions or dreams, laid hands on people during prayer or felt God speak directly to them through the Bible. This scale was more useful than one based on charismatic beliefs, which tended to be less discriminating of genuine charismatics. Thus 65% of 398 participants agreed that they had been baptized in the Holy Spirit, but for most this was a statement of belief about the nature of baptism rather than an expression of a particular charismatic experience. When the same group was asked if they spoke in tongues, 81% answered either 'never' or 'I don't know what this means', suggesting they had a very different understanding of 'baptism in the Spirit' from charismatics.

A section of the questionnaire was devoted to assessing beliefs about miraculous healing and the practice of prayer for healing (see Village 2005c for more details). Participants were offered various scenarios related to incidents of apparent supernatural healing or failure to heal after prayer, and asked to respond to a range of Likert-type items. The supernatural healing scale was a 12-item scale with a high reliability (Cronbach's alpha = .92). A high score represented those who believed that God is able to heal people through miracles today. A further question asked if people had seen or experienced miraculous healing themselves.

The scores for the charismatic scale were positively correlated with the Bible scale, and this trend held across all three of the main traditions (see Fig 8.1). Although a few Anglo-Catholics had relatively conservative beliefs about the Bible but little charismatic expression, there was little evidence for the existence of groups with frequent charismatic expression but liberal Bible beliefs. This association may have been strongly influenced by the churches in the sample, and it would be unwise to draw too much from it. There are certainly conservative evangelical churches which reject charismatic expression, and there may be some Anglo-Catholic or broad-church Anglicans who express their faith charismatically, but who have liberal beliefs about the Bible. Such belief is unusual, which would explain why it was not apparent in this rather limited sample.

The charismatic–evangelical relationship led to a number of other predictable associations (Village 2005b). Charismatic scores were positively correlated

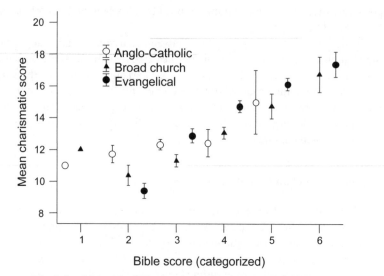

Fig 8.1   Mean (± SE) charismatic score by Bible score

with biblical literalism, Bible-reading frequency, belief in supernatural healing, conservative attitudes to morality and negatively with religious pluralism.[2] These trends held after allowing for church tradition, so in any particular congregation those who had more charismatic experience tended to be more conservative and more evangelical than their fellow churchgoers.

Does this mean that conservative beliefs about the Bible are completely tied to charismatic beliefs, or are these two independent, but correlated, expressions of faith? As I have indicated, it might be difficult to test this without a broader sample from within and beyond the Church of England. However, there is some evidence from factor analysis of the Bible and Lay People dataset that the two forms of expression are not entirely the same (for details of this analysis see Village 2005b). Factor analysis helps to separate variables into groups according to how closely they are correlated with each other (Bryant and Yarnold 1995; Kim and Mueller 1978; Norusis 1994). Five variables were used in this analysis: three measuring belief about the Bible, one measuring belief about supernatural healing and one measuring charismatic practice, mentioned earlier. Although all five variables were inter-correlated, the charismatic and supernatural healing scales were more closely related to each other than to the other three scales. Factor analysis suggested the possibility of two separate but linked types of belief: belief along the conservative/liberal continuum and belief along the charismatic/non-charismatic continuum.

This possible separation of charismatic and conservative belief was also indicated by examining the predictors of each group of variables, using a multivariate analysis of variance. This technique incorporates more than one dependent variable in an

---

2   Correlation coefficients for charismatic score with: biblical literalism: $r = .51, df = 399$, $p < 0.001$; Bible-reading frequency: $r = .48, df = 398, p < 0.001$; belief in supernatural healing: $r = .58, df = 395, p < 0.001$; conservative attitudes to morality: $r = .39, df = 399, p < 0.001$; religious pluralism: $r = -.58, df = 399, p < 0.001$.

analysis of variance, which avoids problems that might arise from doing too many separate analyses. Conservative and charismatic scales were predicted by slightly different factors, further suggesting that they are indicators of different kinds of belief. Conservative Bible belief was stronger in evangelical than in Anglo-Catholic churches; positively correlated with frequency of attendance and age; negatively correlated with educational experience; and higher in those with a psychological-type preference for sensing rather than intuition (see Table 8.1). Charismatic belief was also higher in evangelical than in Anglo-Catholic churches and positively correlated with frequency of attendance, but it was negatively correlated with age, unrelated to education and higher in those with a psychological-type preference for feeling rather than thinking. So, after allowing for church tradition and attendance, biblical conservatives were typically older, sensing-types with less educational experience, whereas charismatics were typically younger, feeling-types.

Table 8.1   Summary of multivariate analyses of variance for conservative and charismatic beliefs

Source of variation	Conservative beliefs	Charismatic beliefs
Church tradition	(+)***	(+)***
Church attendance	(+)**	(+)***
Education	(-)**	
Age	(+)**	(-)***
KTS sensing score	(+)*	
KTS feeling score		(+)**

Note. After Village (2005b). Signs in the parentheses show the direction of the correlation where church tradition scored as in Table 7.2. $^* p < .05$; $^{**} p < .01$; $^{***} p < .001$, otherwise not significant.

Charismatic Experience and Biblical Interpretation

The link between charismatic practice and literal Bible belief was noted in Chapter 4, and was also apparent in the interpretation of the test passage from Mark's Gospel. In broad and evangelical churches, those who frequently experienced speaking in tongues, words of prophecy, religious dreams or visions were most likely to interpret the Bible literally (see above, Table 4.3) and more likely to interpret the test passage literally. This seems to be an example of charismatic experience (or practice) shaping interpretation, though cause and effect is difficult to determine here. One plausible explanation is that charismatic belief shapes both the way that Christians interpret their present-day experience and the way that they interpret the Bible. There is coherence between God experienced personally, God at work in the world and God revealed in scripture, but the key factor is personal experience. This would certainly accord with the distinctive way in which personal experience is primary within Pentecostalism (Jacobsen 2003: 3–5).

What about the effects of more specific experience on the interpretation of a healing story? Not surprisingly, charismatic experience was strongly related to beliefs about miraculous healing today. Those who frequently experienced charismatic phenomena, such as speaking tongues or giving words of prophecy, were likely to believe that God heals miraculously today, to reject non-Christian claims of miraculous healing as spurious or dangerous and to accept the sovereignty of God even in the face of a failure to heal (Village 2005c). Belief in supernatural healing was also related to having seen or experienced such healing personally: those who reported they had done so had significantly higher mean scores on the supernatural scale than those who did not.[3] Again, cause and effect may be difficult to sort out here: are people who believe such healing is possible more likely to ascribe miraculous intervention to an unusual healing, or does experience of such healing engender belief? I could not tell from the evidence available, and I suspect this is a complex question that is not easily answered. What was apparent was that those who reported an experience of miraculous healing were more likely to interpret literally (generally and specifically for the test passage), and had a lower sense of horizon separation than those who had not had this experience (see Table 8.2). The link between experience of and beliefs in miraculous healing meant that the effect of experience disappeared when supernatural belief score was added to the model, and it was difficult to tell whether direct experience of miraculous healing was more important than beliefs about such healing. Nonetheless, the important point is that reported experience of miraculous healing predicts biblical interpretation over and above charismatic experience in general.

Table 8.2   Analyses of variance of literalism and horizon separation scores including experience of miraculous healing

Source of variation	df	Biblical literalism F	Passage literalism F	Horizon separation F
Experienced miraculous healing	1	25.7***	21.2***	15.6***
Theological education	1	5.5*	7.7**	1.4
Education	1	18.1***	2.2	0.2
Charismatic score	1	78.8***	99.2***	38.2***
Error	395	(50.9)	(28.1)	(15.9)

Note. Experience of miraculous healing and theological education were entered as factors, and education and charismatic score entered as covariates, in a general linear model. Values in parentheses are mean square errors. $^*p < .05$; $^{**}p < .01$; $^{***}p < .001$.

The healing section of the questionnaire also included a scenario in which someone who was seriously ill received healing prayer from a church, but subsequently died.

---

[3]   Mean supernatural score for those who had experienced miraculous healing was 51.9 (SD = 5.9, n = 117) compared with 43.9 (SD = 7.0, n = 282) for those who had not, a statistically significant difference (F = 128.1, p < 0.001).

Participants were asked if they had experienced praying for someone who was not healed. If a positive experience of miraculous healing made someone more likely to interpret a biblical healing story literally, would a negative experience of healing prayer make someone less likely to do so? In fact literalism scores were significant *higher* among those who reported failure of healing prayer, primarily because the people who most often reported failure to heal were also those who were most actively engaged in the healing ministry.[4] Those who belonged to a healing prayer group were a subset of the sample that was most likely to have experienced both success and failure in healing. A large number of people rarely engaged in prayer for healing and therefore experienced neither success nor failure. Failure to heal seems to be accepted as part of the healing ministry, and those who pray for others are not put off by the fact that prayers are not always answered as expected. This might be a case where belief about the miraculous is the most important underlying factor that shapes both the interpretation of experience and the interpretation of the Bible. Experiences may be related to beliefs but they do not wholly shape them.

Theological and Practical Implications

The role of the Holy Spirit was not a central theme of the Bible and Lay People study so the empirical evidence is too limited to allow much theological development. However, a key finding is the indication that, despite some strong links, charismatic belief and conservative belief about the Bible are not necessarily the same thing. This empirical evidence feeds into a theological debate that is ongoing within pentecostal and charismatic circles on the role of the Holy Spirit in biblical interpretation. I shall explore this debate briefly before discussing more generally the link between charisma and hermeneutics.

Is There a Distinctive Pentecostal or Charismatic Biblical Hermeneutic?

There has been a great deal of debate in pentecostal circles as to whether or not there is a distinctive way of interpreting the Bible that arises from the movement's particular emphasis on the primacy of the Holy Spirit.[5] Some would prefer not to talk of a specifically 'pentecostal hermeneutic' (Ellington 2001), whereas others argue that applying pentecostal theology consistently must lead to very different approaches to scripture (Smith 1997). The issue is part of the much wider debate on the role of the Holy Spirit in interpretation that has long been an issue for the church.

Luther and his followers used the phrase *per verbum* to express the way that the Spirit works *through* the word to present the Gospel when it is preached or read. This power confronts the listener and demands a response. Calvinists, reluctant to place

---

[4]   Of 144 people who prayed for healing in some sort of group, 65% reported some experience of a failure to heal after prayer, compared with 38% of 249 who did not pray in groups ($\chi^2 = 25.5$, $df = 1$, $p < 0.001$).

[5]   There are useful summaries of this debate in Archer (1996), Brubaker (1997), Hey (2001) and Karkkainen (1998).

too much emphasis on human free will and choice, spoke of the Spirit acting *cum verbo*, that is *with* the word, but distinct from it (Berkhof 1939: 611). Without the Holy Spirit at work in the listener there could be no understanding or conviction of truth. 'The Spirit who inspired the biblical writers must also authenticate the biblical message for anyone trying to understand it today' (Schwölbel 1990: 99). This separation of word and Spirit was developed by Hodge and Warfield at Princeton, who argued that the truth of biblical revelation can be tested by rational criteria, but the Spirit alone prepares the listener to receive the text as the authoritative and saving 'Word of God' (Bray 1996: 556; Hodge and Warfield 1881).

The isolation of rational discernment from Spirit-led conviction made room for critical approaches to scripture among evangelical and fundamentalist scholars. If the word was true it was rationally true, and rational enquiry would confirm this was so. The creationism debate, still very much alive, stems from this idea and has encouraged the application of scientific evidence to prove the literal truth of a particular section of scripture. Creationists are not content to argue that Genesis 1–3 has 'spiritual' truths that can be discerned by true believers: truth means literal truth, so the evidence must exist to verify the account for all open-minded, rational people. By the same token, any evidence to the contrary must be mistaken and misinterpreted by those who hold to the speculative theory of evolution. More widely, the separation of rational study from spiritual revelation allowed evangelical scholarship to engage with historical-critical approaches to the biblical text on their own terms. This trend also led to a greater willingness in some pentecostal circles to accept a more critical and less literal interpretation of scripture. Some pentecostal scholars, wanting to establish scholarly credibility, were inevitably drawn into an understanding of hermeneutics that was essentially modernist and rational (Cargal 1993; Karkkainen 1998).

As Pentecostalism began to engage with academic evangelical scholarship in the mid-twentieth century there was a growing rift between the rather naive, pre-critical approach to scripture found in most congregations and the increasingly scholarly approach of those linked to Bible colleges or universities. Cargal (1993: 163) points to the style of Gordon Fee as representing the sort of scholarly, evangelical hermeneutics that came to dominate pentecostal biblical studies. Although Fee's pentecostal background does emerge in terms of the interests and emphases of his work, much of his methodology is difficult to distinguish from that of mainstream conservative Protestant scholars. His insistence on authorial intent as the key hermeneutical principle directly challenged many of the central pentecostal doctrines, and evoked a rigorous response (Noel 2004). By sparking this debate, Fee and others like him were responsible for endowing pentecostals with a previously unheard of respectability in the academy, which led to a flourish of specifically pentecostal scholarship. So Walter Hollenweger was able to write in 1992: 'Pentecostalism has come of age. It is now possible to be filled with the Spirit, to enjoy the specific Pentecostal charismata and Pentecostal spirituality, to believe in Pentecostal mission, and at the same time to use one's critical faculties to develop them and to use them – as any other charisma for the Kingdom of God' (quoted in Karkkainen 1998).

Not all pentecostals are happy with this state of affairs. A new generation, perhaps influenced by postmodernism, has sought to establish clear water between

evangelical and pentecostal biblical interpretation. This is not a call to abandon
critical scholarship, but a willingness to engage with non-historical, largely reader-
centred approaches. For example, Timothy Cargal (1993) argues for pentecostal,
post-critical use of narrative and other methods that accept the growing move
away from modernity in society at large. 'As a postmodern paradigm increasingly
dominates the thinking of our culture in general, any hermeneutic which cannot
account for its loci of meanings within that postmodern paradigm will become
nonsensical and irrelevant' (p. 187). This is a rather pragmatic view, but also one
that sees postmodernism as more useful to pentecostal hermeneutics that the higher
criticism that evolved from modernity.

In some cases the call for change goes well beyond a mere change in methodology.
Smith (1997) sees the problem in largely epistemological terms. He draws on work
by Stock (1983) on the implications of literacy, and Farley (1982) on the history
of texts in Judaism and early Christianity, to argue that Christianity took on a view
of textuality from Judaism that was essentially incompatible with its own nature
(p. 65). The dominance of textuality, finally established in the eleventh century,
caused the oral to be labelled as 'illiterate' and by association irrational. Smith sees
the dominance of evangelical hermeneutics in Pentecostalism as the subservience
of prophecy to scripture, which is fundamentally at odds with the nature of the
movement: 'A pentecostal evangelical theology is a house divided against itself'
(p. 59).

Although perhaps not willing to go that far, several writers have stressed the
key role of story and testimony in the pentecostal tradition (Archer 2004; Cargal
1993; Ellington 2001; Johns and Johns 1992). If there is an essentially pentecostal
approach then it may be centred on the strongly experiential nature of pentecostal
faith. The Spirit acting in believers is the primary source of motivation and revelation.
Although evangelicals would agree that words about God are no substitute for a
living relationship with God, they are much more reluctant to separate the two.

The debate within Pentecostalism has largely been in America, though it has
echoes in Britain, including among charismatics. Mark Stibbe (1998), replying to
criticism from John Lyons (1998), lists what he sees as seven essential characteristics
of charismatic readings of scripture, namely: experiential, analogical, communal,
Christological, eschatological, emotional and practical. Once again, there is an
emphasis on experience and the effect of reading at an individual and communal level.
Analogical interpretation for Stibbe means that present-day experience is related to
both the 'over-arching meta-narrative of Scripture' and to particular biblical stories.
'[T]he challenge lies in the question "Is there a story of what the Spirit is doing right
now in my life and in my community?"' (p. 185).

What can be concluded from this rather brief review of the debate on hermeneutics
among pentecostals and charismatics? The key issue at stake is whether traditions
that stress the importance of the Holy Spirit as an active force in the life of believers
should be tied to a way of interpreting scripture that has assigned the Spirit to a
secondary role in revealing the will of God. Whatever evangelicals might say about
the underlying importance of the Spirit, in practice the rational exposition of text
comes first. The Spirit may be specifically invoked to aid illumination, or it may be
assumed to be working generally in the life of expositors and believers, but it is the

written text that is the prime source of revelation. In some sense, it really is the *final* authority in all matters of faith and conduct. The pentecostal reaction to this has been to return to experience of the Spirit as the prime element in revealing God. Personal or communal discernment of the Spirit leads to stories that testify to the action of God. Scripture confirms that current experience is analogous to the experiences of God's people in the past.

The empirical evidence from an admittedly small sample is that, in the Church of England at least, charismatics tend to be largely evangelical in their approach to scripture. However, there is also evidence that charismatic and conservative beliefs are not necessarily inextricably linked, and may be shaped by different factors. Can empirical approaches shed some new perspectives on the issue of how Bible reading relates to the work of the Holy Spirit?

Holy Spirit versus Scripture?

James Barr famously pointed out that biblical people were not biblical.[6] His argument was that the first Christians did not have their own scriptures, and therefore had a very different relationship to sacred writings compared with those who today might argue that scripture is the final authority in all matters of faith and conduct. His point is well made and illustrated in several places within scripture itself, where experience beyond the text helps to reinterpret the text. I have previously argued that Jesus himself challenged the interpretative community of his society, and in effect relied on extra-biblical authority to redefine the boundaries of God's people. This debate continued in the post-resurrection community, and several writers have drawn attention to the way that Peter's vision at Joppa and subsequent events lead to a ground-breaking debate by the Jerusalem council (Acts 15:1–29) that redefined the application and understanding of the Torah (Fowl 1998: 101–127; Johnson 1996: 106–108). Paul took up this debate in his mission to the Gentiles. In Galatians, he argues for a thoroughgoing dependence on the in-dwelling Christ rather than the rules of the Torah. In some readings of Galatians, the central issue is seen as one of seeking God's guidance on how to behave, rather than the issue of the means of salvation.[7] Paul's stance seems to be to tell believers to trust to the in-dwelling Christ (Galatians 2:21) and the fruit produced by the Spirit (5:22–3) rather than following moral codes in the Torah.

The extent to which Paul sets up an opposition between reliance on written rules and reliance on the Spirit has been widely debated. A key text in this regard is 2 Corinthians 3:6: 'for the letter kills, but the Spirit gives life'. Although this passage, and the other Pauline texts that make this contrast, have been interpreted in a variety of ways, there is no escaping the central distinction between two different ways

---

[6]   'Thus the time of the Bible was a time when the Bible was not yet there ... Biblical faith, the faith of the men of the Bible, was not in its own nature a scriptural religion' (Barr 1983: 1).

[7]   Barclay (1988), for example, argues that the thrust of the argument in Galatians is less about justification by faith and more about how to make ethical decisions by relying on the Spirit rather than the Law.

of relating to God.[8] Letter represents an attempt to be justified by obeying written rules; Spirit represents a reliance on the in-dwelling Christ. This does not mean that Paul and the other members of the fledgling church abandoned Jewish scriptures, indeed they used them frequently to interpret their experience and to support their arguments (Hays 1989; Hays and Green 1995). The key point is that experience, and specifically the experience of the Spirit of God, was the prime motivator and director of this early community. The scriptures they had were read in the light of their experience, leading to creative reinterpretations of a variety of passages.

The subsequent creation of a canon of scripture, and the much later developments of the Reformation, have given scripture a different position and role among most Christian traditions compared with that of their apostolic forebears, which is the essence of Barr's observation.[9] The question is whether this new relationship is now normative, and whether any return to pre-canonical practice is either possible or desirable. The question has been given an even sharper focus by the rise of the Pentecostal Movement and its challenge to Protestant views of the Bible.

The heart of the issue is the extent to which churches are willing to pay heed to the experience of their members. At one extreme is the word-dominated community in which members are exhorted to follow the call of scripture, shaping their beliefs and behaviours on the truths revealed by the text. These truths are gained through the inspired reading and study of scriptures and their interpretation by individuals or the church. The text is the direct communication of God's will: the Spirit, working through the proclaimed Word or in the life of believers, is the interpreter of the text. At the other extreme is the Spirit-dominated community in which members are exhorted to be filled with the Holy Spirit and live their lives in the power of

---

[8]   Scott Hafemann (1996) gives a detailed overview of the different scholarly opinions of what Paul may have meant by the letter–spirit contrast. The two main theories are that this contrast is about different ways of reading the Law (hermeneutical) or different ways of understanding life under the old and new covenants. Hafeman's own view is that the contrast is essentially between 'Israel, who received the Law of God without the Spirit, and the Church, which now lives by the power of that same Spirit in obedience to the Law' (p. 438). Stephen Westerholm (1984) comes to somewhat similar conclusions after examining the letter–spirit contrast in this passage and in Romans 2:29 and 7:6. Like Hafemann, he concludes that this contrast is not simply about different kinds of reading (i.e. hermeneutics) but about two fundamentally different ways of serving God (i.e. ethics). Similarly, Grindheim (2001) argues that the contrast points to a fundamental difference between the two covenants rather than different ways of reading the Law.

[9]   John Barton (1997) takes slightly different view when he suggests that Christians recognized very early on that what came to be called the New Testament books were important and carried authority. In this (limited) sense, these texts were 'canonized' before they were considered sacred scripture. So, for example, the Apostolic Fathers and Apologists were less likely to allegorize the 'new' Christian writings than they were to allegorize Jewish writings, which indicates that the former were perceived as different in kind from the latter. On this understanding, texts would have been important from the beginning of the Christian church, though the fact remains that the way they were perceived and used was still very different from how they are perceived and used today.

this inspiration.[10] Guidance is directly available from the Spirit of God at work in the believer or through the gifts of prophecy and interpretation given to the church. Scripture bears witness to activity of the Spirit, and gives shape and substance to these activities through analogies and typologies.

The strengths of a word-dominated community are its ability to hold firm to revealed truths in different societies and changing times. Scriptures challenge the fickle nature of human hearts and the abuses of church leaders, demanding an allegiance to God that is ultimately life-giving and transforming. The weaknesses stem from the ease with which written words can become empty ciphers, devoid of any real meaning in the life of believers. Detached, rational examination or unthinking prejudice can replace inspired reading, leading to religion that is empty of divine content. The strengths of a Spirit-dominated community are its ability to rediscover in each circumstance the transforming power of God in the life of believers. The centrality of the direct experience of God requires an intimacy and vigilance, alongside a willingness to listen and respond, that are the hallmarks of true discipleship. The weaknesses stem from the ease with which 'spiritual experience' can become an end itself, leading to self-indulgent worship and self-seeking use of scripture. Current practices are affirmed by over-creative interpretations: inspiration is the smokescreen used to evade the contrary demands of scripture.

These are caricatures, but they perhaps help to articulate some important differences that underlie the essential distinctions between an evangelical and a pentecostal approach to scripture. Both traditions affirm the importance of the Holy Spirit and the importance of scripture, but the relationship of the two is quite different. It is perhaps too easy to argue for a sensible *via media*, in which Word and Spirit are equal partners who both bear witness to one another. This has certainly been tried, mostly by arguing for 'inspired interpretation'. In this paradigm, the same Spirit that inspired the writing of scripture also inspires its interpretation. Some hold to an essentially Calvinist view that such inspiration is the general work of the Spirit in the lives of believers that enables them to perceive the text as the transforming Word (Fuller 1978; Goldingay 1995: 188; Vanhoozer 1998). Others argue for a more specific inspiration that reveals truths otherwise unavailable to readers (Arrington 1994; McLean 1984; Pinnock 1993). Such a position has always been ambivalent for academic scholars, because it implies knowledge or insight that cannot be had by reason. So the trend is to play down such inspiration and make it subservient to the rational exposition of the trained mind. This is an understandable attempt to avoid the excesses of 'spiritual' interpretation, but it has the effect of limiting the work of the Spirit to the power of human reason. Inevitably, if a Spirit-filled exegesis collides with the accepted, rational understanding of the text, the latter will win out. If experience is primary, then it is inevitable that it will sometimes generate interpretations that do violence to the original or plain sense of the text.

---

[10]   There are examples of some sects today that deliberately discourage the use of the Bible in order to focus attention on the direct guidance of God (as revealed through the leadership of the church). Matthew Engelke (2004), for example, studied the Masowe weChishanu church in Zimbabwe, whose members refer to themselves as 'the Christians who don't need the bible'.

In the end, the two approaches are probably best left to live in uneasy tension. New experience must challenge the comfortable status quo; the norms of text and tradition must critique experience and reign in the excesses of the deluded.

Insights from Empirical Study

What does an empirical approach add to this debate? Examining the way that ordinary readers use the Bible can enable a better appraisal of how revelation and guidance from written word and Spirit work in practice. The traditional theological process starts with certain 'givens' such as the nature God, the means of revelation and the nature and purpose of scripture. The relationships of written word, 'living Word' and Spirit are then prescribed mainly though the application of deductive reasoning. The end point may describe how word and Spirit ought to cohere, but this might be very different from what happens in practice. In theory, empirical description and analysis show how congregations or individuals arrive at decisions and what factors guide their actions. We are some way off being able to do this convincingly, but in time there could be adequate ways of describing the links between what believers perceive as 'God speaking through the Bible' and what they perceive as 'God speaking through the Spirit'. Some traditional theologies argue that these two voices must always cohere, whereas others try to give one priority over the other. Empirical studies that start with the lived experience of ordinary believers will tend to stress the way in which those experiences confirm or challenge the religious status quo handed down by tradition. In the same way that the historical study of what actually happened in Acts 12–15 has raised theological questions about the interpretation and reinterpretation of scripture, so empirical study of present-day churches could shed new light and raise new questions for an ongoing debate.

The results reported in this chapter have confirmed that beliefs, experience and interpretation exist in a complex interrelationship. From one point of view, it is prior beliefs and commitments that control both the interpretation of experience and the interpretation of text. This is the postmodern model that says that there is no 'pure' experience and that everything is interpretation. Empirical study, however, resists unwarranted assumptions about cause and effect in observations that are simply correlations. I began this book by pointing out the limits of empirical study in this field, and this is a case where it would be unwise to jump to hasty conclusions without more evidence. At this stage we can note both the complexity and the predictability of some aspects of the interaction of word and Spirit for ordinary Bible readers. What we cannot do empirically yet is to determine whether biblical word interprets spiritual encounter or vice versa.

Further Research

There is clearly scope for widening the scope of the Bible and Lay People study to investigate further the relationship of biblical conservatism to charismatic practice. Of particular interest would be to investigate traditions that have high charismatic practice but which may or may not have an essentially evangelical hermeneutic. The historical evidence is that most would have a conservative rather than liberal belief about the Bible, but there may be important differences from a purely evangelical approach to scripture. For example, instruments would be required to assess the importance of experience or 'community narrative' in the interpretative habits of individuals. Rather than use a test passage, it might be better investigate the passages that have been important to particular individuals in an attempt to identify analogical interpretations and the interaction of text and experience.

The other group of interest in this context would be conservative evangelicals or fundamentalists who have little or no charismatic experience. What is their perception of the role of the Spirit, and does it accord with the kinds of hermeneutical understanding expressed in the writings of scholars from these traditions? Given the widespread and somewhat insidious influence of the Charismatic Movement on a wide range of denominations, it would be interesting to see if its effects are evident in the way that ordinary members use the Bible.

As I have indicated, it is easier to describe correlations between beliefs, experience and biblical interpretation than to establish cause and effect. What may be needed here is more qualitative analysis of case histories, both those that suggest experience creates belief and those that point the other way. This is less about verifying or disproving acts of divine intervention and more about understanding the way that perceptions of scripture are created and changed.

Chapter 9

Towards an Empirical Theology of Scripture

The Bible and Lay People study took a broad approach to investigating how lay people interpret the Bible. This was deliberately so because so little empirical data existed that it would have been unwise to focus the study too narrowly. The aim was to look at a range of interpretative possibilities in relation to a range of extra-biblical variables that might have some predictive capabilities. Inevitably the interpretative possibilities were somewhat limited, and confined to those things that could be quantified and that seemed to be genuine ways in which lay people might interpret the Bible. Literalism, for example, was one of the main interpretative strategies investigated, which immediately highlights the difference between this study and the majority of work on biblical hermeneutics in the academy.

The findings are offered as a starting point for more detailed work in individual areas, which is why I have ended each chapter with suggestions about further research that could be undertaken. In this concluding chapter I want to pull together the main findings, discuss the usefulness of this sort of empirical approach to studying hermeneutics and conclude with some analogies that might be helpful in developing an empirical theology of scripture.

Summary of the Main Findings

Variability

A first thing to conclude is that there was a surprising amount of variability in interpretation, both within and between congregations. The Church of England is generally renowned for being a 'broad church', but even so it is remarkable just how much diversity there is in interpretative practice within a single denomination. As we have seen in Chapter 7, some of this variability is between the different traditions within the Church of England and some is between different congregations in the same tradition. Whether other denominations show such marked differences between their constituent congregations remains to be seen, though I suspect that many mainstream denominations will be similar to the Church of England.

The variability within congregations in this study suggests that even though some 'gathered' churches have distinctive beliefs and practices, they still attract a range of people with different backgrounds, personalities and beliefs. This variability in people produces diversity in interpretative practice with the same congregation. This, it seems to me, can only be a healthy sign because it points to an inclusivity and diversity that is at the heart of the foundational metaphor of the Church as the Body of Christ. The dangers of a narrow, sectarian use of scripture are all too apparent through history, and diversity of approach represents one way in which common sacred texts can speak to different sorts of believers within a unified church.

Predictability

Suggesting that interpretation was 'predictable' might seem a rather pejorative observation. Some uses of the word imply that people might be acting without care or thought, or that they always stick to the safe, the routine and the expected. That is not how an empiricist uses the word. In this context it means that people's behaviours are not random or unexpected, but related to other aspects of their lives. Predictability implies some coherence between attitudes, beliefs and behaviours, and a sense that what people do with the Bible makes sense in a holistic fashion within their lives. In this study it was clear from the evidence presented in Chapter 3 that what readers believed about the Bible was related to how frequently they read it and how they read it. These relationships varied in different traditions, but those who had a 'high' view of scripture as the divine Word tended to live out that belief in the way that they used the Bible in their lives. Those who believed the Bible was more a record of human endeavour with the divine tended to use it less often as a guide to daily living.

In a technical sense, predictability is about the possibility of explaining one set of variables in terms of others: in this case explaining the variability of interpretation in terms of other factors related to people and their churches. The results reported here suggest that factors such as education, personality type, experience and charismatic practice seemed to be more important predictors of biblical interpretation than factors such as sex or age. In some cases, interpretation could be predicted by membership of particular traditions within Anglicanism but, as we saw in Chapter 7, this 'community' effect may often be explained by the way individuals were distributed across congregations. Overall, there was good evidence for the importance of individual differences in shaping interpretation: what individuals bring to the act of reading has an important effect on how they understand the Bible, irrespective of where they worship.

Education emerged as an important factor for shaping literalism and the choice of interpretative horizons. In some cases theological education had a heightening effect over and above general education, though this was a sample of people with rather little experience of such specialized education. This is perhaps an unsurprising finding, but an important one. The analysis in Chapter 4 demonstrated that education has a greater effect on literalism in some traditions than in others, showing that ordinary people can resist certain types of reading if they choose to. In some ways, education could be equated with the loss of 'uncritical' approaches to Bible reading in what scholars now term the loss of 'first naivety'. The recognition that this loss can lead to the 'desert of criticism' is a warning that the church may face an increasing need to help ordinary members deal with their growing exposure to secular education. If the last serious engagement people have with the Bible is when they leave Sunday school they will be ill-equipped to reconcile what they know of the text with how they are taught to understand the world.

In Chapter 2 I discussed the way that biblical scholarship has responded to the reaction against modernity by developing a wide range of new approaches to the study of the Bible. A major development has been the shift of focus to readers and their 'social location', and a key location preoccupying scholars is gender. Feminist Bible readings are now a vital part of the academy, and the stress is on the very different experience of reading Bible between men and women. In this study of ordinary readers, sex was generally a poor predictor of interpretation. Where there were differences between the sexes, they sometimes disappeared if personality type was included in the model. In this sample at least, gender did not seem to be a key factor per se in shaping Bible reading, a reminder again that the preoccupations of the academy do not always translate to ordinary churchgoers. It remains to be seen whether this would have been true if test passages were used that specifically raised issues related to women. It may also be that specifically feminist readings will emerge among ordinary readers in churches as a younger generation that is more aware of gender issues gains numerical dominance in congregations.

Age was also a poor predictor of biblical interpretation. However, even if age is not a fundamental causal agent in shaping interpretation, it may be the most obvious index of other, underlying causal factors. It seems unlikely that age as such would change interpretation, but age is sometimes a good indicator of experience or generational changes that may have profound effects on the way that the Bible is understood. In this sample, younger people tended to be slightly more educated and more charismatic than older people, and this may have created an indirect link between age and interpretation. We happen to be living at a time when there are considerable generational shifts in culture and educational opportunities, which may well create gaps between the way that old and young interpret. In practical terms, knowing how age predicts interpretative practice may be of more use to churches than understanding the underlying causal mechanisms. After all, you can get a pretty good idea of the average age of a congregation just by looking at it, whereas other factors are more difficult to assess. However, as these underlying factors evolve in society at large and in the church in particular, their relationship to age will change, so there will always be value in understanding the primary casual relationships. In years to come, the relationship between age and biblical interpretation in Anglican congregations could be quite different.

Overall, differences between individuals seemed to account for more of the variation in biblical interpretation than differences in their social or denominational location. Obviously the two are linked because people segregate into different sorts of congregations. There was some evidence that congregations or traditions may influence the way that members read, but it was not conclusive and there was sufficient counter-evidence to show that the prime factors shaping people's interpretations were their own beliefs, predispositions and experiences. If personality is a 'given' that remains reasonably constant in any particular individual, then it could be an important predictor of how people interpret the Bible. This might be a direct effect, as was the case in this study, where interpretations were deliberately matched to particular personality types, or it may act indirectly by predisposing people to particular sorts of beliefs or educational experience.

The evidence on the effect of experience on interpretation was rather mixed, and it perhaps depends on what counts as experience. The term could encompass everything that impinges on someone as they go through life: that is anything considered 'nurture' rather than 'nature'. If so, education can be viewed as a 'life experience' with a crucial influence on interpretation. Experience that is more specifically related to the text being read seemed to have some effect when, for example, those who had experienced miraculous healing interpreted a healing story more literally and with less horizon separation than those without that experience. However, in this case 'experience' could itself be a particular interpretation of events that was driven by prior beliefs. What might be useful is to find different sorts of experience that are more easily objectified and to see how these affect reading. In the Bible and Lay People sample, one or two people mentioned that they suffered from epilepsy so that reading the story in Mark 9 as an exorcism was both difficult and threatening. Clearly this sort of experience shapes reading. What is equally intriguing is the way that people resist experience and make it secondary to the reality revealed in the text. This sort of reading is very important in some religious traditions, where the text is prior and shapes the way that the world is viewed and interpreted. If experience is going to be used as a predictor of interpretation then it needs to be tightly defined and measured along with other factors that might control the how much a reader allows experience to shape beliefs.

How Useful is the Empirical Study of Bible Reading?

The obvious rejoinder to this question is 'Useful to whom?' Empirical study is likely to be of some use to those study religion more generally, especially those who value these sorts of methods. It opens up another facet of religion to the reach of social science and psychology, and allows the role of sacred texts to be understood in terms that are intelligible to these arenas of discourse. Empirical study of Bible reading also has a contribution to make to the academic discourse of biblical hermeneutics. It catches the rising tide of interest in readers, and moves discussion of 'real' readers beyond anecdotal observation to more dependable and rigorous analysis. Such study also feeds into the growing disciplines of discourse analysis and the empirical study of reading in general, and could well have a useful contribution to make in these fields. Reading sacred texts brings into play prior commitments in a way that is less obvious in the reading of more 'neutral' material. My main concern here, however, is whether or not such study is of any use for the church. More specifically, is it useful for theologians or for the sort of people who took part in this study?

Empirical study of religion has a general use in holding a mirror up to the church. It may be an imperfect mirror, in which we see ourselves rather darkly, but it is one way of setting aspirations alongside reality. By appealing to the objectivity associated with empiricism, with all its recognized flaws, this sort of study prevents the church from escaping completely into a nether world of idealism and imagined possibilities. A hoped-for and idealized world is vital for people of faith, but it has to have some connection with the world in which we exist. Empirical results may confirm that what ought to be so really is, and thereby affirm the practice of the church; or it might highlight the discrepancy between faith in theory and faith in practice, and therefore challenge either or both. Either way, empirical study helps the church to see itself as others might see it, and hopefully to learn from such a perspective.[1]

In this regard, empirical study of Bible reading shows how the church actually uses the Bible, rather than how it ought to. The data on Bible-reading frequency outlined in Chapter 3 led to discussion on whether individual Bible study was a necessity for true discipleship or a helpful addition for some. Giving voice to the large number of people who could read the Bible but do not moves this kind of discussion forward. In Chapter 7 I suggested that quantifying the variance in measures of biblical interpretation might offer an objective way of assessing the extent of inclusivity or exclusivity within congregations. These are examples of the way in which empirical study of Bible reading might help churches to achieve more critical self-appraisal.

Empiricism also takes seriously the lived experiences of people of faith, and will inevitably tend to privilege them over the prescriptions of tradition. This is both a strength and a weakness. It is a strength because religion is nothing if it is not meaningful in the lives of ordinary religious people. Empirical study of religious experience goes to the heart of the encounter between the divine and the human, which, if it happens at all, happens in the lives of ordinary people. This is surely central to an incarnational faith such as Christianity. The weakness is that privileging human experience can make faith prey to such experience and therefore prone to fashion and individualism. If Christianity is incarnational it is primarily so because of a foundational incarnation, and the faith has laid great stress on particular revelatory events in history. These are what the tradition seeks to preserve alongside, and sometimes despite, the beliefs and experience of the faithful. If empirical study of religion is to be useful it has to allow the everyday experience of faith to engage with that which lies outside the experience of ordinary believers.

Empirical study of Bible reading allows experience to interact with tradition by offering an account of how ordinary people hear, or do not hear, the voice of God in the sacred text. Their interaction with the Bible does not always conform to the expectations of tradition, but they may nonetheless claim divine encounters through and beyond the text. This issue was discussed in Chapter 8 in the context of the relationship between experience and interpretation. I examined this in the light of the 'letter-spirit' debate because this is essentially about the interaction of lived experience with textually revealed truths. This debate is most urgent and focused in Pentecostalism at the moment, but it has widespread implications for the way that the church in general deals with the insights of ordinary people. Are Christians actually 'People of the Book', or are they 'People of the Spirit', and can they be

---

[1]   Postmodernity sometimes denies the possibility of any kind of objective view: this may be so, but perhaps there is benefit in different views, even if they are all tied to some sort of context. Empiricism is still a widely understood and shared context which acts as a link between the worlds of religious faith and secularism.

both? Theoretical answers to this are well worked out, but answering this from the 'ground up' will give a very different perspective.

This last issue raises the question of how God uses scripture to relate to readers. If the Bible is in any sense a vehicle of divine communication, how exactly does this work? Traditional theological explanations evoke the notions of inspiration to explain how the text can mediate the intentions of God and carry divine authority. The focus is on the divine author or the intent encapsulated in the text, both of which are released when the text is read 'in faith'. This might imply the action of the Holy Spirit in inspiring reading, or the unique power of the text itself to inspire the reader.[2] This empirical study has shown that a range of factors beyond the text itself will shape the way that it is understood. If education or personality types really do have the effect of channelling reading in particular directions, what does this mean in terms of communication between God and the reader? Is the text 'fighting' against human nature and nurture, so that the message comes through despite sinful distractions? Or might it be that God is somehow active in lives well before they encounter the text, so that the text resonates with a wider divine revelation? Empirical study of ordinary reading highlights the bald fact that people are different and these differences explain different encounters with scripture. For some commentators this diversity is simply evidence of the corrupting effect of the world. If it is so, then the corruption is widespread and endemic to the church. If there are readings that are the only true readings, they belong to a tiny minority, even within the church. Is there a more generous way of understanding the individual variations in reading among ordinary readers that can both celebrate diversity and honour the truth? It is to this that I turn in the final section.

An Empirical Theology of Scripture?

It is premature to develop rounded theology of scripture based on empirical observation of ordinary readers. The empirical evidence is still too fragmentary to permit such an undertaking, which would have to have considerable confidence that it could draw on reliable evidence of Bible reading across a wide range of traditions and biblical material. What I intend here is to suggest ways that such a theology might be able to do justice to both the importance of scripture for the Christian faith and the diversity of practice among ordinary readers. I will do this by using two analogies, one based the scientific observations of light, and the other based on a New Testament parable.

Any prescriptive account of Bible reading (and I take the term 'theology' to imply some sort of prescription) has to account for the sort of variety and predictability found in this study. Leslie Francis, who has spent some years investigating the relationship between personality and religion, has drawn on foundational theological texts such as the creation story in Genesis to argue for the Godliness of human diversity (Francis 2004: 147). If God created humans in distinct kinds, male and

---

[2]   David Law (2001) argues that scripture is inspired because it contains 'ciphers' that mediate the divine through existential encounter when the text is read.

female, then this may be analogous to other kinds of human diversity such as that reflected in ethnicity or personality, which are 'God-givens' that God saw as good (Genesis 1:31). Theologies based on empirical observation of humans have to account for the goodness and value of this innate diversity, which precedes the stories of the Fall (Genesis 3) and the Tower of Babel (Genesis 11:1–9). The latter story might cast doubt on the value of diversity, which seems in this context to be a curse rather than a blessing. Nonetheless, this diversity is not lost when Babel encounters Pentecost: there is a shared understanding between those who hear the Spirit-filled disciples, despite their diversity of tongues (Acts 2:1–12). Can the diverse ways in which the Bible is interpreted be understood as a God-given necessity, related to the innate diversity of creation?

An analogy that has been famously used to describe human diversity is the rainbow. Desmond Tutu spoke of South Africa as 'The Rainbow Nation', a single phrase that turned the tragedy of division into the celebration of diversity. Rainbows are formed by refracted light, an observation made by Isaac Newton in 1665 as he experimented with prisms. Newton found that a single beam of white light passing through a prism was split into the familiar colours of the rainbow. White light that appeared to be monochrome was actually made up of different colours. Perhaps Bible reading acts on the eternal Word as a prism acts on light. The Word of God encounters human diversity and is translated it into different 'words' through the lens of individual differences, revealing a collage of meaning. For some the word is 'blue', for others it is 'green' or 'yellow' or 'red'. If you look at a white light through a prism it will appear different colours, depending on where you place your eye. Unless the actions of the prism are understood, observers will assume that the source of the light is coloured. Those who only look in the blue zone will be utterly convinced that the source of light is blue; those in the red zone will believe the source is red. This analogy has links to the contextualism of the more radical forms of postmodernity where there is no 'meta-narrative', only the locally contingent manifestations of truth. In the analogy there would be no white light source, only coloured light that changes depending on where you stand: in effect, the prism creates its own light. In Bible-reading terms, this is equivalent to taking away any central coherence or divine origin from the text and making individuals, or individual reading communities, the source of the message. In fact, the analogy challenges this view: a prism does not create light, it refracts it. Human diversity may shape the Word into words, but these words are not entirely of human making.

An empirical *theology* of scripture accepts the existence of a coherent divine Word that embraces the whole activity of God communicating though and beyond scripture, including the reality that this Word may become radically contextualized. The various 'words' created by human activity say something, but not everything, about the divine Word. The objectivity that is inherent in an empirical approach to Bible reading resists the prescriptive task that might too easily cast aside particular words. Instead, the task consists of trying to describe and understand different ways of reading, both in their own terms and in relation to other ways of reading. This is analogous to both standing in one part of the rainbow, where everything is a single colour, and standing back and observing the whole rainbow.[3] Postmodernity critiques the idea that empiricists can ever 'stand back and observe', for there is no neutral space from which to do so. <u>An empirical stance, however, does not entirely abandon the idea that some ways of observing are more objective than others. In that sense it is modernist and unashamedly so.</u> It is important to note, however, that an empirical theology of Scripture is based on observation of various 'words', and not any claim of having an objective view of the Word itself. In our analogy, an empirical stance is not one that seeks the objective space from which to observe the light source; it is content to live this side of the prism and observe the rainbow.

The other surprising observation that Newton made was that once light was refracted into colours, these coloured beams could be recombined into white light again. This was not easy and required considerable precision because all the constituent parts had to be present to make white light again. Perhaps the analogy will stretch to the suggestion that although ordinary Bible readers may, by dint of their individuality, create particular and limited meaning from what they read, combining insights from a range of readers might achieve a closer proximity to the eternal Word than by insisting that the Word means this particular word and only this. The end result will always be an imperfect recombination, but that should not stop the church trying to listen carefully to what the Spirit is saying through ordinary readers. Empirical theology starts with this listening, but has to have some way of evaluating what is heard.

<u>This brings me to my second analogy and final conclusion.</u> The New Testament Parable of the Talents is found in Matthew 25:14–30 and Luke 19:11–27. The parable exists in two slightly different forms, though both are centred on the giving of money to slaves and what they then do with it.[4] The account in Matthew is probably nearer the original, and seems to be an illustration of the sort of behaviour expected of disciples. Clearly the talents are symbolic of other things: this is not a lesson on the virtues of capitalism, but is instead looking at what disciples do with what they are given. What they are given varies from one to another, but there is no explanation of why this should be so. One has five talents, one two and the other just one. When the master returns they are judged against what they have done with what they had. So the words used to the slave with five talents who made five more and the words used to the slave with two who made two more are identical: 'Well done, good and trustworthy slave; you have been trustworthy in a few things, I will put you in charge of many things; enter into the joy of your master'. The implication is that, had the remaining slave doubled his solitary talent, he too would have been treated in the

---

[3]   These ways of study are referred to as 'emic' (from within) and 'etic' (from outside), terms first coined by the anthropologist and linguist Kenneth Pike (1967).

[4]   The Lukan account has additional material about a nobleman leaving to engage with his enemies, which is probably a redaction of a story that was originally much like the Matthean version (Nolland 1993: 910–12). The *talanton* mentioned in Matthew was a large amount of money, much more than the *mina* mentioned in Luke. In Luke, ten servants are given one *mina* each, and we hear of three who have made differing amounts. In Matthew, three servants are given different amounts and we hear of two who doubled their capital and one who left it unchanged.

same way. As it is, what he received from the master is returned unchanged, having been carefully guarded but never used.

If we apply this to a theology of scripture, it seems to offer a way of evaluating different practice, while at the same time being aware of the diversity that exists both within and between academy and church. The talents initially refer to that which we are given. Each reader comes to the Bible with different talents,[5] which in this context might refer to the sort of characteristics that this study has shown will shape the way that they read. These may be innate characteristics such as sex or personality type; or they may be acquired characteristics such as education, beliefs or experience. These are 'givens', and in the context of the parable they are most definitely God-given. The Matthean account is particularly interesting because it seems to highlight the difference between what has been given to each slave. Perhaps this is a perceptive awareness of the bald fact of individual difference that is the reality of life. It may seem unfair for the master to give different amounts to different slaves, but that is what he does. It may be annoying and frustrating that people are different and do very different things with scripture, but they do. It may seem unfair that some people have a better start in life, and better opportunities along the way, especially if these are understood to be in some sense within the gifting of God. Yet that is the perspective of this Kingdom parable, and it is the undeniable observation of life.

The parable is chiefly concerned with what the slaves do with what they are given and how this is judged. There are no details, only the end result, but there is clearly a contrast between the willingness of the first two slaves to take risks and the inordinate caution of the last. When it comes to scripture, perhaps the key ethical demand is that we use what we have to enhance what we are. If, as this study suggests, what people do with scripture is at least partly controlled by who they are and what they have, then a Kingdom judgement is one that takes this into account. The master commends both slaves equally because of what they did, not for what they achieved in absolute terms. Being willing to apply personalities, education or experiences as valuable tools in the act of Bible reading requires disciples to see God's action in their lives before and beyond the encounter with scripture. God does not necessarily speak though the Bible into the godless lives of believers: any encounter of God in scripture is surely linked to a wider experience of God. Such experience could be found in the sacred inspiration of the Spirit, or it could be found in the more mundane realities that are common to the rest of humanity.

In this context, the censure of the slave who buried his talent comes as a stark warning, but what exactly is this warning? By analogy, 'burying your talents' is to ignore or avoid the risky business of using who you are, or what you have, when you interpret the Bible. It is pretending that God prefers us to read by ignoring all that we have been given, pushing it to one side and making sure that it will not be altered by our reading. The parable suggests that such 'safe' reading is not Kingdom reading because it is too fearful and not faithful. The master expects us to take risks and to return to him more than he gave us.

---

[5] According to the *Oxford English Dictionary*, the figurative use of the word talent, to refer to natural abilities, seems to have sprung directly from its use in the parable.

If this parable is used to shape an empirical theology of scripture, then it speaks of a kind of reading that is unafraid to accept the God of individual differences, unafraid to bring our individuality to the encounter with scripture and unafraid to be changed by that encounter. In many ways, this is totally unlike the kind of reading so long championed by the academy. It is the sort of reading that the academy is beginning to understand as carrying intellectual honesty and virtue. It is the sort of reading that perhaps comes most naturally to ordinary Bible readers.

Appendix

Mark 9:14–29

When they came to the disciples, they saw a great crowd around them, and some scribes arguing with them. When the whole crowd saw him, they were immediately overcome with awe, and they ran forward to greet him. He asked them, 'What are you arguing about with them?' Someone from the crowd answered him, 'Teacher, I brought you my son; he has a spirit that makes him unable to speak; and whenever it seizes him, it dashes him down; and he foams and grinds his teeth and becomes rigid; and I asked your disciples to cast it out, but they could not do so'. He answered them, 'You faithless generation, how much longer must I be among you? How much longer must I put up with you? Bring him to me'. And they brought the boy to him. When the spirit saw him, immediately it convulsed the boy, and he fell on the ground and rolled about, foaming at the mouth. Jesus asked the father, 'How long has this been happening to him?' And he said, 'From childhood. It has often cast him into the fire and into the water, to destroy him; but if you are able to do anything, have pity on us and help us'. Jesus said to him, 'If you are able!—All things can be done for the one who believes'. Immediately the father of the child cried out, 'I believe; help my unbelief!' When Jesus saw that a crowd came running together, he rebuked the unclean spirit, saying to it, 'You spirit that keeps this boy from speaking and hearing, I command you, come out of him, and never enter him again!' After crying out and convulsing him terribly, it came out, and the boy was like a corpse, so that most of them said, 'He is dead'. But Jesus took him by the hand and lifted him up, and he was able to stand. When he had entered the house, his disciples asked him privately, 'Why could we not cast it out?' He said to them, 'This kind can come out only through prayer'.

Bibliography

Adam, A. K. M. (1990). 'The sign of Jonah: a Fish-eye view'. *Semeia*, 51: 177–91.
—— (1995). *What is Postmodern Biblical Criticism?* Minneapolis, MN: Fortress Press.
—— (2004). 'Integral and differential hermeneutics'. In *The Meanings We Choose: Hermeneutical Ethics, Indeterminacy and the Conflict of Interpretations*, ed. C. H. Cosgrove. London and New York: T & T Clark, pp. 24–38.
Aichele, G., Burnett, F. W., Castelli, E. A., Fowler, R. M., et al. (eds) (1995). *The Post-Modern Bible*. New Haven, CT and London: Yale University Press.
Aiken, L. R. (1996). *Rating Scales and Checklists: Evaluating Behavior, Personality and Attitudes*. New York: John Wiley & Sons.
Allport, G. W. (1950). *The Individual and his Religion: A Psychological Interpretation*. New York: Macmillan.
Alvesson, M. (2002). *Postmodernism and Social Research*. Milton Keynes: Open University Press.
Ammerman, N. T. (1982). 'Operationalizing evangelicalism: an amendment'. *Sociological Analysis*, 43: 170–72.
Anderson, A. (2004). *An Introduction to Pentecostalism: Global Charismatic Christianity*. Cambridge: Cambridge University Press.
Anderson, J. C., and Moore, S. D. (eds) (1992). *Mark and Method: New Approaches in Biblical Studies*. Minneapolis, MN: Fortress Press.
Anderson, J. C., and Staley, J. L. (eds) (1995). *Taking It Personally: Autobiographical Biblical Criticism* (*Semeia*, vol. 72). Atlanta, GA: Scholars Press.
Archbishop of Canterbury's Commission on Urban Priority Areas (1985). *Faith in The City: A Call for Action by Church and Nation*. London: Church House Publishing.
Archbishop's Commission on Rural Areas (1990). *Faith in the Countryside*. Worthing: Churchman Publishing.
Archbishop's Council (2004). *Mission-Shaped Church: Church Planting and Fresh Expressions of Church in a Changing Context*. London: Church House Publishing.
Archer, K. J. (1996). 'Pentecostal hermeneutics: retrospect and prospect'. *Journal of Pentecostal Theology*, 8: 63–81.
—— (2004). 'Pentecostal story: the hermeneutic filter for the making of meaning'. *Pneuma: The Journal of the Society for Pentecostal Studies*, 26: 36–59.
Arnau, R. C., Green, B. A., Rosen, D. H., Gleaves, D. H., et al. (2003). 'Are Jungian preferences really categorical?: An empirical investigation using taxometric analysis'. *Personality and Individual Differences*, 34: 233–51.
Arndt, W. F., and Gingrich, F. W. (1979). *A Greek–English Lexicon of the New Testament*. Chicago: University of Chicago Press.

Arrington, F. L. (1994). 'The use of the bible by Pentecostals'. *Pneuma: The Journal of the Society for Pentecostal Studies*, 16: 101–107.

Astley, J. (2002). *Ordinary Theology: Looking, Listening, and Learning in Theology.* Aldershot & Burlington, VT: Ashgate.

Baker, J. (1996). 'Churchmanship'. In *Celebrating the Anglican Way*, ed. I. Bunting. London: Hodder & Stoughton, pp. 110–24.

Ballard, P., and Pritchard, J. (1996). *Practical Theology in Action.* London: SPCK.

Barclay, J. M. G. (1988). *Obeying the Truth: A Study of Paul's Ethics in Galatians.* Edinburgh: T & T Clark.

Barr, J. (1973). *The Bible in the Modern World.* London: SCM Press.

—— (1981). *Fundamentalism.* London: SCM Press.

—— (1983). *Holy Scripture: Canon, Authority, Criticism.* Oxford: Clarendon Press.

Barton, J. (1997). *The Spirit and the Letter: Studies in the Biblical Canon.* London: SPCK.

—— (ed.) (1998). *The Cambridge Companion to Biblical Interpretation.* Cambridge and New York: Cambridge University Press.

Barton, S. C. (1995). 'Historical criticism and social-scientific perspectives in New Testament study'. In *Hearing the New Testament: Strategies for Interpretation*, ed. J. B. Green. Grand Rapids, MI: Eerdmans, pp. 61–89.

Bassett, R. L., Mathewson, K., and Gailitis, A. (1993). 'Recognising the person in biblical interpretation: an empirical study'. *Journal of Psychology and Christianity*, 12: 38–46.

Baylor University (2005) *The Baylor Religion Survey.* Waco, TX: Baylor Institute for Studies of Religion.

Bayne, R. (1997). *The Myers–Briggs Type Indicator: A Critical Review and Practical Guide.* Cheltenham: Stanley Thornes.

Beal, T. K., and Linafelt, T. (eds) (2006). *Mel Gibson's Bible: Religion, Popular Culture, and the Passion of the Christ.* Chicago: University of Chicago Press.

Belcher, R. P. (1980). *A Layman's Guide to the Inerrancy Debate.* Chicago: Moody Press.

Berger, K. (2003). *Identity and Experience in the New Testament.* Minneapolis: Fortress Press.

Berger, P. L. (1967). *The Sacred Canopy: Elements of Sociological Theory of Religion.* Garden City, NY: Doubleday.

—— (1969). *The Social Reality of Religion.* London: Faber & Faber.

—— (1971). *A Rumour of Angels: Modern Society and the Rediscovery of the Supernatural.* Harmondsworth: Penguin.

—— (1992). *A Far Glory: The Quest for Faith in an Age of Credulity.* New York: Doubleday.

Berkhof, L. (1939). *Systematic Theology.* Edinburgh: Banner of Truth Trust.

Bess, T. L., and Harvey, R. J. (2002). 'Bimodal score distributions and the Myers–Briggs type indicator: fact or artefact?' *Journal of Personality Assessment*, 78: 176–86.

Boone, K. C. (1989). *The Bible Tells Them So: The Discourse of Protestant Fundamentalism.* Albany, NY: State University of New York Press.

Braaten, C. E., and Jenson, R. W. (eds) (2002). *The Strange New Word of the Gospel: Re-Evangelizing in the Postmodern World*. Grand Rapids, MI: Eerdmans.

Bray, G. (1996). *Biblical Interpretation Past and Present*. Leicester: Apollos / IVP.

Brewer, W. F. (1996). 'Good and bad story endings and story completeness'. In *Empirical Approaches to Literature and Aesthetics*, ed. R. J. Kreuz and M. S. MacNealy. Norwood, NJ: Ablex Publishing Corporation, pp. 261–74.

Brierley, P. (1999). *Religious Trends No. 2*. London: Christian Research.

—— (2000). *The Tide Is Running Out*. London: Christian Research.

Broadbent, D. E. (1958). *Perception and Communication*. New York: Pergamon Press.

Brown, C. G. (2001). *The Death of Christian Britain: Understanding Secularisation, 1800–2000*. London & New York: Routledge.

Brubaker, M. R. (1997). 'Postmodernism and Pentecostals'. *Evangelical Journal*, 15: 33–45.

Bruce, S. (2002). *God is Dead: Secularization in the West*. Oxford and Malden, MA: Blackwell Publishers.

Brueggemann, W. (1997). 'Biblical theology appropriately postmodern'. *Biblical Theology Bulletin*, 27: 4–9.

Bryant, F. B., and Yarnold, P. R. (1995). 'Principal-components analysis and exploratory and confirmatory factor analysis'. In *Reading and Understanding Multivariate Statistics*, ed. L. G. Grimm and P. R. Yarnold. Washington, DC: American Psychological Association, pp. 99–136.

Bultmann, R. (1972). *New Testament and Mythology*. London: SPCK.

—— (1985). *New Testament and Mythology and Other Basic Writings*. London: SCM Press.

Burke, T. J., and Elliott, J. K. (eds) (2003). *Paul and the Corinthians: Studies on a Community in Conflict*. Leiden and Boston, MA: Brill.

Campbell, R. A. (1991). 'Does Paul acquiesce on divisions at the Lord's Supper?' *Novum Testamentum*, 33: 61–70.

Capps, D. (1981). *Biblical Approaches to Pastoral Counseling*. Philadelphia: Westminster.

—— (1984). 'The Bible's role in pastoral care and counseling: four basic principles'. *Journal of Psychology and Christianity*, 3: 5–15.

Cargal, T. B. (1993). 'Beyond the fundamentalist–modernist controversy: Pentecostals and hermeneutics in a postmodern age'. *Pneuma: The Journal of the Society for Pentecostal Studies*, 15: 163–88.

Carpenter, J. (1997). *Revive Us Again: The Reawakening of American Fundamentalism*. Oxford: Oxford University Press.

Cartledge, M. J. (1999). 'Empirical theology: inter- or intra- disciplinary?' *Journal of Beliefs and Values*, 20: 98–104.

Childs, B. S. (1993). *Biblical Theology of the Old and New Testaments*. Minneapolis: Fortress Press.

Clines, D. J. A. (1997). *The Bible and the Modern World*. Sheffield: Sheffield Academic Press.

Coggins, R. J., and Houlden, J. L. (eds) (1990). *A Dictionary of Biblical Interpretation*. London: SCM Press.

Conn, H. M. (ed.) (1988). *Inerrancy and Hermeneutic*. Grand Rapids, MI: Baker Book House.

Corbishley, T. (1963). *The Spiritual Exercises of Saint Ignatius*. Wheathamstead: Anthony Clarke.

Cox, J. (2003). 'Master narratives of long-term religious change'. In *The Decline of Christendom in Western Europe, 1750–2000*, ed. H. McLeod and W. Ustorf. Cambridge: Cambridge University Press, pp. 201–217.

Cupitt, D. (1997). *After God: The Future of Religion*. London: Weidenfeld and Nicolson.

Davies, P. R. (1995). *Whose Bible Is It Anyway?* Sheffield: Sheffield Academic Press.

Davis, T. W. (2004). *Shifting Sands: The Rise and Fall of Biblical Archaeology*. Oxford and New York: Oxford University Press.

Dempster, M. (1993). 'Paradigm shifts and hermeneutics: confronting issues old and new'. *Pneuma: The Journal of the Society for Pentecostal Studies*, 15: 129–36.

Dixon, R. D., Jones, L. P., and Lowery, R. C. (1992). 'Biblical authority questions: two choices in identifying conservative Christian subcultures'. *Sociological Analysis*, 53: 63–72.

Dockery, D. S. (ed.) (1995). *The Challenge of Postmodernism: An Evangelical Engagement*. Wheaton, IL: Bridgepoint / Victor.

Dorfman, M. H. (1996). 'Evaluating the interpretive community: evidence from expert and novice readers'. *Poetics*, 23: 453–70.

Dunn, J. D. G. (1988). *Word Biblical Commentary: Romans 1–8*. Dallas, TX: Word Books.

Dyson, A. (1985). 'The bishop of Durham and all that'. *Modern Churchman*, 27: 1–2.

Edwards, J. K. (2005). *Effective First-Person Biblical Preaching: The Steps from Text to Narrative Sermon*. New York: HarperCollins Publishers.

Ellens, J. H., and Rollins, W. G. (eds) (2004). *Psychology and the Bible: A New Way to Read the Scriptures*, vol. 1: *From Freud to Kohut*. Westport, CT: Praeger.

Ellington, S. A. (2001). 'History, story, and testimony: locating truth in a Pentecostal hermeneutic'. *Pneuma: The Journal of the Society for Pentecostal Studies*, 23: 245–63.

Engelke, M. (2004). 'Text and performance in an African church: The Book, "live and direct"'. *American Ethnologist*, 31: 76–91.

Escott, P. (2001). *Faith in Life*. London: Churches Information for Mission.

Esler, P. F. (1994). *The First Christians in their Social Worlds: Social-Scientific Approaches to New Testament Interpretation*. London and New York: Routledge.

Eysenck, H. J., and Wilson, G. D. (1973). *The Experimental Study of Freudian Theories*. London: Methuen.

—— and Keane, M. T. (2000). *Cognitive Psychology: A Student's Handbook*. Hove: Psychology Press Ltd.

Farley, E. (1982). *Ecclesial Reflection: An Anatomy of Theological Method*. Philadelphia: Fortress Press.

Fee, G. D. (1987). *The First Epistle to the Corinthians*. Grand Rapids, MI: Eerdmans.

Feinberg, P. D. (1980). 'The meaning of inerrancy'. In *Inerrancy*, ed. N. L. Geisler. Grand Rapids, MI: Academie Books / Zondervan, pp. 267–306.

Fish, S. (1980). *Is There a Text in This Class?* Cambridge, MA and London: Harvard University Press.

—— (1989). *Doing what Comes Naturally: Change, Rhetoric and the Practice of Theory in Literary and Legal Studies*. Oxford: Clarendon Press.

—— (1994). *There's no such Thing as Free Speech*. Oxford and New York: Oxford University Press.

—— (1995). *Professional Correctness: Literary Studies and Political Change*. New York: Clarendon Press.

Fishbein, M., and Ajzen, I. (1975). *Belief, Attitude, Intention and Behaviour.* Reading, MA: Addison-Wesley.

Fisher, E., Astley, J., and Wilcox, C. (1992). 'A survey of Bible reading practice and attitudes to the Bible among Anglican congregations'. In *The Contours of Christian Education*, eds. J. Astley and D. Day. Great Wakering: McCrimmon Publishing, pp. 382–95.

Fisher, S., and Greenberg, R. P. (1985). *The Scientific Credibility of Freud's Theories and Therapy*. New York: Columbia University Press.

Flemming, D. (2002). 'Contextualizing the Gospel in Athens: Paul's Areopagus address as a paradigm for missionary communication'. *Missiology*, 30: 199–214.

Ford, D., and Stanton, G. (eds) (2003). *Reading Texts, Seeking Wisdom: Scripture and Theology*. London: SCM.

Forstorp, P.-A. (1990). 'Receiving and responding: ways of taking from the Bible'. In *Bible Reading in Sweden: Studies Related to the Translation of the New Testament*, ed. G. Hansson. Stockholm: Almqvist & Wiksell International, pp. 149–69.

Fowl, S. E. (1998). *Engaging Scripture*. Oxford: Blackwell.

—— (ed.) (1997). *The Theological Interpretation of Scripture: Classic and Contemporary Readings*. Oxford and Malden, MA: Blackwell.

Fowler, R. M., Blumhofer, E., and Segovia, F. F. (eds) (2004). *New Paradigms for Bible Study*. London and New York: T & T Clark.

Francis, L. J. (1978). 'Attitude and longitude: a study in measurement'. *Character Potential*, 8: 119–30.

—— (1984). 'Dimensions of Christian belief'. *Educational Studies*, 10: 103–11.

—— (1989). 'Drift from the churches: secondary school pupil's attitudes toward Christianity'. *British Journal of Religious Education*, 11: 76–86.

—— (1992). 'Reliability and validity of the Francis scale of attitudes towards Christianity'. *Panorama*, 4: 17–19.

—— (1997). *Personality Type and Scripture: Exploring St Mark's Gospel*. London: Mowbray.

—— (2001). 'Personality type and communicating the Gospel'. *Modern Believing*, 42: 32–46.

—— (2002). 'Personality theory and empirical theology'. *Journal of Empirical Theology*, 15: 37–53.

—— (2003). 'Psychological type and biblical hermeneutics: SIFT method of preaching'. *Rural Theology*, 1: 13–23.

—— (2004). 'Personality theory, empirical theology and normativity'. In *Normative and Empirical Research in Theology*, ed. J. A. Van der Ven and M. Scherer-Rath. Leiden: Brill, pp. 137–58.

—— (2005). *Faith and Psychology: Personality, Religion and the Individual.* London: Darton, Longman & Todd.

—— and Atkins, P. (2000). *Exploring Luke's Gospel: A Guide to the Gospel Readings in the Revised Common Lectionary.* London: Continuum / Mowbray.

—— and Atkins, P. (2001). *Exploring Matthew's Gospel: A Guide to the Gospel Readings in the Revised Common Lectionary.* London: Continuum.

—— and Atkins, P. (2002). *Exploring Mark's Gospel: An Aid for Readers and Preachers Using Year B of the Revised Common Lectionary.* London: Continuum / Mowbray.

——, Craig, C. L. and Robbins, M. (2005). 'Two different operationalisations of psychological type: comparing the Myers–Briggs Type Indicator and the Keirsey Temperament Sorter'. *Journal of Analytical Psychology*, unpublished.

—— and Jones, S. H. (1997). 'Personality and charismatic experience among adult Christians'. *Pastoral Psychology*, 45: 421–8.

—— and Jones, S. H. (1998). 'Personality and Christian belief among adult churchgoers'. *Journal of Psychological Type*, 47: 5–11.

——, Lewis, J. M., Philipchalk, R., Brown, L. B., et al. (1995). 'The internal consistency, reliability and construct validity of the Francis scale of attitude toward Christianity (adult) among undergraduate students in the UK, USA, Australia and Canada'. *Personality and Individual Differences*, 19: 949–53.

—— and Louden, S. H. (2000). 'Mystical orientation and psychological type: a study among student and adult churchgoers'. *Transpersonal Psychology Review*, 4: 36–42.

—— Robbins, M., and Astley, J. (2005). *Fragmented Faith? Exposing the Fault-Lines in the Church of England.* Milton Keynes: Paternoster Press.

—— and Ross, F. J. (1997). 'The perceiving function and Christian spirituality: distinguishing between sensing and intuition'. *Pastoral Sciences*, 16: 93–103.

—— and Stubbs, M. T. (1987). 'Measuring attitudes towards Christianity: from childhood to adulthood'. *Personality and Individual Differences*, 8: 741–3.

Freeman, K. W. (1996). 'Toward a *sensus fidelium* for an evangelical church: postconservatives and postliberals on reading Scripture'. In *The Nature of Confession: Evangelicals and Postliberals in Conversation*, ed. T. R. Phillips and D. L. Okholm. Downers Grove, IL: InterVarsity Press, pp. 162–79.

Frymire, J. W. (2006). *Preaching the Story: How to Communicate God's Word through Narrative Sermons.* Anderson, IN: Warner Press Publishers.

Fulbrook, M. (2002). *Historical Theory.* London and New York: Routledge.

Fulkerson, M. M. (1998). '"Is there a (non-sexist) bible in this church?" A feminist case for the priority of interpretive communities'. *Modern Theology*, 14: 225–42.

Fuller, D. P. (1978). 'The Holy Spirit's role in biblical interpretation'. Grand Rapids, MI: Eerdmans, pp. 189–98.

Fullerton, J. T., and Hunsberger, B. E. (1982). 'A unidimensional measure of Christian orthodoxy'. *Journal for the Scientific Study of Religion*, 21: 317–26.

Funk, R. W. (2001). 'The Jesus Seminar and the quest'. In *Jesus Then and Now: Images of Jesus in History and Christology*, eds. M. W. Meyer and C. T. Hughes. Harrisburg, PA: Trinity Press International, pp. 130–39.

—— (ed.) (1998). *The Acts of Jesus: The Search for the Authentic Deeds of Jesus.* San Francisco: HarperSanFrancisco.

Funk, R. W. and Hoover, R. W. (eds) (1993). *The Five Gospels: The Search for the Authentic Words of Jesus. A New Translation and Commentary.* New York: Macmillan.

Furlong, M. (2000). *C of E: The State it's In.* London: Hodder & Stoughton.

Gadamer, H.-G. (1979). *Truth and Method.* London: Sheed & Ward.

Garber, Z. (2006). *Mel Gibson's Passion: The Film, the Controversy, and its Implications.* West Lafayette, IN: Purdue University Press.

Geisler, N. L. (1980). *Inerrancy.* Grand Rapids, MI: Academie Books / Zondervan.

Gill, R. (1993). *The Myth of the Empty Church.* London: SPCK.

—— (2003). *The 'Empty' Church Revisited.* Aldershot & Burlington VT: Ashgate.

—— Hadaway, C. K., and Marler, P. L. (1998). 'Is religious belief declining in Britain?' *Journal for the Scientific Study of Religion*, 37: 507–516.

Gillingham, S. E. (1998). *One Bible, Many Voices.* London: SPCK.

Goldingay, J. (1994). *Models for Scripture.* Carlisle and Grand Rapids, MI: Paternoster Press and Eerdmans.

—— (1995). *Models for the Interpretation of Scripture.* Carlisle and Grand Rapids, MI: Paternoster Press and Eerdmans.

Goldsmith, M., and Wharton, M. (1993). *Knowing Me – Knowing You.* London: SPCK.

Goodliff, P. (1998). *Care in a Confused Climate: Pastoral Care and Postmodern Culture.* London: Darton, Longman and Todd.

Graesser, A. C., and Klettke, B. (2001). 'Agency, plot, and the structural affect theory of literary story comprehension'. In *The Psychology and Sociology of Literature*, ed. D. Schram and G. Steen. Amsterdam: Benjamins, pp. 57–70.

Green, J. B. (2002). 'Scripture and theology: failed experiments, fresh perspectives'. *Interpretation*, 56: 5–20.

—— and Turner, M. (2000). *Between Two Horizons: Spanning New Testament Studies and Systematic Theology.* Grand Rapids, MI: Eerdmans.

Grindheim, S. (2001). 'The law kills but the gospel gives life: the letter–spirit dualism in 2 Corinthians 3:5–18'. *Journal for the Study of the New Testament*, 84: 97–115.

Gulley, N. R. (1995). 'Reader-response theories in postmodern hermeneutics: a challenge to Evangelical theology'. In *The Challenge of Postmodernism: An Evangelical Engagement*, ed. D. S. Dockery. Wheaton, IL: Bridgepoint / Victor, pp. 208–238.

Gumbel, N. (1993). *Questions of Life.* Eastbourne: Kingsway Publications.

—— (1994). *Telling Others: The Alpha Initiative.* Eastbourne: Kingsway Publications.

—— (1999). *Alpha Course Manual.* London: HTB Publications.

Gunstone, J. (1989). *Signs and Wonders: The Wimber Phenomenon.* London: Darton, Longman & Todd.

Hafemann, S. J. (1996). *Paul, Moses and the History of Israel: The Letter/Spirit Contrast and the Argument from Scripture in 2 Corinthians 3.* Peabody, MA: Hendrickson.

Hakemulder, J. (2001). 'How to make alle Menschen Brüder'. In *The Psychology and Sociology of Literature*, ed. D. Schram and G. Steen. Amsterdam: Benjamins, pp. 225–42.

—— (2006). 'Literature: empirical studies'. In *Encyclopaedia of Language and Linguistics*, vol. 10, ed. K. Brown. Boston, MA: Elsevier, pp. 274–80.

Hanauer, D. (1995). 'Literary and poetic text categorization judgements'. *Journal of Literary Semantics*, 24: 187–210.

Harrington, H., and Patten, R. (1994). 'Pentecostal hermeneutics and postmodern literary theory'. *Pneuma: The Journal of the Society for Pentecostal Studies*, 16: 109–114.

Harrison, J. (1983). *Attitudes to the Bible God Church.* Unpublished research report. Swindon: Bible Society.

Harrison, T. (1985). *The Durham Phenomenon.* London: Darton, Longman and Todd.

Hartberg, T. (1980) *Attitude Research in the Bible Society.* MSc: unpublished.

Hayes, J. H. (ed.) (1999). *Dictionary of Biblical Interpretation.* Nashville, TN: Abingdon Press.

Haynes, S. R., and McKenzie, S. C. (eds) (1999). *To Each His Own Meaning: An Introduction to Biblical Criticisms and their Applications.* Louisville, KY: Westminster John Knox Press.

Hays, R. B. (1989). *Echoes of Scripture in the Letters of Paul.* New Haven: Yale University Press.

—— and Green, J. B. (1995). 'The use of the Old Testament by New Testament writers'. In *Hearing the New Testament: Strategies for Interpretation*, ed. J. B. Green. Grand Rapids, MI: Eerdmans, pp. 222–38.

Heelas, P., and Woodhead, L. (2004). *Spiritual Revolution: Why Religion Is Giving Way to Spirituality.* Oxford: Blackwell.

Hey, S. (2001). 'Changing roles of Pentecostal hermeneutics'. *Evangelical Review of Theology*, 25: 210–18.

Hill, P. C., and Hood, R. W. (eds) (1999). *Measures of Religiosity.* Birmingham, AL: Religious Education Press.

Hocken, P. (1997). *Streams of Renewal.* Carlisle: Paternoster.

—— (2002). 'Charismatic movements'. In *The New International Dictionary of Pentecostal and Charismatic Movements*, ed. S. M. Burgess and E. M. van der Maas. Grand Rapids, MI: Zondervan, pp. 477–519.

Hodge, A. A., and Warfield, B. B. (1881). 'Inspiration'. *The Presbyterian Review*, 2: 225–60.

Hodgson, P. E. (2005). *Theology and Modern Physics.* Aldershot and Burlington VT: Ashgate.

Holland, N. (1975). *5 Readers Reading.* New Haven: Yale University Press.

Houlden, J. L. (ed.) (1995). *The Interpretation of the Bible in the Church.* London: SCM.

Huggett, J. (1986). *Listening to God.* London: Hodder & Stoughton.

—— (1989). *Open to God.* London: Hodder & Stoughton.

Hunt, R. A. (1972). 'Mythological-symbolic religious commitment. The LAM scales'. *Journal for the Scientific Study of Religion*, 10: 42–52.

Hunt, S. (2000). 'All things bright and beautiful: the rise of the Anglican charismatic church'. *Journal of Empirical Theology*, 13: 16–34.

Hurd, J. C. (1965). *The Origin of 1 Corinthians.* London: SPCK.

Hylson-Smith, K. (1989). *Evangelicals in the Church of England 1734–1984.* Edinburgh: T & T Clark.

—— (1993). *High Churchmanship in the Church of England from the Sixteenth Century to the late Twentieth Century.* Edinburgh: T & T Clark.

Iser, W. (1978). *The Act of Reading: A Theory of Aesthetic Response.* Baltimore and London: John Hopkins University Press.

Jacobsen, D. G. (2003). *Thinking in the Spirit: Theologies of the Early Pentecostal Movement.* Bloomington, IN: Indiana University Press.

James, W. (1902). *The Varieties of Religious Experience: A Study in Human Nature.* New York: Random House.

Jelen, T. G. (1989a). 'Biblical literalism and inerrancy: does the difference make a difference?' *Sociological Analysis*, 49: 421–9.

—— (ed.) (1989b). *Religion and Political Behavior in the United States.* New York: Praeger.

Jelen, T. G., Wilcox, C., and Smidt, C. E. (1990). 'Biblical literalism and inerrancy: a methodological investigation'. *Sociological Analysis*, 51: 307–313.

Jenkins, K. (1995). *On "What is History?": From Carr and Elton to Rorty and White.* London and New York: Routledge.

Jobling, D., Pippin, T., and Schleifer, R. (eds) (2001). *The Postmodern Bible Reader.* Oxford and Malden, MA: Blackwell.

Johns, L., and Johns, C. (1992). 'Yielding to the Spirit: a pentecostal approach to group Bible study'. *Journal of Pentecostal Theology*, 1: 109–134.

Johnson, C. B. (1983). *The Psychology of Biblical Interpretation.* Grand Rapids, MI: ℕℝ Zondervan Corporation.

Johnson, L. T. (1996). *Scripture and Discernment.* Nashville, TN: Abingdon Press.

Johnston, G. (2001). *Preaching to a Postmodern World: A Guide to Reaching Twenty-First-Century Listeners.* Leicester: Inter-Varsity Press.

Johnstone, B. (2002). *Discourse Analysis.* Malden, MA: Blackwell.

Jung, C. G. (1921). *Psychologische Typen.* Zurich: Rascher Verlag.

—— (1971). *Psychological Types: The Collected Works.* Vol. 6. London: Routledge and Kegan Paul.

Karkkainen, V.-M. (1998). 'Pentecostal hermeneutics in the making: on the way from fundamentalism to postmodernism'. *Journal of the European Theological Association*, 18: 76–115.

Keegan, T. J. (1995). 'Biblical criticism and the challenge of postmodernism'. *Biblical Interpretation*, 3: 1–14.

Keirsey, D. (1998). *Please Understand Me II: Temperament, Character and Intelligence.* Del Mar, CA: Prometheus Nemesis.

—— and Bates, M. (1978). *Please Understand Me.* Del Mar, CA: Prometheus Nemesis.

Kendall, E. (1998). *Myers–Briggs Type Indicator: Step 1 Manual Supplement.* Palo Alto, CA: Consulting Psychologists Press.

Kille, D. A. (2001). *Psychological Biblical Criticism.* Minneapolis: Fortress Press.

——(2004). 'Reading the Bible in three dimensions: psychological biblical interpretation'. In *Psychology and the Bible*, vol. 1: *Freud to Kohut*, ed. J. H. Ellens and W. G. Rollins. Westport, CT: Praeger, pp. 17–32.

Kim, J.-O., and Mueller, C. W. (1978). *Introduction to Factor Analysis: What It Is and How to Do It.* Beverly Hills, CA: Sage Publications.

Kitzberger, I. R. (ed.) (1999). *The Personal Voice in Biblical Interpretation.* London and New York: Routledge.

Kline, P. (1972). *Fact and Fantasy in Freudian Theory.* London: Methuen.

Kolbrener, W. (1996). 'No "elsewhere": Fish, Soloveitchik and the unavoidability of interpretation'. *Literature and Theology*, 10: 171–90.

Kovacs, J. L. (ed.) (2005). *1 Corinthians: Interpreted by Early Christian Commentators.* Grand Rapids, MI: Eerdmans.

Kreuz, R. J., and MacNealy, M. S. (eds) (1996). *Empirical Approaches to Literature and Aesthetics.* Norwood, NJ: Ablex Publishing Corporation.

Law, D. R. (2001). *Inspiration.* London and New York: Continuum.

Lee, R. M. (1993). *Doing Research on Sensitive Topics.* London: Sage.

Lieb, M. (2002). 'How Stanley Fish works'. *Journal of Religion*, 82: 252–9.

Likert, R. (1932). *A Technique for the Measurement of Attitudes.* New York: Columbia University Press.

Lindbeck, G. A. (1984). *The Nature of Doctrine: Religion and Theology in a Postliberal Age.* Philadelphia: Westminster Press.

——(1989). 'Scripture, consensus, and community'. In *Biblical Interpretation in Crisis: The Ratzinger Conference on Bible and Church*, ed. R. J. Neuhaus. Grand Rapids, MI: Eerdmans.

Lonsdale, D. (2000). *Eyes to See, Ears to Hear: An Introduction to Ignatian Spirituality.* London: Darton Longman & Todd.

Loomis, M., and Singer, J. (1980). 'Testing the bipolarity assumption in Jung's typology'. *Journal of Analytical Psychology*, 25: 351–6.

Losie, L. A. (2004). 'Paul's speech on the Areopagus: a model of cross-cultural evangelism: Acts 17:16–34'. In *Mission in Acts: Ancient Narratives in Contemporary Context*, ed. R. L. Gallagher and P. Hertig. Maryknoll, NY: Orbis Books, pp. 221–38.

Lyon, D. (1999). *Postmodernity.* Milton Keynes: Open University Press.

——(2000). *Jesus in Disneyland: Religion in Postmodern Times.* Cambridge: Polity Press.

Lyons, J. (1998). 'The Fourth Wave and the approaching millennium: some problems with Charismatic hermeneutics'. *Anvil*, 15: 169–80.

Macquarrie, J. (1960). *The Scope of Demythologizing: Bultmann and his Critics.* London: SCM.

Madsen, D. L. (1994). *Rereading Allegory: A Narrative Approach to Genre.* New York: St Martins Press.

Marshall, D. G. (1995). 'Reading and interpretive communities'. In *The Discerning Reader: Christian Perspectives on Literature and Theory*, ed. D. Barratt, R.

Pooley and L. Ryken. Leicester and Grand Rapids, MI: Apollos and Baker Book House, pp. 69–84.

Massey, J. (2006). *Stewards of Story.* London: SPCK.

McCartney, D., and Clayton, C. (1994). *Let the Reader Understand: A Guide to Interpreting and Applying the Bible.* Grand Rapids, MI: Baker Books.

McLean, M. (1984). 'Toward a Pentecostal hermeneutic'. *Pneuma: The Journal of the Society for Pentecostal Studies*, 6: 35–56.

Menzies, R. (1994). 'Jumping off the postmodern bandwagon'. *Pneuma: The Journal of the Society for Pentecostal Studies*, 16: 115–20.

Metzger, B. M., and Coogan, M. D. (eds) (2001). *The Oxford Guide to Ideas and Issues of the Bible.* Oxford and New York: Oxford University Press.

Michaels, W. B. (1977). 'The interpreter's self: Peirce on the Cartesian "subject"'. *Georgia Review*, 31: 383–402.

Moore, S. D. (1986). 'Negative hermeneutics, insubstantial texts: Stanley Fish and the biblical interpreter'. *Journal of the American Academy of Religion*, 54: 707–719.

Morgan, R. (1990). 'Biblical theology'. In *A Dictionary of Biblical Interpretation*, ed. R. J. Coggins and J. L. Houlden. London: SCM Press, pp. 86–9.

—— with Barton, J. (1988). *Biblical Interpretation.* Oxford: Oxford University Press.

Munslow, A. (1997). *Deconstructing History.* London and New York: Routledge.

Murray, S. (2004). *Post-Christendom: Church and Mission in a Strange New World.* Milton Keynes: Authentic Media.

Myers, I. B. (1993). *Introduction to Type.* Oxford: Oxford Psychologists Press.

—— and McCaulley, M. H. (1985). *Manual: A Guide to the Development and Use of the Myers–Briggs Type Indicator.* Palo Alto, CA: Consulting Psychologists Press.

—— and Myers, P. B. (1980). *Gifts Differing.* Palo Alto, CA: Consulting Psychologists Press.

Noble, P. R. (1994). 'Hermeneutics and post-modernism: can we have a radical reader-response theory? Part I'. *Religious Studies*, 30: 419–36.

—— (1995). 'Hermeneutics and post-modernism: can we have a radical reader-response theory? Part II'. *Religious Studies*, 31: 1–22.

—— (1996). 'Fish and the Bible: should reader-response theories "catch on"?' *Heythrop Journal*, 37: 456–67.

Noel, B. T. (2004). 'Gordon Fee and the challenge to Pentecostal hermeneutics: thirty years later'. *Pneuma: The Journal of the Society for Pentecostal Studies*, 26: 60–80.

Nolland, J. (1993). *Word Biblical Commentary: Luke 18:35–24:53.* Dallas: Word Books.

Norusis, M. (1994). *SPSS Professional Statistics 6.1.* Chicago: SPSS Inc.

Oppenheim, A. N. (1992). *Questionnaire Design, Interviewing and Attitude Measurement.* London and New York: Pinter Publishers.

Osgerby, B. (2004). *Youth Media.* London and New York: Routledge.

Palmer, M. F. (1997). *Freud and Jung on Religion.* London and New York: Routledge.

Parsons, W. B., and Jonte-Pace, D. (2001). 'Mapping religion and psychology'. In *Religion and Psychology: Mapping the Terrain*, ed. D. Jonte-Pace and W. B. Parsons. London and New York: Routledge, pp. 1–10.

Penchansky, D. (1995). *The Politics of Biblical Theology: A Postmodern Reading.* Macon, GA: Mercer University Press.

Petersen, L. R. (2001). 'Religion, plausibility structures, and education's effect on attitudes toward elective abortion'. *Journal for the Scientific Study of Religion*, 40: 187–204.

Phillips, T. R., and Okholm, D. L. (eds) (1996). *The Nature of Confession: Evangelicals and Postliberals in Conversation.* Downers Grove, IL: InterVarsity Press.

Pike, K. L. (1967). *Language in Relation to a Unified Theory of Structure of Human Behavior.* The Hague: Mouton.

Pinnock, C. H. (1993). 'The role of the Spirit in interpretation'. *Journal of the Evangelical Theology Society*, 36: 491–7.

Quinn, M. T., Lewis, R. J., and Fischer, K. L. (1992). 'A cross-correlation of the Myers-Briggs and the Keirsey instruments'. *Journal of College Student Development*, 33: 279–80.

Randall, K. (2005). *Evangelicals Etcetera: Conflict and Conviction in the Church of England's Parties.* Aldershot and Burlington, VT: Ashgate.

Richter, P. (1995). 'Social-scientific criticism of the New Testament: an appraisal and extended example'. In *Approaches to New Testament Study*, ed. S. E. Porter and D. Tombs. Sheffield: Sheffield Academic Press, pp. 266–309.

Ricoeur, P. (1981). *Hermeneutics and the Human Sciences: Essays on Language, Action and Interpretation.* Cambridge: Cambridge University Press.

—— (1991). *From Text to Action: Essays in Hermeneutics, II.* London: Athlone.

Robinson, J. A. T. (1963). *Honest to God.* London: SCM Press.

 Rollins, W. G. (1999). *Soul and Psyche: The Bible in Psychological Perspective.* Minneapolis: Fortress Press.

Saye, S. (1996). 'The wild and crooked tree: Barth, Fish and interpretive communities'. *Modern Theology*, 12: 435–58.

Schram, D., and Steen, G. (eds) (2001). *The Psychology and Sociology of Literature.* Amsterdam: Benjamins.

Schwölbel, C. (1990). 'Calvin'. In *A Dictionary of Biblical Interpretation*, ed. R. J. Coggins and J. L. Houlden. London: SCM Press, pp. 98–101.

Scotland, N. (2003). 'Evangelicalism and the Charismatic Movement (UK)'. In *The Futures of Evangelicalism: Issues and Prospects*, ed. C. G. Bartholomew, R. Parry and A. V. West. Leicester: Inter-Varsity Press, pp. 271–301.

Segovia, F. F. (1995a). '"And they speak in other tongues": competing modes of discourse in contemporary biblical studies'. In *Reading from This Place: Social Location and Biblical Interpretation in Global Perspective*, vol. 1, ed. F. F. Segovia and M. A. Tolbert. Minneapolis: Fortress Press, pp. 1–34.

—— (1995b). 'Cultural studies and contemporary biblical criticism: ideological criticism as a mode of discourse'. In *Reading from This Place: Social Location and Biblical Interpretation in Global Perspective*, vol. 2, pp. 1–17.

—— and Tolbert, M. A. (eds) (1995a). *Reading from This Place: Social Location and Biblical Interpretation in Global Perspective*, vol. 1. Minneapolis: Fortress Press.

—— and Tolbert, M. A. (eds) (1995b). *Reading from This Place: Social Location and Biblical Interpretation in Global Perspective*, vol. 2. Minneapolis: Fortress Press.

Shillington, V. G. (2002). *Reading the Sacred Text: An Introduction to Biblical Studies.* London and New York: T & T Clark.

Simms, K. (2003). *Paul Ricoeur.* London and New York: Routledge.

Singer, J., Loomis, M., Kirkhart, E., and Kirkhart, L. (1996). *The Singer–Loomis Type Deployment Inventory: Version 4.1.* Gresham, OR: Moving Boundaries Inc.

Slack, J. (1990). Chapter 11, 'Attention'. In *Introduction to Psychology*, vol. 2, ed. I. Roth. Hove and Milton Keynes: Lawrence Erlbaum Associates & Open University Press, pp. 528–69.

Smidt, C. (1989). 'Identifying Evangelical respondents: an analysis of "born-again" and Bible questions used across different surveys'. In *Religion and Political Behavior in the United States*, ed. T. Jelen. New York and Westport, CT: Praeger, pp. 23–43.

Smith, J. K. A. (1997). 'The closing of the book: Pentecostals, Evangelicals, and the sacred writings'. *Journal of Pentecostal Theology*, 11: 49–71.

Snodgrass, K. R. (2000). 'From allegorizing to allegorizing: a history of the interpretation of the parables of Jesus'. In *The Challenge of Jesus' Parables*, ed. R. N. Longenecker. Grand Rapids, MI and Cambridge: Eerdmans, pp. 3–29.

Spector, P. E. (1992). *Summated Rating Scale Construction.* London: Sage.

Steven, J. H. S. (2002). *Worship in the Spirit: Charismatic Worship in the Church of England.* Carlisle and Waynesboro, GA: Paternoster Press.

Stibbe, M. (1998). 'This is that: some thoughts concerning Charismatic hermeneutics'. *Anvil*, 15: 181–93.

Stiver, D. R. (1995). 'The uneasy alliance between evangelicalism and postmodernism: a reply to Anthony Thiselton'. In *The Challenge of Postmodernism: An Evangelical Engagement*, ed. D. S. Dockery. Wheaton, IL: Bridgepoint / Victor, pp. 239–53.

Stobart, E. (2006). *Child Abuse Linked to Accusations of "Possession" and "Witchcraft". Research Report 750.* London: Department for Education and Skills.

Stock, B. (1983). *The Implications of Literacy.* Princeton: Princeton University Press.

Stout, J. (1982). 'What is the meaning of a text?' *New Literary History*, 14: 1–12.

Summerfield, C., and Gill, B. (eds) (2005). *Social Trends No. 35.* London: Office for National Statistics.

Svensson, C. (1990). 'The Bible and the real reader: world view and interpretive strategies'. In *Bible Reading in Sweden: Studies Related to the Translation of the New Testament*, ed. G. Hansson. Stockholm: Almqvist & Wiksell International, pp. 117–48.

Synan, V. (1997). *The Holiness-Pentecostal Tradition: Charismatic Movements in the Twentieth Century.* Grand Rapids, MI: Eerdmans.

—— (ed.) (2001). *The Century of the Holy Spirit: 100 years of Pentecostal and Charismatic Renewal, 1901–2001.* Nashville, TN: Thomas Nelson.

Tate, W. R. (1994). *Reading Mark from the Outside.* San Francisco: Christian Universities Press.

—— (1997). *Biblical Interpretation.* Peabody, MA: Hendrickson.

Thiselton, A. C. (1980). *The Two Horizons.* Exeter: Paternoster Press.

—— (1992). *New Horizons in Hermeneutics.* London: HarperCollins.

—— (1998). 'Biblical studies and theoretical hermeneutics'. In *The Cambridge Companion to Biblical Interpretation*, ed. J. Barton. Cambridge: Cambridge University Press, pp. 95–113.

—— (2000). *The First Epistle to the Corinthians.* Grand Rapids, MI and Carlisle: Eerdmans and Paternoster.

Thompson, B. (1996). *Personal Preferences Self-Description Questionnaire.* College Station, TX: Psychometrics Group.

Tompkins, J. P. (ed.) (1980). *Reader-Response Criticism. From Formalism to Post-Structuralism.* Baltimore and London: John Hopkins University Press.

Travis, S. H. (1994). *The Bible as a Whole.* Oxford: Bible Reading Fellowship.

Tucker, I. F., and Gillespie, B. V. (1993). 'Correlations among three measures of personality type'. *Perceptual and Motor Skills*, 77: 650.

van der Lans, J. (1990). 'Interpretation of religious language and cognitive style: a pilot study with the LAM-scale'. *International Journal for the Psychology of Religion*, 1: 107–123.

van der Ven, J. A. (1998). *Practical Theology: An Empirical Approach.* Leuven: Peeters.

van Dijk, T. A. (ed.) (1997). *Discourse studies: A Multidisciplinary Introduction.* London: Sage Publications.

van Peer, W., and Stoeger, I. (2001). 'Psychoanalysts and daydreaming'. In *The Psychology and Sociology of Literature*, ed. D. Schram and G. Steen. Amsterdam: Benjamins, pp. 185–200.

Vanhoozer, K. J. (1998). *Is There a Meaning in this Text?* Leicester: Apollos / IVP.

—— (ed.) (2003). *The Cambridge Companion to Postmodern Theology.* Cambridge: Cambridge University Press.

Village, A. (2005a). 'Assessing belief about the Bible: a study among Anglican laity'. *Review of Religious Research*, 46: 243–54.

—— (2005b). 'Christian belief about the Bible and the Holy Spirit in relation to psychological type'. *Research in the Social Scientific Study of Religion*, 16: 1–16.

—— (2005c). 'Dimensions of belief about miraculous healing'. *Mental Health, Religion and Culture*, 8: 97–107.

—— (2005d). 'Factors shaping biblical literalism: A study among Anglican laity'. *Journal of Beliefs and Values*, 26: 29–38.

—— (2006). 'Biblical interpretative horizons and ordinary readers: an empirical study'. *Research in the Social Scientific Study of Religion*, 17: 157–76.

—— (2007). 'Feeling in and falling out: sense of belonging and frequency of disagreeing among Anglican congregations'. *Archive for the Psychology of Religion*, 29: 268–88.

—— and Francis, L. J. (2005). 'The relationship of psychological type preferences to biblical interpretation'. *Journal of Empirical Theology*, 18: 74–89.

—— Francis, L. J., and Craig, C. L. (2007). 'Church tradition and psychological type preferences among Anglicans in England'. *Journal of Anglican Studies*, in press.

Watson, F. (1994). *Text, Church and World.* Edinburgh: T & T Clark.

—— (1997). *Text and Truth: Redefining Biblical Theology.* Edinburgh: T & T Clark.

Webster, J. (2003). *Holy Scripture: A Dogmatic Sketch.* Cambridge: Cambridge University Press.

Weinsheimer, J. C. (1985). *Gadamer's Hermeneutics: A Reading of Truth and Method.* New Haven and London: Yale University Press.

Wells, A., and Matthews, G. (1994). *Attention and Emotion: A Clinical Perspective.* Hove: Lawrence Erlbaum Associates.

Westerholm, S. (1984). 'Letter and Spirit: the foundation of Pauline ethics'. *New Testament Studies*, 30: 229–48.

White, L. M., and Yarbrough, O. L. (eds) (1995). *The Social World of the First Christians: Essays in Honor of Wayne A. Meeks.* Minneapolis: Fortress Press.

Whitelam, K. W. (1998). 'The social world of the Bible'. In *The Cambridge Companion to Biblical Interpretation*, ed. J. Barton. Cambridge: Cambridge University Press, pp. 35–49.

Whitman, J. (1987). *Allegory: The Dynamics of an Ancient and Mediaeval Technique.* Oxford: Oxford University Press.

Wilcox, C. (1992). *God's Warriors: The Christian Right in Twentieth-Century America.* Baltimore: John Hopkins University Press.

Wilkinson, L. (1997). 'Hermeneutics and the postmodern reaction against "truth"'. In *The Act of Bible Reading*, ed. E. Dyck. Carlisle: Paternoster Press / IVP, pp. 114–47.

Wilson, B. R. (1966). *Religion in a Secular Society: A Sociological Comment.* London: Watts.

Wimber, J., and Springer, K. (1986). *Power Healing.* London: Hodder & Stoughton.

Wimsatt, W. K., and Beardsley, M. (1971). 'The intentional fallacy'. In *The Verbal Icon: Studies in the Meaning of Poetry*, ed. W. K. Wimsatt. London: Methuen, pp. 1–18.

Witherington III, B. (1995). *Conflict and Community in Corinth: A Socio-rhetorical Commentary on 1 and 2 Corinthians.* Grand Rapids, MI and Carlisle: Eerdmans and Paternoster.

Woodward, J., and Pattison, S. (eds) (2000). *The Blackwell Reader in Pastoral and Practical Theology.* Oxford and Malden, MA: Blackwell.

Wulff, D. M. (2001). 'Psychology of religion: empirical approaches'. In *Religion and Psychology: Mapping the Terrain*, ed. D. Jonte-Pace and W. B. Parsons. London and New York: Routledge, pp. 15–29.

Young, F. M. (1993). 'Allegory and the ethics of reading'. In *The Open Text*, ed. F. Watson. London: SCM Press, pp. 103–120.

—— (2003). 'Alexandrian and Antiochene exegesis'. In *A History of Biblical Interpretation*, ed. A. J. Hauser and D. F. Watson. Grand Rapids, MI: Eerdmans, pp. 334–54.

Index

and horizon 86–7, 89, 162
experience of 145, 150–51, 162
and interpretation 145, 150
praying for 11, 69, 145, 147, 150–51
scale 13–14, 86–7, 133–4, 147–8
hermeneutics *see also* biblical interpretation
and biblical studies
academic 19–23
horizons of meaning 77–81
pentecostal or charismatic 151–7
historical criticism, *see* biblical studies,
historical
Holy Spirit *see* Bible reading and the Holy
Spirit
horizons, interpretative
in biblical studies 79–81
in hermeneutics 77–9
and ordinary readers 81–90
preference for 82, 84–9, 131–3
separation of 81–2, 83–4, 86–7, 90–94,
95, 150, 131–3, 135

imagination and reading 116–9
interpretative community 71, 122, 125–43,
154
and church tradition 131–3, 134, 135–8
congregations as 126, 130–31, 137–8,
139–42
definition of 127–31
effect on interpretation 130, 131–7
empirical study of 130–31
and social communities 129, 139–42
theological response to 138–42

Jung, Carl 14, 97–9, 105, 108, 123

Keirsey Temperament Sorter (KTS) 14, 110,
113–15, 133–4, 149

LAM scales 35, 61–2
letter versus spirit 154–7, 163–4
liberalism 15, 22, 29, 34–6, 39–42, 51, 55,
70, 109, 114, 147
literacy 4, 52–3, 101–102, 126, 153
literalism 57–63, 71–4, 92–4, 127, 146, 159
in academic studies 57–60
in Bible and Lay People Study 62–6
and biblical horizons 86–90
and charismatic practice 148–51
among churchgoers 12, 59–70, 159
factors predicting 66–9, 150, 160

further research on 62, 74–5, 142–3
and interpretative communities 131–4,
135–7
measurement of 14, 35, 38, 61–4, 68
scale 62–6
theologies of 71–4
literary criticism, *see also* biblical studies,
literary 101, 128

MBTI *see* Myers–Briggs typology
miraculous healing, *see* healing,
supernatural
modernity 19–22, 28, 91, 93, 152–3, 166
and secularization 23–5
Myers–Briggs typology 105–106, 110, 111

narrative 94, 116–19, 153, 158

ordinary Bible readers, definition of 1
see also Bible reading, academic versus
lay

parables
interpretation of 38, 62–3, 66
Pentecostalism 25, 26, 146, 149, 155
and biblical interpretation 146, 151–4,
156, 163
personality 97, 103–122
assessing 14, 103–106
preferences and interpretation 12, 94,
102, 113–16, 120–23, 160–62,
164–5, 168
and religion 104–09
pilot studies 11–13, 36–9, 62, 66, 84
postmodernity 19–20, 24–5, 28, 81, 91, 128,
152–3, 157, 161, 165–6
practical theology 2, 6
prayer for healing 11, 89, 90, 95, 145, 147,
151
psychological type 105–111, 151
categories 106–108
dominant function 107–108, 115, 118
judging processes 105, 107, 109, 117–18
perceiving processes 105–106, 109, 118,
119–20
and preferred interpretation 110–16
and reader imagination 116–19, 123
versus trait models 104–105, 108
psychology
and the Bible 99–100, 102–103, 123–4
cognitive 101, 120, 124